THE
THEORY
OF
MORAL SENTIMENTS;
OR,
AN ESSAY
TOWARDS
An ANALYSIS of the PRINCIPLES by which MEN naturally judge concerning the CONDUCT and CHARACTER, first of their NEIGHBOURS, and afterwards of THEMSELVES.
TO WHICH IS ADDED,
A DISSERTATION
ON THE
ORIGIN OF LANGUAGES.

BY ADAM SMITH, L.L.D. F.R.S.
Formerly Professor of Philosophy in the University of Glasgow; and Author of the Nature and Cause of the Wealth of Nations.
THE SIXTH EDITION.
DUBLIN:
Printed for J. BEATTY and C. JACKSON, No. 32, SKINNER-ROW.
M,DCC,LXXVII.

CONTENTS.

PART I.

Of the Propriety of Action.

SECTION I.

Of Merit and Demerit; or of the objects of reward and punishment.

SECTION I.

Chap. I. That whatever appears to be the proper object of gratitude, appears to deserve reward; and that, in the same manner, whatever appears to be the proper object of resentment, appears to deserve punishment

PART III.

Of the foundation of our judgments concerning our own sentiments and conduct, and of the sense of duty.

PART IV.

Of the effect of utility upon the sentiments of approbation.

PART VI.

PART V.

Of Systems of Moral Philosophy.

Of the influence of custom and fashion upon the sentiments of moral approbation and disapprobation.

SECTION I.

PART I.
Of the PROPRIETY of ACTION.

Consisting of three Sections.

SECTION I.
Of the SENSE of PROPRIETY.

CHAP. I.
Of SYMPATHY.

How selfish soever man may be supposed, there are evidently some principles in his nature, which interest him in the fortune of others, and render their happiness necessary to him, though he derives nothing from it, except the pleasure of seeing it. Of this kind is pity or compassion, the emotion which we feel for the misery of others, when we either see it, or are made to conceive it in a very lively manner. That we often derive sorrow from the sorrow of others, is a matter of fact too obvious to require any instances to prove it; for this sentiment, like all the other original passions of human nature, is by no means confined to the virtuous and humane, though they perhaps may feel it with the most exquisite sensibility. The greatest ruffian, the most hardened violator of the laws of society, is not altogether without it.

As we have no immediate experience of what other men feel, we can form no idea of the manner in which they are affected, but by conceiving what we ourselves should feel in the like situation. Though our brother is upon the rack, as long as we ourselves are at our ease, our senses will never inform us of what he suffers. They never did and never can carry us beyond our own person, and it is by the imagination only that we can form any conception of what are his sensations. Neither can that faculty help us to this any other way, than by representing to us what would be our own, if we were in his case. It is the impressions of our own senses only, not those of his, which our imaginations copy. By the imagination we place ourselves in his situation, we conceive ourselves enduring all the same torments, we enter as it were into his body and become in some measure him, and thence form some idea of his sensations and even feel something which, though weaker in degree, is not altogether unlike them. His agonies, when they are thus brought home to ourselves, when we have thus adopted and made them our own, begin at last to affect us, and we then tremble and shudder at the thought of what he feels. For as to be in pain or distress of any kind excites the most excessive sorrow, so to conceive or to imagine that we are in it, excites some degree of the same emotion, ₃in proportion to the vivacity or dullness of the conception.

That this is the source of our fellow-feeling for the misery of others, that it is by changing places in fancy with the sufferer, that we come either to conceive or to be affected by what he feels, may be demonstrated by many obvious observations, if it should not be thought sufficiently evident of itself. When we see a stroke aimed and just ready to fall upon the leg or arm of another person, we naturally shrink and draw back our own leg or our own arm; and when it does fall, we feel it in some measure, and are hurt by it as well as the sufferer. The mob, when they are gazing at a dancer on the slack rope, naturally writhe and twist and balance their own bodies, as they see him do, and as they feel that they themselves must do if in his situation. Persons of delicate fibres and a weak constitution of body, complain that in looking on the sores and ulcers which are exposed by beggars in the streets, they are apt to feel an itching or uneasy sensation in the correspondent part of their own bodies. The horror which they conceive at the misery of those wretches affects that particular part in themselves more than any other; because that horror arises from conceiving what they themselves would suffer, if they really were the wretches whom they are looking upon, and if that particular part in themselves was actually affected in the same miserable manner. The very force of this conception is sufficient, in their feeble frames, to produce that itching or uneasy sensation complained of. Men of the most robust make, observe that in looking upon sore eyes they often feel a very sensible soreness in their own, which proceeds ₄from the same reason; that organ being in the strongest man more delicate than any other part of the body is in the weakest.

Neither is it those circumstances only, which create pain or sorrow, that call forth our fellow-feeling. Whatever is the passion which arises from any object in the person principally concerned, an analogous emotion springs up, at the thought of his situation, in the breast of every attentive spectator. Our joy for the deliverance of those heroes of tragedy or romance who interest us, is as sincere as our grief for their distress, and our fellow-feeling with their misery is not more real than that with their happiness. We enter into their gratitude towards those faithful friends who did not desert them in their difficulties; and we heartily go along with their resentment against those perfidious traitors who injured, abandoned, or deceived them. In every passion of which the mind of man is susceptible, the emotions of the by-stander always correspond to what, by bringing the case home to himself, he imagines, should be the sentiments of the sufferer.

Pity and compassion are words appropriated to signify our fellow-feeling with the sorrow of others. Sympathy, though its meaning was, perhaps, originally the same, may now, however, without much impropriety, be made use of to denote our fellow-feeling with any passion whatever.

Upon some occasions sympathy may seem to arise merely from the view of a certain emotion in another person. The passions, upon some occasions, may seem to be transfused from one man to another, ₅instantaneously, and antecedent to any knowledge of what excited them in the person principally concerned. Grief and joy, for example, strongly expressed in the look and gestures of any one, at once affect the spectator with some degree of a like painful or agreeable emotion. A smiling face is, to every body that sees it, a chearful object; as a sorrowful countenance, on the other hand, is a melancholy one.

This, however, does not hold universally, or with regard to every passion. There are some passions of which the expressions excite no sort of sympathy, but before we are acquainted with what gave occasion to them, serve rather to disgust and provoke us against them. The furious behavior of an angry man is more likely to exasperate us against himself than against his enemies. As we are unacquainted with his provocation, we cannot bring his case home to ourselves, nor conceive any thing like the passions which it excites. But we plainly see what is the situation of those with whom he is angry, and to what violence they may be exposed from so enraged an adversary. We readily, therefore, sympathize with their fear or resentment, and are immediately disposed to take part against the man from whom they appear to be in so much danger.

If the very appearances of grief and joy inspire us with some degree of the like emotions, it is because they suggest to us the general idea of some good or bad fortune that has befallen the person in whom we observe them: and in these passions this is sufficient to have some little influence upon us. The effects of grief and joy terminate in the person who feels those emotions, of which the expressions do not, like those of resentment, suggest to us the idea of any other person for whom we are concerned, and whose interests are opposite to his. The general idea of good or bad fortune, therefore, creates some concern for the person who has met with it, but the general idea of provocation excites no sympathy with the anger of the man who has received it. Nature, it seems, teaches us to be more averse to enter into this passion, and, till informed of its cause, to be disposed rather to take part against it.

Even our sympathy with the grief or joy of another, before we are informed of the cause of either, is always extremely imperfect. General lamentations, which express nothing but the anguish of the sufferer, create rather a curiosity to inquire into his situation, along with some disposition to sympathize with him, than any actual sympathy that is very sensible. The first question which we ask is, What has befallen you? Till this be answered, tho' we are uneasy both from the vague idea of his misfortune, and still more from torturing ourselves with conjectures about what it may be, yet our fellow-feeling is not very considerable.

Sympathy, therefore, does not arise so much from the view of the passion, as from that of the situation which excites it. We sometimes feel for another, a passion of which he himself seems to be altogether incapable; because when we put ourselves in his case, that passion arises in our breast from the imagination, though it does not in his from the reality. We blush for the impudence and rudeness of another, though he himself appears to have no sense of the impropriety of his own behavior; because we cannot help feeling with what confusion we ourselves should be covered, had we behaved in so absurd a manner.

Of all the calamities to which the condition of mortality exposes mankind, the loss of reason appears, to those who have the least spark of humanity, by far the most dreadful, and they behold that last stage of human wretchedness with deeper commiseration than any other. But the poor wretch, who is in it, laughs and sings perhaps, and is altogether insensible of his own misery. The anguish which humanity feels, therefore, at the sight of such an object, cannot be the reflection of any sentiment of the sufferer. The compassion of the spectator must arise altogether from the consideration of what he himself would feel if he was reduced to the same unhappy situation, and, what perhaps is impossible, was at the same time able to regard it with his present reason and judgment.

What are the pangs of a mother when she hears the moanings of her infant that during the agony of disease cannot express what it feels? In her idea of what it suffers, she joins, to its real helplessness, her own consciousness of that helplessness, and her own terrors for the unknown consequences of its disorder; and out of all these, forms, for her own sorrow, the most complete image of misery and distress. The infant, however, feels only the uneasiness of the present instant, which can never be great. With regard to the future it is perfectly secure, and in its thoughtlessness and want of foresight possesses an antidote against fear and anxiety, [8] the great tormentors of the human breast, from which reason and philosophy will in vain attempt to defend it when it grows up to a man.

We sympathize even with the dead, and overlooking what is of real importance in their situation, that awful futurity which awaits them, we are chiefly affected by those circumstances which strike our senses, but can have no influence upon their happiness. It is miserable, we think, to be deprived of the light of the sun; to be shut out from life and conversation; to be laid in the cold grave, a prey to corruption and the reptiles of the earth; to be no more thought of in this world, but to be obliterated in a little time from the affections and almost from the memory of their dearest friends and relations. Surely, we imagine, we can never feel too much for those who have suffered so dreadful a calamity. The tribute of our fellow-feeling seems doubly due to them now, when they are in danger of being forgot by every body; and, by the vain honors which we pay to their memory, we endeavor, for our own misery, artificially to keep alive our melancholy remembrance of their misfortune. That our sympathy can afford them no consolation seems to be an addition to their calamity; and to think that all we can do is unavailing, and that, what alleviates all other distress, the regret, the love, and the lamentations of their friends, can yield no comfort to them, serves only to exasperate our sense of their misery. The happiness of the dead, however, most assuredly, is affected by none of these circumstances; nor is it the thought of these things which can ever [9] disturb the profound security of their repose. The idea of that dreary and endless melancholy, which the fancy naturally ascribes to their condition, arises altogether from our joining to the change which has been produced upon them, our own consciousness of that change, from our putting ourselves in their situation, and from our lodging, if I may be allowed to say so, our own living souls in their inanimated bodies, and thence conceiving what would be our emotions in this case. It is from this very illusion of the imagination, that the foresight of our own dissolution is so terrible to us, and that the idea of those circumstances, which undoubtedly can give us no pain when we are dead, makes us miserable while we are alive. And from thence arises one of the most important principles in human nature, the dread of death, the great poison to the happiness, but the great restraint upon the injustice of mankind, which, while it afflicts and mortifies the individual, guards and protects the society.

CHAP. II.
Of the Pleasure of mutual Sympathy.

But whatever may be the cause of sympathy, or however it may be excited, nothing pleases us more than to observe in other men a fellow-feeling with all the emotions of our own breast; nor are we ever so much shocked as by the appearance of the contrary. Those who are fond of deducing all our sentiments from certain refinements of self-love, [10] think themselves at no loss to account, according to their own principles, both for this pleasure and this pain. Man, say they, conscious of his own weakness and of the need which he has for the assistance of others, rejoices whenever he observes that they adopt his own passions, because he is then assured of that assistance; and grieves whenever he observes the contrary, because he is then assured of their opposition. But both the pleasure and the pain are always felt so instantaneously, and often upon such frivolous occasions, that it seems evident that neither of them can be derived from any such self-interested consideration. A man is mortified when, after having endeavored to divert the company, he looks round and sees that no body laughs at his jests but himself. On the contrary, the mirth of the company is highly agreeable to him, and he regards this correspondence of their sentiments with his own as the greatest applause.

Neither does his pleasure seem to arise altogether from the additional vivacity which his mirth may receive from sympathy with theirs, nor his pain from the disappointment he meets with when he misses this pleasure; though both the one and the other, no doubt, do in some measure. When we have read a book or poem so often that we can no longer find any amusement in reading it by ourselves, we can still take pleasure in reading it to a companion. To him it has all the graces of novelty; we enter into the surprise and admiration which it naturally excites in him, but which it is no longer capable of exciting in us; we consider all the ideas which it presents rather in the light in which they appear to him, than in that in which they appear [11] to ourselves, and we are amused by sympathy with his amusement which thus enlivens our own. On the contrary, we should be vexed if he did not seem to be entertained with it, and we could no longer take any pleasure in reading it to him. It is the same case here. The mirth of the company, no doubt, enlivens our own mirth, and their silence, no doubt, disappoints us. But though this may contribute both to the pleasure which we derive from the one, and to the pain which we feel from the other, it is by no means the sole cause of either; and this correspondence of the sentiments of others with our own appears to be a cause of pleasure, and the want of it a cause of pain, which cannot be accounted for in this manner. The sympathy, which my friends express with my joy, might, indeed, give me pleasure by enlivening that joy: but that which they express with my grief could give me none, if it served only to enliven that grief. Sympathy, however, enlivens joy and alleviates grief. It enlivens joy by presenting another source of satisfaction; and it alleviates grief by insinuating into the heart almost the only agreeable sensation which it is at that time capable of receiving.

It is to be observed accordingly, that we are still more anxious to communicate to our friends our disagreeable than our agreeable passions, that we derive still more satisfaction from their sympathy with the former than from that with the latter, and that we are still more shocked by the want of it.

How are the unfortunate relieved when they have sound out a person to whom they can communicate the cause of their sorrow? Upon his sympathy [12] they seem to disburthen themselves of a part of their distress: he is not improperly said to share it with them. He not only feels a sorrow of the same kind with that which they feel, but as if he had derived a part of it to himself, what he feels seems to alleviate the weight of what they feel. Yet by relating their misfortunes, they in some measure renew their grief. They awaken in their memory the remembrance of those circumstances which occasion their affliction. Their tears accordingly flow faster than before, and they are apt to abandon themselves to all the weakness of sorrow. They take pleasure, however, in all this, and, it is evident, are sensibly relieved by it; because the sweetness of his sympathy more than compensates the bitterness of that sorrow, which, in order to excite that sympathy, they had thus enlivened and renewed. The cruelest insult, on the contrary, which can be offered to the unfortunate, is to appear to make light of their calamities. To seem not to be affected with the joy of our companions is but want of politeness; but not to wear a serious countenance when they tell us their afflictions, is real and gross inhumanity.

Love is an agreeable, resentment a disagreeable passion; and accordingly we are not half so anxious that our friends should adopt our friendships, as that they should enter into our resentments. We can forgive them though they seem to be little affected with the favors which we may have received, but lose all patience if they seem indifferent about the injuries which may have been done to us: nor are we half so angry with them for not entering into our gratitude, as for not sympathizing with our [13] resentment. They can easily avoid being friends to our friends, but can hardly avoid being enemies to those with whom we are at variance. We seldom resent their being at enmity with the first, though upon that account we may sometimes affect to make an awkward quarrel with them; but we quarrel with them in good earnest if they live in friendship with the last. The agreeable passions of love and joy can satisfy and support the heart without any auxiliary pleasure. The bitter and painful emotions of grief and resentment more strongly require the healing consolation of sympathy.

As the person who is principally interested in any event is pleased with our sympathy, and hurt by the want of it, so we, too, seem to be pleased when we are able to sympathize with him, and to be hurt when we are unable to do so. We run not only to congratulate the successful, but to condole with the afflicted; and the pleasure which we find in the conversation of one whom in all the passions of his heart we can entirely sympathize with, seems to do more than compensate the painfulness of that sorrow with which the view of his situation affects us. On the contrary, it is always disagreeable to feel that we cannot sympathize with him, and instead of being pleased with this exemption from sympathetic pain, it hurts us to find that we cannot share his uneasiness. If we hear a person loudly lamenting his misfortunes, which, however, upon bringing the case home to ourselves, we feel, can produce no such violent effect upon us, we are shocked at his grief; and, because we cannot enter into it, call it pusillanimity and weakness. It gives us the spleen, on the other hand, to see another too happy [14] or too much elevated, as we call it, with any little piece of good fortune. We are disobliged even with his joy, and, because we cannot go along with it, call it levity and folly. We are even put out of humor if our companion laughs louder or longer at a joke than we think it deserves; that is, than we feel that we ourselves could laugh at it.

CHAP. III.
Of the manner in which we judge of the propriety or impropriety of the affections of other men, by their concord or dissonance with our own.

When the original passions of the person principally concerned are in perfect concord with the sympathetic emotions of the spectator, they necessarily appear to this last just and proper, and suitable to their objects; and, on the contrary, when, upon bringing the case home to himself, he finds that they do not coincide with what he feels, they necessarily appear to him unjust and improper, and unsuitable to the causes which excite them. To approve of the passions of another, therefore, as suitable to their objects, is the same thing as to observe that we entirely sympathize with them; and not to approve of them as such, is the same thing as to observe that we do not entirely sympathize with them. The man who resents the injuries that have been done to me, and observes that I resent them precisely as he does, necessarily approves of my resentment. The man whose sympathy keeps time to my grief, cannot but admit the reasonableness of my sorrow. He who admires the same poem, or the same picture, and admires them exactly as I do, must surely allow the justness of my admiration. He who laughs at the same joke, and laughs along with me, cannot well deny the propriety of my laughter. On the contrary, the person who, upon these different occasions, either feels no such emotion as that which I feel, or feels none that bears any proportion to mine, cannot avoid disapproving my sentiments on account of their dissonance with his own. If my animosity goes beyond what the indignation of my friend can correspond to; if my grief exceeds what his most tender compassion can go along with; if my admiration is either too high or too low to tally with his own; if I laugh loud and heartily when he only smiles, or, on the contrary, only smile when he laughs loud and heartily; in all these cases, as soon as he comes from considering the object, to observe how I am affected by it, according as there is more or less disproportion between his sentiments and mine, I must incur a greater or less degree of his disapprobation: and upon all occasions his own sentiments are the standards and measures by which he judges of mine.

To approve of another man's opinions is to adopt those opinions, and to adopt them is to approve of them. If the same arguments which convince you convince me likewise, I necessarily approve of your conviction; and if they do not, I necessarily disapprove of it: neither can I possibly conceive that I should do the one without the other. To approve or disapprove, therefore, of the opinions of others is acknowledged, by every body, to mean no more than to observe their agreement or disagreement with our own. But this is equally the case with regard to our approbation or disapprobation of the sentiments or passions of others.

There are, indeed, some cases in which we seem to approve without any sympathy or correspondence of sentiments, and in which, consequently, the sentiment of approbation would seem to be different from the perception of this coincidence. A little attention, however, will convince us that even in these cases our approbation is ultimately founded upon a sympathy or correspondence of this kind. I shall give an instance in things of a very frivolous nature, because in them the judgments of mankind are less apt to be perverted by wrong systems. We may often approve of a jest, and think the laughter of the company quite just and proper, though we ourselves do not laugh, because, perhaps, we are in a grave humour, or happen to have our attention engaged with other objects. We have learned, however, from experience, what sort of pleasantry as upon most occasions capable of making us laugh, and we observe that this is one of that kind. We approve, therefore, of the laughter of the company, and feel that it is natural and suitable to its object; because, though in our present mood we cannot easily enter into it, we are sensible that upon most occasions we should very heartily join in it.

The same thing often happens with regard to all the other passions. A stranger passes by us in the [17] street with all the marks of the deepest affliction; and we are immediately told that he has just received the news of the death of his father. It is impossible that, in this case, we should not approve of his grief. Yet it may often happen, without any defect of humanity on our part, that, so far from entering into the violence of his sorrow, we should scarce conceive the first movements of concern upon his account. Both he and his father, perhaps, are intirely unknown to us, or we happen to be employed about other things, and do not take time to picture out in our imagination the different circumstances of distress which must occur to him. We have learned, however, from experience, that such a misfortune naturally excites such a degree of sorrow, and we know that if we took time to consider his situation, fully and in all its parts, we should, without doubt, most sincerely sympathize with him. It is upon the consciousness of this conditional sympathy, that our approbation of his sorrow is founded, even in those cases in which that sympathy does not actually take place; and the general rules derived from our preceding experience of what our sentiments would commonly correspond with, correct upon this, as upon many other occasions, the impropriety of our present emotions.

The sentiment or affection of the heart from which any action proceeds, and upon which its whole virtue or vice must ultimately depend, may be considered under two different aspects, or in two different relations; first, in relation to the cause which excites it, or the motive which gives occasion to it; and secondly, in relation to the end which it proposes, or the effect which it tends to produce.

[18] In the suitableness or unsuitableness, in the proportion or disproportion which the affection seems to bear to the cause or object which excites it, consists the propriety or impropriety, the decency or ungracefulness of the consequent action.

In the beneficial or hurtful nature of the effects which the affection aims at, or tends to produce, consists the merit or demerit of the action, the qualities by which it is entitled to reward, or is deserving of punishment.

Philosophers have, of late years, considered chiefly the tendency of affections, and have given little attention to the relation which they stand in to the cause which excites them. In common life, however, when we judge of any person's conduct, and of the sentiments which directed it, we constantly consider them under both these aspects. When we blame in another man the excesses of love, of grief, of resentment, we not only consider the ruinous effects which they tend to produce, but the little occasion which was given for them. The merit of his favourite, we say, is not so great, his misfortune is not so dreadful, his provocation is not so extraordinary, as to justify so violent a passion. We should have indulged, we say; perhaps, have approved of the violence of his emotion, had the cause been in any respect proportioned to it.

When we judge in this manner of any affection, as proportioned or disproportioned to the cause which excites it, it is scarce possible that we should make use of any other rule or canon but the correspondent affection in ourselves. If, upon bringing the case [19] home to our own breast, we find that the sentiments which it gives occasion to, coincide and tally with our own, we necessarily approve of them as proportioned and suitable to their objects; if otherwise, we necessarily disapprove of them, as extravagant and out of proportion.

Every faculty in one man is the measure by which he judges of the like faculty in another. I judge of your sight by my sight, of your ear by my ear, of your reason by my reason, of your resentment by my resentment, of your love by my love. I neither have nor can have any other way of judging about them.

CHAP. IV.
The same subject continued.

We may judge of the propriety or impropriety of the sentiments of another person by their correspondence or disagreement with our own, upon two different occasions; either, first, when the objects which excite them are considered without any peculiar relation, either to themselves or to the person whose sentiments we judge of; or, secondly, when they are considered as peculiarly affecting one or other of us.

1. With regard to those objects which are considered without any peculiar relation either to ourselves or to the person whose sentiments we judge of; wherever his sentiments intirely correspond with our own, we ascribe to him the qualities of taste and good judgment. The beauty of a plain, the greatness of a mountain, the ornaments of a building, the expression of a picture, the composition of a discourse, the conduct of a third person, the proportions of different quantities and numbers, the various appearances which the great machine of the universe is perpetually exhibiting, with the secret wheels and springs which produce them; all the general subjects of science and taste, are what we and our companions regard, as having no peculiar relation to either of us. We both look at them from the same point of view, and we have no occasion for sympathy, or for that imaginary change of situations from which it arises, in order to produce, with regard to these, the most perfect harmony of sentiments and affections. If, notwithstanding, we are often differently affected, it arises either from the different degrees of attention, which our different habits of life allow us to give easily to the several parts of those complex objects, or from the different degrees of natural acuteness in the faculty of the mind to which they are addressed.

When the sentiments of our companion coincide with our own in things of this kind, which are obvious and easy, and in which, perhaps, we never found a single person who differed from us, though we, no doubt, must approve of them, yet he seems to deserve no praise or admiration on account of them. But when they not only coincide with our own, but lead and direct our own; when in forming them he appears to have attended to many things which we had overlooked, and to have adjusted them to all the various circumstances of their objects; we not only approve of them, but wonder and are surprised at their uncommon and unexpected acuteness and comprehensiveness, and he appears to deserve a very high degree of admiration and applause. For approbation heightened by wonder and surprise, constitutes the sentiment which is properly palled admiration, and of which applause is the natural expression. The decision of the man who judges that exquisite beauty is preferable to the grossest deformity, or that twice two are equal to four, must certainly be approved of by all the world, but will not, surely, be much admired. It is the acute and delicate discernment of the man of taste, who distinguishes the minute, and scarce perceptible, differences of beauty and deformity; it is the comprehensive accuracy of the experienced mathematician, who unravels, with ease, the most intricate and perplexed proportions; it is the great leader in science and taste, the man who directs and conducts our own sentiments, the extent and superior justness of whose talents astonish us with wonder and surprise, who excites our admiration and seems to deserve our applause: and upon this foundation is grounded the greater part of the praise which is bestowed upon what are called the intellectual virtues.

The utility of those qualities, it may be thought, is what first recommends them to us; and, no doubt, the consideration of this, when we come to attend to it, gives them a new value. Originally, however, 22 we approve of another man's judgment, not as something useful, but as right, as accurate, as agreeable to truth and reality: and it is evident we attribute those qualities to it for no other reason but because we find that it agrees with our own. Taste, in the same manner, is originally approved of, not as useful, but as just, as delicate, and as precisely suited to its object. The idea of the utility of all qualities of this kind, is plainly an after-thought, and not what first recommended them to our approbation.

2. With regard to those objects, which affect in a particular manner either ourselves or the person whose sentiments we judge of, it is at once more difficult to preserve this harmony and correspondence, and at the same time, vastly more important. My companion does not naturally look upon the misfortune that has befallen me, or the injury that has been done me, from the same point of view in which I consider them. They affect me much more nearly. We do not view them from the same station, as we do a picture, or a poem, or a system of philosophy, and are, therefore, apt to be very differently affected by them. But I can much more easily overlook the want of this correspondence of sentiments with regard to such indifferent objects as concern neither me nor my companion, than with regard to what interests me so much as the misfortune that has befallen me, or the injury that has been done me. Though you despise that picture, or that poem, or even that system of philosophy, which I admire, there is little danger of our quarrelling upon that account. Neither of us can reasonably be much interested about them. They ought all of them to be matters of great indifference to us 23 both; so that, though our opinions may be opposite, our affections may still be very nearly the same. But it is quite otherwise with regard to those objects by which either you or I are particularly affected. Though your judgment in matters of speculation, though your sentiments in matters of taste, are quite opposite to mine, I can easily overlook this opposition; and if I have any degree of temper, I may still find some entertainment in your conversation, even upon those very subjects. But if you have either no fellow-feeling for the misfortunes I have met with, or none that bears any proportion to the grief which distracts me, or if you have either no indignation at the injuries I have suffered, or none that bears any proportion to the resentment which transports me, we can no longer converse upon these subjects. We become intolerable to one another. I can neither support your company, nor you mine. You are confounded at my violence and passion, and I am enraged at your cold insensibility and want of feeling.

In all such cases, that there may be some correspondence of sentiments between the spectator and the person principally concerned, the spectator must, first of all, endeavour, as much as he can, to put himself in the situation of the other, and to bring home to himself every little circumstance of distress which can possibly occur to the sufferer. He must adopt the whole case of his companion with all its minutest incidents; and strive to render as perfect as possible, that imaginary change of situation upon which his sympathy is founded.

After all this, however, the emotions of the spectator will still be very apt to fall short of the violence [24] of what is felt by the sufferer. Mankind, though naturally sympathetic, never conceive, for what has befallen another, that degree of passion which naturally animates the person principally concerned. That imaginary change of situation, upon which their sympathy is founded, is but momentary. The thought of their own safety, the thought that they themselves are not really the sufferers, continually intrudes itself upon them; and though it does not hinder them from conceiving a passion somewhat analogous to what is felt by the sufferer, hinders them from conceiving any thing that approaches to the same degree of violence. The person principally concerned is sensible of this, and, at the same time passionately desires a more complete sympathy. He longs for that relief which nothing can afford him but the entire concord of the affections of the spectators with his own. To see the emotions of their hearts, in every respect, beat time to his own, in the violent and disagreeable passions, constitutes his sole consolation. But he can only hope to obtain this by lowering his passion to that pitch, in which the spectators are capable of going along with him. He must flatten, if I may be allowed to say so, the sharpness of its natural tone, in order to reduce it to harmony and concord with the emotions of those who are about him. What they feel, will, indeed, always be, in some respects, different from what he feels, and compassion can never be exactly the same with original sorrow; because the secret consciousness that the change of situations, from which the sympathetic sentiment arises, is but imaginary, not only lowers it in degree, but in some measure, varies it in kind, and gives it a quite different [25] modification. These two sentiments, however, may, it is evident, have such a correspondence with one another, as is sufficient for the harmony of society. Though they will never be unisons, they may be concords, and this is all that is wanted or required.

In order to produce this concord, as nature teaches the spectators to assume the circumstances of the person principally concerned, so she teaches this last in some measure to assume those of the spectators. As they are continually placing themselves in this situation, and thence conceiving emotions similar to what he feels; so he is as constantly placing himself in theirs, and thence conceiving some degree of that coolness about his own fortune, with which he is sensible that they will view it. As they are constantly considering what they themselves would feel, if they actually were the sufferers, so he is as constantly led to imagine in what manner he would be affected if he was only one of the spectators of his own situation. As their sympathy makes them look at it, in some measure, with his eyes, so his sympathy makes him look at it, in some measure, with theirs, especially when in their presence and acting under their observation: and as the reflected passion, which he thus conceives, is much weaker than the original one, it necessarily abates the violence of what he felt before he came into their presence, before he began to recollect in what manner they would be affected by it, and to view his situation in this candid and impartial light.

[26] The mind, therefore, is rarely so disturbed, but that the company of a friend will restore it to some degree of tranquillity and sedateness. The breast is, in some measure, calmed and composed the moment we come into his presence. We are immediately put in mind of the light in which he will view our situation, and we begin to view it ourselves in the

same light; for the effect of sympathy is instantaneous. We expect less sympathy from a common acquaintance than from a friend: we cannot open to the former all those little circumstances which we can unfold to the latter: we assume, therefore, more tranquillity before him, and endeavour to fix our thoughts upon those general outlines of our situation which he is willing to consider. We expect still less sympathy from an assembly of strangers, and we assume, therefore, still more tranquillity before them, and always endeavour to bring down our passion to that pitch, which the particular company we are in may be expected to go along with. Nor is this only an assumed appearance: for if we are at all masters of ourselves, the presence of a mere acquaintance will really compose us, still more than that of a friend; and that of an assembly of strangers still more than that of an acquaintance.

Society and conversation, therefore, are the most powerful remedies for restoring the mind to its tranquillity, if, at any time, it has unfortunately lost it; as well as the best preservatives of that equal and happy temper, which is so necessary to self-satisfaction and enjoyment. Men of retirement and speculation, who are apt to sit brooding at home 27 over either grief or resentment, though they may often have more humanity, more generosity, and a nicer sense of honour, yet seldom possess that equality of temper which is so common among men of the world.

CHAP. V.
Of the amiable and respectable virtues.

Upon these two different efforts, upon that of the spectator to enter into the sentiments of the person principally concerned, and upon that of the person principally concerned, to bring down his emotions to what the spectator can go along with, are founded two different sets of virtues. The soft, the gentle, the amiable virtues, the virtues of candid condescension and indulgent humanity, are founded upon the one: the great, the awful and respectable, the virtues of self-denial, of self-government, of that command of the passions which subjects all the movements of our nature to what our own dignity and honour, and the propriety of our own conduct require, derive their origin from the other.

How amiable does he appear to be, whose sympathetic heart seems to re-echo all the sentiments of those with whom he converses, who grieves for their calamities, who resents their injuries, and rejoices 28 at their good fortune! When we bring home to ourselves the situation of his companions, we enter into their gratitude, and feel what consolation they must derive from the tender sympathy of so affectionate a friend. And for a contrary reason, how disagreeable does he appear to be, whose hard and obdurate heart feels for himself only, but is altogether insensible of the happiness or misery of others! We enter, in this case too, into the pain which his presence must give to every mortal with whom he converses, to those especially with whom we are most apt to sympathize, the unfortunate and the injured.

On the other hand, what noble propriety and grace do we feel in the conduct of those who, in their own case, exert that recollection and self-command which constitute the dignity of every passion, and which bring it down to what others can enter into? We are disgusted with that clamorous grief, which, without any delicacy, calls upon our compassion with sighs and tears and importunate lamentations. But we reverence that reserved, that silent and majestic sorrow, which discovers itself only in the swelling of the eyes, in the quivering of the lips and cheeks, and in the distant, but affecting, coldness of the whole behaviour. It imposes the like silence upon us. We regard it with respectful attention, and watch with anxious concern over our whole behaviour, lest by any impropriety we should disturb that concerted tranquillity, which it requires so great an effort to support.

The insolence and brutality of anger, in the same manner when we indulge its fury without check or 29 restraint, is, of all subjects, the most detestable. But we admire that noble and generous resentment which governs its pursuit of the greatest injuries, not by the rage which they are apt to excite in the breast of the sufferer, but by the indignation which they naturally call forth in that of the impartial spectator; which allows no word, no gesture, to escape it beyond what this more equitable sentiment would dictate; which never, even in thought, attempts any greater vengeance, nor desires to inflict any greater punishment, than what every indifferent person would rejoice to see executed.

And hence it is, that to feel much for others and little for ourselves, that to restrain our selfish, and to indulge our benevolent affections, constitutes the perfection of human nature; and can alone produce among mankind that harmony of sentiments and passions in which consist their whole grace and propriety. As to love our neighbour as we love ourselves is the great law of christianity, so it is the great precept of nature to love ourselves only as we love our neighbour, or what comes to the same thing, as our neighbour is capable of loving us.

As taste and good judgment, when they are considered as qualities which deserve praise and admiration, are supposed to imply a delicacy of sentiment and an acuteness of understanding not commonly to be met with; so the virtues of sensibility and self-command are not apprehended to consist in the ordinary, but in the uncommon degrees of those qualities. The amiable virtue of humanity requires, surely, a sensibility, much beyond what is possessed by the rude vulgar of mankind. The great and 30 exalted virtue of magnanimity undoubtedly demands much more than that degree of self-command, which the weakest of mortals are capable of exerting. As in the common degree of the intellectual qualities, there are no abilities; so in the common degree of the moral, there is no virtue. Virtue is excellence, something uncommonly great and beautiful, which rises far above what is vulgar and ordinary. The amiable virtues consist in that degree of sensibility which surprises by its exquisite and unexpected delicacy and tenderness. The awful and respectable, in that degree of self-command which astonishes by its amazing superiority over the most ungovernable passions of human nature.

There is, in this respect, a considerable difference between virtue and mere propriety; between those qualities and actions which deserve to be admired and celebrated, and those which simply deserve to be approved of. Upon many occasions, to act with the most perfect propriety, requires no more than that common and ordinary degree of sensibility or self-command which the most worthless of mankind are possessed of, and sometimes even that degree is not necessary. Thus, to give a very low instance, to eat when we are hungry, is certainly, upon ordinary occasions, perfectly right and proper, and cannot miss being approved of as such by every body. Nothing, however, could be more absurd than to say it is virtuous.

On the contrary, there may frequently be a considerable degree of virtue in those actions, which fall short of the most perfect propriety; because they may still approach nearer to perfection than 31 could well be expected upon occasions in which it was so extremely difficult to attain it: and this is very often the case upon those occasions which require the greatest exertions of self-command. There are some situations which bear so hard upon human nature, that the greatest degree of self-government, which can belong to so imperfect a creature as man, is not able to stifle, altogether, the voice of human weakness, or reduce the violence of the passions to that pitch of moderation, in which the impartial spectator can entirely enter into them. Though in those cases, therefore, the behaviour of the sufferer fall short of the most perfect propriety, it may still deserve some applause, and even in a certain sense, may be denominated virtuous. It may still manifest an effort or generosity and magnanimity of which the greater part of men are incapable; and though it fails of absolute perfection, it may be a much nearer approximation towards perfection, than what, upon such trying occasions, is commonly either to be found or to be expected.

In cases of this kind, when we are determining the degree of blame or applause which seems due to any action, we very frequently make use of two different standards. The first is the idea of complete propriety and perfection, which, in those difficult situations, no human conduct ever did, or even can come up to; and in comparison with which the actions of all men must for ever appear blameable and imperfect. The second is the idea of that degree of proximity or distance from this complete perfection, which the actions of the greater part of men commonly arrive at. Whatever goes beyond this degree, how far soever it may be removed 32 from absolute perfection, seems to deserve applause; and whatever falls short of it, to deserve blame.

It is in the same manner that we judge of the productions of all arts which address themselves to the imagination. When a critic examines the work of any of the great masters for poetry or painting, he may sometimes examine it by an idea of perfection, in his own mind, which neither that nor any other human work will ever come up to; and as long as he compares it with this standard, he can see nothing in it but faults and imperfections. But when he come to consider the rank which it ought to hold among other works of the same kind, he necessarily compares it with a very different standard, the common degree of excellence which is usually attained in this particular art; and when he judges of it by this new measure, it may often appear to deserve the highest applause, upon account of its approaching much nearer to perfection than the greater part of those works which can be brought into competition with it.

33

SECTION II.
Of the degrees of the different passions which are consistent with propriety.

INTRODUCTION.

The propriety of every passion excited by objects peculiarly related to ourselves the pitch which the spectator can go along with, must lie, it is evident, in certain mediocrity. If the passion is too high, or if it is too low, he cannot enter into it. Grief and resentment for private misfortunes and injuries may easily, for example, be too high, and in the greater part of mankind they are so. They may likewise, though this more rarely happens, be too low. We denominate the excess, weakness and fury: and we call the defect, stupidity, insensibility, and want of spirit. We can enter into neither of them, but are astonished and confounded to see them.

This mediocrity, however, in which the point of propriety consists, is different in different passions. It is high in some, and low in others. There are some passions which it is indecent to express very strongly, even upon those occasions, in which it is ⟨34⟩ acknowledged that we cannot avoid feeling them in the highest degree. And there are others of which the strongest expressions are upon many occasions extremely graceful, even though the passions themselves do not, perhaps, arise so necessarily. The first are those passions with which, for certain reasons, there is little or no sympathy: the second are those with which, for other reasons, there is the greatest. And if we consider all the different passions of human nature, we shall find that they are regarded as decent, or indecent, just in proportion as mankind are more or less disposed to sympathize with them.

CHAP. I.
Of the passions which take their origin from the body.

1.It is indecent to express any strong degree of those passions which arise from a certain situation or disposition of the body; because the company, not being in the same disposition, cannot be expected to sympathize with them. Violent hunger, for example, though upon many occasions not only natural, but unavoidable, is always indecent, and to eat voraciously is universally regarded as a piece of ill manners. There is, however, some degree of sympathy, even with hunger. It is agreeable to see our companions eat with a good appetite, and all ⟨35⟩ expressions of loathing are offensive. The disposition of body which is habitual to a man in health, makes his stomach easily keep time, if I may be allowed so coarse an expression, with the one, and not with the other. We can sympathize with the distress which excessive hunger occasions when we read the description of it in the journal of a siege, or of a sea voyage. We imagine ourselves in the situation of the sufferers, and thence readily conceive the grief, the fear and consternation, which must necessarily distract them. We feel, ourselves, some degree of those passions, and therefore sympathize with them: but as we do not grow hungry by reading the description, we cannot properly, even in this case, be said to sympathize with their hunger.

It is the same case with the passion by which Nature unites the two sexes. Though naturally the most furious of all passions, all strong expressions of it are upon every occasion indecent, even between persons in whom its most complete indulgence is acknowledged by all laws, both human and divine, to be perfectly innocent. There seems, however, to be some degree of sympathy even with this passion. To talk to a woman as we should to a man is improper: it is expected that their company should inspire us with more gaiety, more pleasantry, and more attention; and an entire insensibility to the fair sex, renders a man contemptible in some measure even to the men.

Such is our aversion for all the appetites which take their origin from the body: all strong expressions of them are loathsome and disagreeable. According 36 to some ancient philosophers, these are the passions which we share in common with the brutes, and which having no connexion with the characteristical qualities of human nature, are upon that account beneath its dignity. But there are many other passions which we share in common with the brutes, such as resentment, natural affection, even gratitude, which do not, upon that account, appear to be so brutal. The true cause of the peculiar disgust which we conceive for the appetites of the body when we see them in other men, is that we cannot enter into them. To the person himself who feels them, as soon as they are gratified, the object that excited them ceases to be agreeable: even its presence often becomes offensive to him; he looks round to no purpose for the charm which transported him the moment before, and he can now as little enter into his own passion as another person. When we have dined, we order the covers to be removed; and we should treat in the same manner the objects of the most ardent and passionate desires, if they were the objects of no other passions but those which take their origin from the body.

In the command of those appetites of the body consists that virtue which is properly called temperance. To restrain them within those bounds, which regard to health and fortune prescribes, is the part of prudence. But to confine them within those limits, which grace, which propriety, which delicacy, and modesty, require, is the office of temperance.

2. It is for the same reason that to cry out with bodily pain, how intolerable soever, appears always 37 unmanly and unbecoming. There is, however, a good deal of sympathy even with bodily pain. If, as has already been observed, I see a stroke aimed, and just ready to fall upon the leg or arm, of another person, I naturally shrink and draw back my own leg, or my own arm; and when it does fall, I feel it in some measure, and am hurt by it as well as the sufferer. My hurt, however, is, no doubt, excessively slight, and, upon that account, if he makes any violent out-cry, as I cannot go along with him, I never fail to despise him. And this is the case of all the passions which take their origin from the body: they excite either no sympathy at all, or such a degree of it, as is altogether disproportioned to the violence of what is felt by the sufferer.

It is quite otherwise with those passions which take their origin from the imagination. The frame of my body can be but little affected by the alterations which are brought about upon that of my companion: but my imagination is more ductile, and more readily assumes, if I may so, the shape and configuration of the imaginations of those with whom I am familiar. A disappointment in love, or ambition, will, upon this account, call forth more sympathy than the greatest bodily evil. Those passions arise altogether from the imagination. The person who has lost his whole fortune, if he is in health, feels nothing in his body. What he suffers is from the imagination only, which represents to him the loss of his dignity, neglect from his friends, contempt from his enemies, dependence, want, and misery, coming fast upon him; and we sympathize with him more strongly upon this account, because our imaginations can more readily mould themselves 38 upon his imagination, than our bodies can mould themselves upon his body.

The loss of a leg may generally be regarded as a more real calamity than the loss of a mistress. It would be a ridiculous tragedy, however, of which the catastrophe was to turn upon a loss of that kind. A misfortune of the other kind, how frivolous soever it may appear to be, has given occasion to many a fine one.

Nothing is so soon forgot as pain. The moment it is gone the whole agony of it is over, and the thought of it can no longer give us any sort of disturbance. We ourselves cannot then enter into the anxiety and anguish which we had before conceived. An unguarded word from a friend will occasion a more durable uneasiness. The agony which this creates is by no means over with the word. What at first disturbs us is not the object of the senses, but the idea of the imagination. As it is an idea, therefore, which occasions our uneasiness, till time and other accidents have in some measure effaced it from our memory, the imagination continues to fret and rankle within, from the thought of it.

Pain never calls forth any very lively sympathy unless it is accompanied with danger. We sympathize with the fear, though not with the agony of the sufferer. Fear, however, is a passion derived altogether from the imagination, which represents, with an uncertainty and fluctuation that increases our anxiety, not what we really feel, but what we may hereafter possibly suffer. The gout or the tooth-ache, though exquisitely painful, excite very little sympathy; more dangerous diseases, though accompanied with very little pain, excite the highest.

Some people faint and grow sick at the sight of a chirurgical operation, and that bodily pain which is occasioned by tearing the flesh, seems, in them, to excite the most excessive sympathy. We conceive in a much more lively and distinct manner, the pain which proceeds from an external cause, than we do that which arises from an internal disorder. I can scarce form an idea of the agonies of my neighbour when he is tortured with the gout, or the stone; but I have the clearest conception of what he must suffer from an incision, a wound, or a fracture. The chief cause, however, why such objects produce such violent effects upon us, is their novelty. Once who has been witness to a dozen dissections, and as many amputations, sees, ever after, all operations of this kind with great indifference, and often with perfect insensibility. Though we have read or seen represented more than five hundred tragedies, we shall seldom feel so entire an abatement of our sensibility to the object which they represent to us.

In some of the Greek tragedies there is an attempt to excite compassion, by the representation of the agonies of bodily pain. Philoctetes cries out and faints from the extremity of his sufferings. Hippolytus and Hercules are both introduced as expiring under the severest tortures, which, it seems, even the fortitude of Hercules was incapable of supporting. In all these cases, however, it is not the pain which interests us, but some other circumstance. It is not the sore foot, but the solitude, of Philoctetes which affects us, and diffuses over that charming tragedy, that romantic wildness, which is so agreeable to the imagination. The agonies of Hercules and Hippolytus are interested only because we foresee that death is to be the consequence. If those heroes were to recover, we should think the representation of their sufferings perfectly ridiculous. What a tragedy would that be of which the distress consisted in a colic. Yet no pain is more exquisite. These attempts to excite compassion by the representation of bodily pain, may be regarded as among the greatest breaches of decorum of which the Greek theatre has set the example.

The little sympathy which we feel with bodily pain is the foundation of the propriety of constancy and patience in enduring it. The man, who under the severest tortures allows no weakness to escape him, vents no groan, gives way to no passion which we do not entirely enter into, commands our highest admiration. His firmness enables him to keep time with our indifference and insensibility. We admire and entirely go along with the magnanimous effort which he makes for this purpose. We approve of his behaviour, and from our experience of the common weakness of human nature, we are surprised, and wonder how he should be able to act so as to deserve approbation. Approbation, mixed and animated by wonder and surprise, constitutes the sentiment which is properly called admiration, of which, applause is the natural expression, as has already been observed.

41

CHAP. II.
Of those passions which take their origin from a particular turn or habit of the imagination.

Even of the passions derived from the imagination, those which take their origin from a peculiar turn or habit it has acquired, though they may be acknowledged to be perfectly natural, are, however, but little sympathized with. The imaginations of mankind, not having acquired that particular turn, cannot enter into them; and such passions, though they may be allowed to be almost unavoidable in some part of life, are always in some measure ridiculous. This is the case with that strong attachment which naturally grows up between two persons of different sexes, who have long fixed their thoughts upon one another. Our imagination not having run in the same channel with that of the lover, we cannot enter into the eagerness of his emotions. If our friend has been injured, we readily sympathize with his resentment, and grow angry with the very person with whom he is angry. If he has received a benefit, we readily enter into his gratitude, and have a very high sense of the merit of his benefactor. But if he is in love, though we may think his passion just as reasonable as any of the kind, yet we never think ourselves bound to conceive a passion of the same kind, and for the same person for whom he has conceived it. The passion appears to every body, but the man who feels it, entirely disproportioned 42 to the value of the object; and love, though it is pardoned in a certain age because we know it is natural, is always laughed at, because we cannot enter into it. All serious and strong expressions of it appear ridiculous to a third person; and though a lover may be good company to his mistress, he is so to nobody else. He himself is sensible of this; and as long as he continues in his sober senses, endeavours to treat his own passion with raillery and ridicule. It is the only style in which we care to hear of it; because it is the only style in which we ourselves are disposed to talk of it. We grow weary of the grave, pedantic, and long-sentenced love of Cowley and Propertius, who never have done with exaggerating the violence of their attachments; but the gaiety of Ovid, and the gallantry of Horace, are always agreeable.

But though we feel no proper sympathy with an attachment of this kind, though we never approach even in imagination towards conceiving a passion for that particular person, yet as we either have conceived, or may be disposed to conceive, passions of the same kind, we readily enter into those high hopes of happiness which are proposed from its gratification, as well as into that exquisite distress which is feared from its disappointment. It interests us not as a passion, but as a situation that gives occasion to other passions which interest us; to hope, to fear, and to distress of every kind: in the same manner as in a description of a sea voyage, it is not the hunger which interests us, but the distress which that hunger occasions. Though we do not properly enter into the attachment of the lover, we readily go along with those expectations of romantic happiness which he derives from it. We feel how natural it is for the mind, in a certain situation, relaxed with indolence, and fatigued with the violence of desire, to long for serenity and quiet, to hope to find them in the gratification of that passion which distracts it, and to frame to itself the idea of that life of pastoral tranquillity and retirement which the elegant, the tender, and the passionate Tibullus takes so much pleasure in deferring; a life like what the poets describe in the Fortunate Islands, a life of friendship, liberty, and repose; free from labour, and from care, and from all the turbulent passions which attend them. Even scenes of this kind interest us most, when they are painted rather as what is hoped, than as what is enjoyed. The grossness of that passion which mixes with, and is, perhaps, the foundation of love, disappears when its gratification is far off and at a distance; but renders the whole offensive, when described as what is immediately possessed. The happy passion, upon this account, interests us much less than the fearful and the melancholy. We tremble for whatever can disappoint such natural and agreeable hopes: and thus enter into all the anxiety, and concern, and distress of the lover.

Hence it is, that, in some modern tragedies and romances, this passion appears so wonderfully interesting. It is not so much the love of Castalio and Monimia which attaches us in the Orphan, as the distress which that love occasions. The author who should introduce two lovers, in a scene of perfect security, expressing their mutual fondness for one another, would excite laughter, and not sympathy. If a scene of this kind is ever admitted into a tragedy, it is always, in some measure, improper, and is endured, not from any sympathy with the passion that is expressed in it, but from concern for the dangers and difficulties with which the audience foresee that its gratification is likely to be attended.

The reserve which the laws of society impose upon the fair sex, with regard to this weakness, renders it more peculiarly distressful in them, and, upon that very account, more deeply interesting. We are charmed with the love of Phædra, as it is expressed in the French tragedy of that name, notwithstanding all the extravagance and guilt which attends it. That very extravagance and guilt may be said, in some measure, to recommend it to us. Her fear, her shame, her remorse, her horror, her despair, become thereby more natural and interesting. All the secondary passions, if I may be allowed to call them so, which arise from the situation of love, become necessarily more furious and violent: and it is with these secondary passions only that we can properly be said to sympathize.

Of all the passions, however, which are so extravagantly disproportioned to the value of their objects, love is the only one that appears, even to the weakest minds, to have any thing in it that is either graceful or agreeable. In itself, first of all, though it may be ridiculous, it is not naturally odious; and though its consequences are often fatal and dreadful, its intentions are seldom mischievous. And then, though there is little propriety in the passion itself, there is a good deal in some of those which always accompany it. There is in love a strong mixture of humanity, generality, kindness, friendship, esteem; passions with which, of all others, for reasons which shall be explained immediately, we have the greatest propensity to sympathize, even notwithstanding we are sensible that they are, in some measure, excessive. The sympathy which we feel with them, renders the passion which they accompany less disagreeable, and supports it in our imagination, notwithstanding all the vices which commonly go along with it; though in the one sex it necessarily leads to ruin and infamy; and though in the other, where it is apprehended to be least fatal, it is almost always attended with an incapacity for labour, a neglect of duty, a contempt of fame, and even of common reputation. Notwithstanding all this, the degree of sensibility and generosity with which it is supposed to be accompanied, renders it to many the object of vanity; and they are fond of appearing capable of feeling what would do them no honour if they had really felt it.

It is for a reason of the same kind, that a certain reserve is necessary when we talk of our own friends, our own studies, our own professions. All these are objects which we cannot expect should interest our companions in the same degree in which they interest us. And it is for want of this reserve, that the one half of mankind make bad company to the other. A philosopher is company to a philosopher only; the member of a club, to his own little knot of companions.

46

CHAP. III.
Of the unsocial passions.

There is another set of passions, which though derived from the imagination, yet before we can enter into them, or regard them as graceful or becoming, must always be brought down to a pitch much lower than that to which undisciplined nature would raise them. These are hatred and resentment, with all their different modifications. With regard to all such passions, our sympathy is divided between the person who feels them and the person who is the object of them. The interests of these two are directly opposite. What our sympathy with the person who feels them would prompt us to wish for, our fellow-feeling with the other would lead us to fear. As they are both men, we are concerned for both, and our fear for what the one may suffer, damps our resentment for what the other has suffered. Our sympathy, therefore, with the man who has received the provocation, necessarily falls short of the passion which naturally animates him, not only upon account of those general causes which render all sympathetic passions inferior to the original ones, but upon account of that particular cause which is peculiar to itself, our opposite sympathy 47 with another person. Before resentment, therefore, can become graceful and agreeable, it must be more humbled and brought down below that pitch to which it would naturally rise, than almost any other passion.

Mankind, at the same time, have a very strong sense of the injuries that are done to another. The villain, in a tragedy or romance, is as much the object of our indignation, as the hero is that of our sympathy and affection. We detest Iago as much as we esteem Othello; and delight as much in the punishment of the one, as we are grieved at the distress of the other. But though mankind have so strong a fellow-feeling with the injuries that are done to their brethren, they do not always resent them the more that the sufferer appears to resent them. Upon most occasions, the greater his patience, his mildness, his humanity, provided it does not appear that he wants spirit, or that fear was the motive of his forbearance, the higher the resentment against the person who injured him. The amiableness of the character exasperates their sense of the atrocity of the injury.

These passions, however, are regarded as necessary parts of the character of human nature. A person becomes contemptible who tamely sits still, and submits to insults, without attempting either to repel or to revenge them. We cannot enter into his indifference and insensibility: we call his behaviour mean-spiritedness, and are as really provoked by it as by the insolence of his adversary. Even the mob are enraged to see any man submit patiently to affronts and ill usage. They desire to see this insolence resented, 48 and resented by the person who suffers from it. They cry to him with fury, to defend, or to revenge himself. If his indignation rouses at last, they heartily applaud, and sympathize with it. It enlivens their own indignation against his enemy, whom they rejoice to see him attack in turn, and are as really gratified by his revenge, provided it is not immoderate, as if the injury had been done to themselves.

But though the utility of those passions to the individual, by rendering it dangerous to insult or injure him, be acknowledged; and though their utility to the public, as the guardians of justice, and of the equality of its administration, be not less considerable, as shall be shewn hereafter; yet there is still something disagreeable in the passions themselves, which makes the appearance of them in other men the natural object of our aversion. The expression of anger towards any body present, if it exceeds a bare intimation that we are sensible of his ill usage, is regarded not only as an insult to that particular person, but as a rudeness to the whole company. Respect for them ought to have restrained us from giving way to so boisterous and offensive an emotion. It is the remote effects of these passions which are agreeable; the immediate effects are mischief to the person against whom they are directed. But it is the immediate, and not the remote effects of objects which render them agreeable or disagreeable to the imagination. A prison is certainly more useful to the public than a palace; and the person who founds the one is generally directed by a much juster spirit of patriotism, than he who builds the other. But the immediate effects of a prison, the 49 confinement of the wretches shut up in it, are disagreeable; and the imagination either does not take time to trace out the remote ones, or sees them at too great a distance to be much affected by them. A prison, therefore, will always be a disagreeable object; and the fitter it is for the purpose for which it was intended, it will be the more so. A palace, on the contrary, will always be agreeable; yet its remote effects may often be inconvenient to the public. It may serve to promote luxury, and set the example of the dissolution of manners. Its immediate effects, however, the conveniency, the pleasure, and the gaiety of the people who live in it, being all agreeable, and suggesting to the imagination a thousand agreeable ideas, that faculty generally rests upon them, and seldom goes further in tracing its more distant consequences. Trophies of the instruments of music or of agriculture, imitated in painting or in stucco, make a common and an agreeable ornament of our halls and dining-rooms. A trophy of the same kind, composed of the instruments of surgery, of dissecting and amputation-knives, of saws for cutting the bones, of trepanning instruments, &c. would be absurd and shocking. Instruments of surgery, however, are always more finely polished, and generally more nicely adapted to the purposes for which they are intended, than instruments of agriculture. The remote effects of them too, the health of the patient, is agreeable, yet as the immediate effect of them is pain and suffering, the sight of them always displeases us. Instruments of war are agreeable, though their immediate effect may seem to be in the same manner pain and suffering. But then it is the pain and suffering of our enemies, with whom we have no sympathy. [50]With regard to us, they are immediately connected with the agreeable ideas of courage, victory, and honour. They are themselves, therefore, supposed to make one of the noblest parts of dress, and the imitation of them one of the finest ornaments of architecture. It is the same case with the qualities of the mind. The ancient stoics were of opinion, that as the world was governed by the all-ruling providence of a wise, powerful, and good God, every single event ought to be regarded, as making a necessary part of the plan of the universe, and as tending to promote the general order and happiness of the whole: that the vices and follies of mankind, therefore, made as necessary a part of this plan as their wisdom or their virtue; and by that eternal art which educes good from ill, were made to tend equally to the prosperity and perfection of the great system of nature. No speculation of this kind, however, how deeply soever it might be rooted in the mind, could diminish our natural abhorrence for vice, whose immediate effects are so destructive, and whose remote ones are too distant to be traced by the imagination.

It is the same case with those passions we have been just now considering. Their immediate effects are so disagreeable, that even when they are most justly provoked, there is still something about them which disgusts us. These, therefore, are the only passions of which the expressions, as I formerly observed, do not dispose and prepare us to sympathize with them, before we are informed of the cause which excites them. The plaintive voice of misery, when heard at a distance, will not allow us to be indifferent about the person from whom it comes. [51]As soon as it strikes our ear, it interests us in his fortune, and, if continued, forces us almost involuntarily to fly to his assistance. The sight of a smiling countenance, in the same manner, elevates even the pensive into that gay and airy mood, which disposes him to sympathize with, and share the joy which it expresses; and he feels his heart, which with thought and care was before that shrunk and depressed, instantly expanded and elated. But it is quite otherwise with the expressions of hatred and resentment. The hoarse, boisterous, and discordant voice of anger, when heard at a distance, inspires us either with fear or aversion. We do not fly towards it, as to one who cries out with pain and agony. Women, and men of weak nerves, tremble and are overcome with fear, though sensible that themselves are not the objects of the anger. They conceive fear, however, by putting themselves in the situation of the person who is so. Even those of stouter hearts are disturbed; not indeed enough to make them afraid, but enough to make them angry; for anger is the passion which they would feel in the situation of the other person. It is the same case with hatred. Mere expressions of spite inspire it against no body, but the man who uses them. Both these passions are by nature the objects of our aversion. Their disagreeable and boisterous appearance never excites, never prepares, and often disturbs our sympathy. Grief does not more powerfully engage and attract us to the person in whom we observe it, than these, while we are ignorant of their cause, disgust and detach us from him. It was, it seems, the intention of Nature, that those rougher and more unamiable emotions, which drive men from one another, should be less easily and more rarely communicated.

[52]When music imitates the modulations of grief or joy, it either actually inspires us with those passions, or at least puts us in the mood which disposes us to conceive them. But

when it imitates the notes of anger, it inspires us with fear. Joy, grief, love, admiration, devotion, are all of them passions which are naturally musical. Their natural tones are all soft, clear, and melodious; and they naturally express themselves in periods which are distinguished by regular pauses, and which upon that account are easily adapted to the regular returns of the correspondent airs of a tune. The voice of anger, on the contrary, and of all the passions which are akin to it, is harsh and discordant. It periods too are all irregular, sometimes very long, and sometimes very short, and distinguished by no regular pauses. It is with difficulty, therefore, that music can imitate any of those passions; and the music which does imitate them is not the most agreeable. A whole entertainment may consist, without any impropriety, of the imitation of the social and agreeable passions. It would be a strange entertainment which consisted altogether of the imitations of hatred and resentment.

If those passions are disagreeable to the spectator, they are not less so to the person who feels them. Hatred and anger are the greatest poison to the happiness of a good mind. There is, in the very feeling of those passions, something harsh, jarring, and convulsive, something that tears and distracts the breast, and is altogether destructive of that composure and tranquillity of mind which is so necessary to happiness, and which is best promoted by the contrary passions of gratitude and love. It is not the value of what they lose by the perfidy and ingratitude of those they live with, which the generous and humane are most apt to regret. Whatever they may have lost, they can generally be very happy without it. What most disturbs them is the idea of perfidy and ingratitude exercised towards themselves; and the discordant and disagreeable passions which this excites, constitutes, in their own opinion, the chief part of the injury which they suffer.

How many things are requisite to render the gratification of resentment compleatly agreeable, and to make the spectator thoroughly sympathize with our revenge? The provocation must first of all be such that we should become contemptible, and be exposed to perpetual insults, if we did not, in some measure, resent it. Smaller offences are always better neglected; nor is there any thing more despicable than that froward and captious humour which takes fire upon every slight occasion of quarrel. We should resent more from a sense of the propriety of resentment, from a sense that mankind expect and require it of us, than because we feel in ourselves the furies of that disagreeable passion. There is no passion, of which the human mind is capable, concerning whose justness we ought to be so doubtful, concerning whose indulgence we ought so carefully to consult our natural sense of propriety, or so diligently to consider what will be the sentiments of the impartial spectator. Magnanimity, or a regard to maintain our own rank and dignity in society, is the only motive which can ennoble the expressions of this disagreeable passion. This motive must characterize our whole stile and deportment. These must be plain, open, and direct; determined without positiveness, and elevated without insolence; not only free from petulance and low scurrility, but generous, candid, and full of all proper regards, even for the person who has offended us. It must appear, in short, from our whole manner, without our labouring affectedly to express it, that passion has not extinguished our humanity; and that if we yield to the dictates of revenge, it is with reluctance, from necessity, and in consequence of great and repeated provocations. When resentment is guarded and qualified in this manner, it may be admitted to be even generous and noble.

CHAP. IV.
Of the social passions.

As it is a divided sympathy which renders the whole set of passions just now mentioned, upon most occasions, so ungraceful and disagreeable; so there is another set opposite to these, which a redoubled sympathy renders almost always peculiarly agreeable and becoming. Generosity, humanity, kindness, compassion, mutual friendship and esteem, all the social and benevolent affections, when expressed in the countenance or behaviour, even towards [55] those who are peculiarly connected with ourselves, please the indifferent spectator upon almost every occasion. His sympathy with the person who feels those passions, exactly coincides with his concern for the person who is the object of them. The interest, which, as a man, he is obliged to take in the happiness of this last, enlivens his fellow-feeling with the sentiments of the other, whose emotions are employed about the same object. We have always, therefore, the strongest disposition to sympathize with the benevolent affections. They appear in every respect agreeable to us. We enter into the satisfaction both of the person who feels them, and of the person who is the object of them. For as to be the object of hatred and indignation gives more pain than all the evils which a brave man can fear from his enemies; so there is a satisfaction in the consciousness of being beloved, which, to a person of delicacy and sensibility, is of more importance to happiness than all the advantage which he can expect to derive from it. What character is so detectable as that of one who takes pleasure to sow dissension among friends, and to turn their most tender love into mortal hatred? Yet wherein does the atrocity of this so much abhorred injury consist? Is it in depriving them of the frivolous good offices, which had their friendship continued, they might have expected from one another? It is in depriving them of that friendship itself, in robbing them of each others affections, from which both derived so much satisfaction; it is in disturbing the harmony of their hearts, and putting an end to that happy commerce which had before subsisted between them. These affections, that harmony, this commerce, are felt, not only by the tender and the delicate, but by [56] the rudest vulgar of mankind, to be of more importance to happiness than all the little services which could be expected to flow from them.

The sentiment of love is, in itself, agreeable to the person who feels it. It sooths and composes the breast, seems to favour the vital motions, and to promote the healthful state of the human constitution; and it is rendered still more delightful by the consciousness of the gratitude and satisfaction which it must excite in him who is the object of it. Their mutual regard renders them happy in one another, and sympathy, with this mutual regard, makes them agreeable to every other person. With what pleasure do we look upon a family, through the whole of which reign mutual love and esteem, where the parents and children are companions for one another, without any other difference than what is made by respectful affection on the one side, and kind indulgence on the other; where freedom and fondness, mutual raillery, and mutual kindness, show that no opposition of interest divides the brothers, nor any rivalship of favour sets the sisters at variance, and where every thing presents us with the idea of peace, chearfulness, harmony, and contentment? On the contrary, how uneasy are we made when we go into a house in which jarring contention sets one half of those who dwell in it against the other; where amidst affected smoothness and complaisance, suspicious looks and sudden starts of passion betray the mutual jealousies which burn within them, and which are every moment ready to burst out through all the restraints which the presence of the company imposes?

Those amiable passions, even when they are acknowledged to be excessive, are never regarded with aversion. There is something agreeable even in the weakness of friendship and humanity. The too tender mother, the too indulgent father, the too generous and affectionate friend, may sometimes, perhaps, on account of the softness of their natures, be looked upon with a species of pity, in which, however, there is a mixture of love, but can never be regarded with hatred and aversion, nor even with contempt, unless by the most brutal and worthless of mankind: It is always with concern, with sympathy and kindness, that we blame them for the extravagance of their attachment. There is a helplessness in the character of extreme humanity which more than any thing interests our pity. There is nothing in itself which renders it either ungraceful or disagreeable. We only regret that it is unfit for the world, because the world is unworthy of it, and because it must expose the person who is endowed with it as a prey to the perfidy and ingratitude of insinuating falsehood, and to a thousand pains and uneasinesses, which, of all men, he the least deserves to feel, and which generally too he is, of all men, the least capable of supporting. It is quite otherwise with hatred and resentment. Too violent a propensity to those detestable passions, renders a person the object of universal dread and abhorrence, who, like a wild beast, ought, we think, to be hunted out of all civil society.

CHAP. V.
Of the selfish passions.

Besides those two opposite sets of passions, the social and unsocial, there is another which holds a sort of middle place between them; is never either so graceful as is sometimes the one set, nor is ever so odious as is sometimes the other. Grief and joy, when conceived upon account of our own private good or bad fortune, constitute this third set of passions. Even when excessive, they are never so disagreeable as excessive resentment, because no opposite sympathy can ever interest us against them: and when most suitable to their objects they are never so agreeable as impartial humanity and just benevolence; because no double sympathy can ever interest us for them. There is, however, this difference between grief and joy, that we are generally most disposed to sympathize with small joys and great sorrows. The man, who, by some sudden revolution of fortune, is lifted up all at once into a condition of life, greatly above what he had formerly lived in, may be assured that the congratulations of his best friends are not all of them perfectly sincere. An upstart, though of the greatest merit, is generally disagreeable, and a sentiment of envy commonly prevents us from heartily sympathizing with his joy. If he has any judgment he is sensible of this, and instead of appearing to be elated with his good fortune, he endeavours, as much as he can, to smother his joy, and keep down that elevation of mind with which his new circumstances naturally inspire him. He affects the same plainness of dress, and the same modesty of behaviour, which became him in his former station. He redoubles his attention to his old friends, and endeavours more than ever to be humble, assiduous, and complaisant. And this is the behaviour which in his situation we most approve of; because we expect, it seems, that he should have more sympathy with our envy and aversion to his happiness, than we have with his happiness. It is seldom that with all this he succeeds. We suspect the sincerity of his humility, and he grows weary of this constraint. In a little time, therefore, he generally leaves all his old friends behind him, some of the meanest of them excepted, who may, perhaps, condescend to become his dependents: nor does he always acquire any new ones; the pride of his new connections is as much affronted at finding him their equal, as that of his old ones had been by his becoming their superior: and it requires the most obstinate and persevering modesty to atone for this mortification to either. He generally grows weary too soon, and is provoked, by the sullen and suspicious pride of the one, and by the saucy contempt of the other, to treat the first with neglect, and the second with petulance, till at last he grows habitually insolent, and forfeits the esteem of all. If the chief part of human happiness arises from the consciousness of being beloved, as I believe it does, those sudden changes of fortune seldom contribute much to happiness. He is happiest who advances more gradually to greatness, [60] whom the public destines to every step of his preferment long before he arrives at it, in whom, upon that account, when it comes, it can excite no extravagant joy, and with regard to whom it cannot reasonably create either any jealousy in those he overtakes, or any envy in those he leaves behind.

Mankind, however, more readily sympathize with those smaller joys which flow from less important causes. It is decent to be humble amidst great prosperity; but we can scarce express too much satisfaction in all the little occurrences of common life, in the company with which we spent the evening last night, in the entertainment that was set before us, in what was said and what was done, in all the little incidents of the present conversation, and in all those frivolous nothings which fill up the void of human life. Nothing is more graceful than habitual chearfulness, which is always founded upon a peculiar relish for all the little pleasures which common occurrences afford. We readily sympathize with it: it inspires us with the same joy, and makes every trifle turn up to us in the same agreeable aspect in which it presents itself to the person endowed with this happy disposition. Hence it is that youth, the season of gaiety, so easily engages our affections. That propensity to joy which seems even to animate the bloom, and to sparkle from the eyes of youth and beauty, though in a person of the same sex, exalts, even the aged, to a more joyous mood than ordinary. They forget, for a time, their infirmities, and abandon themselves to those agreeable ideas and emotions to which they have long been strangers, but which, when the presence [61] of so much happiness recalls them to their breast, take their place there, like old acquaintance, from whom they are sorry to have ever been parted, and whom they embrace more heartily upon account of this long separation.

It is quite otherwise with grief. Small vexations excite no sympathy, but deep affliction calls forth the greatest. The man who is made uneasy by every little disagreeable incident, who is hurt if either the cook or the butler have failed in the least article of their duty, who feels every defect in the highest ceremonial of politeness, whether it be shewn to himself or to any other person, who takes it amiss that his intimate friend did not bid him good-morrow when they met in the forenoon, and that his brother hummed a tune all the time he himself was telling a story; who is put out of humour by the badness of the weather when in the country, by the badness of the roads when upon a journey, and by the want of company, and dullness of all public diversions when in town; such a person, I say, though he should have some reason, will seldom meet with much sympathy. Joy is a pleasant emotion, and we gladly abandon ourselves to it upon the slightest occasion. We readily, therefore, sympathize with it in others, whenever we are not prejudiced by envy. But grief is painful, and the mind, even when it is our own misfortune, naturally resists and recoils from it. We would endeavour either not to conceive it at all, or to shake it off as soon as we have conceived it. Our aversion to grief will not, indeed, always hinder us from conceiving it in our own case upon very trifling occasions, [62]but it constantly prevents us from sympathizing with it in others when excited by the like frivolous causes: for our sympathetic passions are always less irresistible than our original ones. There is, besides, a malice in mankind, which not only prevents all sympathy with little uneasinesses, but renders them in some measure diverting. Hence the delight which we all take in raillery, and in the small vexation which we observe in our companion, when he is pushed, and urged, and teased upon all sides. Men of the most ordinary good-breeding dissemble the pain which any little incident may give them; and those who are more thoroughly formed to society, turn, of their own accord, all such incidents into raillery, as they know their companions will do for them. The habit which a man, who lives in the world, has acquired of considering how every thing that concerns himself will appear to others, makes those frivolous calamities turn up in the same ridiculous light to him, in which he knows they will certainly be considered by them.

Our sympathy, on the contrary, with deep distress, is very strong and very sincere. It is unnecessary to give an instance. We weep even at the feigned representation of a tragedy. If you labour, therefore, under any signal calamity, if by some extraordinary misfortune you are fallen into poverty, into diseases, into disgrace and disappointment; even though your own fault may have been, in part, the occasion, yet you may generally depend upon the sincerest sympathy of all your friends, and, as far as interest and honour will permit, [63]upon their kindest assistance too. But if your misfortune is not of this dreadful kind, if you have only been a little baulked in your ambition, if you have only been jilted by your mistress, or are only hen-pecked by your wife, lay your account with the raillery of all your acquaintance.

[64]

SECTION III.
Of the effects of prosperity and adversity upon the judgment of mankind with regard to the propriety of action; and why it is more easy to obtain their approbation in the one state than in the other.

CHAP. I.
That though our sympathy with sorrow is generally a more lively sensation than our sympathy with joy, it commonly falls much more short

of the violence of what is naturally felt by the person principally concerned.

Our sympathy with sorrow, though not more real, has been more taken notice of than our sympathy with joy. The word sympathy, in its most proper and primitive signification, denotes our fellow-feeling with the sufferings, not that with the enjoyments, of others. A late ingenious and subtile philosopher thought it necessary to prove, by arguments, that we had a real sympathy with joy, and that congratulation was a principle of human nature. Nobody, I believe, ever thought it necessary to prove that compassion was such.

First of all, our sympathy with sorrow is, in some sense, more universal than that with joy. Though [65] sorrow is excessive, we may still have some fellow-feeling with it. What we feel does not, indeed, in this case, amount to that complete sympathy, to that perfect harmony and correspondence of sentiments which constitutes approbation. We do not weep, and exclaim, and lament, with the sufferer. We are sensible, on the contrary, of his weakness, and of the extravagance of his passion, and yet often feel a very sensible concern upon his account. But if we do not entirely enter into, and go along with, the joy of another, we have no sort of regard or fellow-feeling for it. The man who skips and dances about with that intemperate and senseless joy which we cannot accompany him in, is the object of our contempt and indignation.

Pain besides, whether of mind or body, is a more pungent sensation than pleasure, and our sympathy with pain, though it falls greatly short of what is naturally felt by the sufferer, is generally a more lively and distinct perception than our sympathy with pleasure, though this last often approaches more nearly, as I shall show immediately, to the natural vivacity of the original passion.

Over and above all this, we often struggle to keep down our sympathy with the sorrow of others. Whenever we are not under the observation of the sufferer, we endeavour, for our own sake, to suppress it as much as we can, and we are not always successful. The opposition which we make to it, and the reluctance with which we yield to it, necessarily oblige us to take more particular notice of it. But we never have occasion to make this opposition to our sympathy with joy. If there is any envy in the case, [66] we never feel the least propensity towards it; and if there is none, we give way to it without any reluctance. On the contrary, as we are always ashamed of our own envy, we often pretend, and sometimes really wish to sympathize with the joy of others, when by that disagreeable sentiment we are disqualified from doing so. We are glad, we say, on account of our neighbour's good fortune, when in our hearts, perhaps, we are really sorry. We often feel a sympathy with sorrow when we wish to be rid of it; and we often miss that with joy when we would be glad to have it. The obvious observation, therefore, which it naturally falls in our way to make, is that our propensity to sympathize with sorrow must be very strong, and our inclination to sympathize with joy very weak.

Notwithstanding this prejudice, however, I will venture to affirm, that, when there is no envy in the case, our propensity to sympathize with joy is much stronger than our propensity to sympathize with sorrow; and that our fellow-feeling for the agreeable emotion approaches much more nearly to the vivacity of what is naturally felt by the persons principally concerned, than that which we conceive for the painful one.

We have some indulgence for that excessive grief which we cannot entirely go along with. We know what a prodigious effort is requisite before the sufferer can bring down his emotions to compleat harmony and concord with those of the spectator. Though he fails, therefore, we easily pardon him. But we have no such indulgence for the intemperance of joy; because we are not conscious that any such vast effort is requisite to bring it down to what we can entirely enter into. The man who, under the greatest calamities, can command his sorrow, seems worthy of the highest admiration; but he who, in the fulness of prosperity, can in the same manner master his joy, seems hardly to deserve any praise. We are sensible that there is a much wider interval in the one case than in the other, between what is naturally felt by the person principally concerned, and what the spectator can entirely go along with.

What can be added to the happiness of the man who is in health, who is out of debt, and has a clear conscience? To one in this situation, all accessions of fortune may properly be said to be superfluous; and if he is much elevated upon account of them, it must be the effect of the most frivolous levity. This situation, however, may very well be called the natural and ordinary state of mankind. Notwithstanding the present misery and depravity of the world, so justly lamented, this really is the state of the greater part of men. The greater part of men, therefore, cannot find any great difficulty in elevating themselves to all the joy which any accession to this situation can well excite in their companion.

But though little can be added to this state, much may be taken from it. Though between this condition and the highest pitch of human prosperity, the interval is but a trifle; between it and the lowest depth of misery the distance is immense and prodigious. Adversity, on this account, necessarily depresses the mind of the sufferer much more below its natural state, than prosperity can elevate him above it. The spectator, therefore, must find it much more difficult to sympathize entirely, and keep perfect time, with his sorrow, than thoroughly to enter into his joy, and must depart much further from his own natural and ordinary temper of mind in the one case than in the other. It is on this account, that, though our sympathy with sorrow is often a more pungent sensation than our sympathy with joy, it always falls much more short of the violence of what is naturally felt by the person principally concerned.

It is agreeable to sympathize with joy; and wherever envy does not oppose it, our heart abandons itself with satisfaction to the highest transports of that delightful sentiment. But it is painful to go along with grief, and we always enter into it with reluctance. When we attend to the representation of a tragedy, we struggle against that sympathetic sorrow which the entertainment inspires as long as we can, and we give way to it at last only when we can no longer avoid it: we even then endeavour to cover our concern from the company. If we shed any tears, we carefully conceal them, and are afraid lest the spectators, not entering into this excessive tenderness, should regard it as effeminacy and weakness. The wretch whose misfortunes call upon our compassion feels with what reluctance we are likely to enter into his sorrow, and therefore proposes his grief to us with fear and hesitation: he even smothers the half of it, and is ashamed, upon account of this hard-heartedness of mankind, to give vent to the fulness of his affliction. It is otherwise with the man who riots in joy and success. Wherever envy does not interest us against him, he expects our compleatest sympathy. He does not fear, therefore, to announce himself with shouts of exultation, in full confidence that we are heartily disposed to go along with him.

1. It has been objected to me that as I found the sentiment of approbation, which is always agreeable, upon sympathy, it is inconsistent with my system to admit any disagreeable sympathy. I answer, that in the sentiment of approbation there are two things to be taken notice of; first the sympathetic passion of the spectator; and, secondly, the emotion which arises from his observing the perfect coincidence between this sympathetic passion in himself, and the original passion in the person principally concerned. This last emotion, in which the sentiment of approbation properly consists, is always agreeable and delightful. The other may either be agreeable or disagreeable, according to the nature of the original passion, whose feature it must always, in some measure, retain. Two sounds I suppose, may, each of them, taken singly, be austere, and yet, if they are perfect concords, the perception of their harmony and coincidence may be agreeable.

Why should we be more ashamed to weep than to laugh before company? We may often have as real occasion to do the one as to do the other: But we always feel that the spectators are more likely to go along with us in the agreeable, than in the painful emotion. It is always miserable to complain, even when we are oppressed by the most dreadful calamities. But the triumph of victory is not always ungraceful. Prudence, indeed, would often advise us to bear prosperity with more moderation; because prudence would teach us to avoid that envy which this very triumph is, more than any thing, apt to excite.

How hearty are the acclamations of the mob, who never bear any envy to their superiors, at a triumph or a public entry? And how sedate and moderate is commonly their grief at an execution? Our sorrow at a funeral generally amounts to no more than affected gravity; but our mirth at a christening or a marriage, is always from the heart, and without any affectation. Upon these, and all such joyous occasions, our satisfaction, though not so [70] durable, is often as lively as that of the persons principally concerned. Whenever we cordially congratulate our friends, which, however, to the disgrace of human nature, we do but seldom, their joy literally becomes our joy: we are for the moment, as happy as they are: our heart swells and overflows with real pleasure: joy and complacency sparkle from our eyes, and animate every feature of our countenance, and every gesture of our body.

But, on the contrary, when we condole with our friends in their afflictions, how little do we feel, in comparison of what they feel? We sit down by them, we look at them, and while they relate to us the circumstances of their misfortune, we listen to them with gravity and attention. But while their narration is every moment interrupted by those natural bursts of passion which often seem almost to choak them in the midst of it; how far are the languid emotions of our hearts from keeping time to the transports of theirs? We may be sensible, at the same time, that their passion is natural, and no greater than what we ourselves might feel upon the like occasion. We may even inwardly reproach ourselves with our own want of sensibility, and perhaps on that account, work ourselves up into an artificial sympathy, which, however, when it is raised, is always the slightest and most transitory imaginable; and generally, as soon as we have left the room, vanishes, and is gone for ever. Nature, it seems, when she has loaded us with our own sorrows, thought that they were enough, and therefore did not command us to take any further share in those of others, than what was necessary to prompt us to relieve them.

[71] It is on account of this dull sensibility to the afflictions of others, that magnanimity amidst great distress appears always so divinely graceful. His behaviour is genteel and agreeable who can maintain his chearfulness amidst a number of frivolous disasters. But he appears to be more than mortal who can support in the same manner the most dreadful calamities. We feel what an immense effort is requisite to silence those violent emotions which naturally agitate and distract those in his situation. We are amazed to find that he

can command himself so intirely. His firmness, at the same time, perfectly coincides with our insensibility. He makes no demand upon us for that more exquisite degree of sensibility which we find, and which we are mortified to find, that we do not possess. There is the most perfect correspondence between his sentiments and ours, and on that account the most perfect propriety in his behaviour. It is a propriety too, which, from our experience of the usual weakness of human nature, we could not reasonably have expected he should be able to maintain. We wonder with surprise and astonishment at that strength of mind which is capable of so noble and generous an effort. The sentiment of compleat sympathy and approbation, mixed and animated with wonder and surprise, constitutes what is properly called admiration, as has already been more than once taken notice of. Cato, surrounded on all sides by his enemies, unable to resist them, and disdaining to submit to them, and reduced by the proud maxims of that age, to the necessity of destroying himself; yet never shrinking from his misfortunes, never supplicating with the lamentable voice of wretchedness, those miserable sympathetic tears which we are always so unwilling to give; but on the contrary, arming himself with manly fortitude, and the moment before he executes his fatal resolution, giving, with his usual tranquillity, all necessary orders for the safety of his friends; appears to Seneca, that great preacher of insensibility, a spectacle which even the gods themselves might behold with pleasure and admiration.

Whenever we meet, in common life, with any examples of such heroic magnanimity, we are always extremely affected. We are more apt to weep and shed tears for such as, in this manner, seem to feel nothing for themselves, than for those who give way to all the weakness of sorrow: and in this particular case, the sympathetic grief of the spectator appears to go beyond the original passion in the person principally concerned. The friends of Socrates all wept when he drank the last potion, while he himself expressed the gayest and most chearful tranquillity. Upon all such occasions the spectator makes no effort, and has no occasion to make any, in order to conquer his sympathetic sorrow. He is under no fear that it will transport him to any thing that is extravagant and improper; he is rather pleased with the sensibility of his own heart, and gives way to it with complacence and self-approbation. He gladly indulges, therefore, the most melancholy views which can naturally occur to him, concerning the calamity of his friend, for whom, perhaps, he never felt so exquisitely before, the tender and tearful passion of love. But it is quite otherwise with the person principally concerned. He is obliged as much as possible, to turn away his eyes from whatever is either naturally terrible or disagreeable in his situation. Too serious an attention to those circumstances, he fears, might make so violent an impression upon him, that he could no longer keep within the bounds of moderation, or render himself the object of the complete sympathy and approbation of the spectators. He fixes his thoughts, therefore, upon those only which are agreeable; the applause and admiration which he is about to deserve by the heroic magnanimity of his behaviour. To feel that he is capable of so noble and generous an effort, to feel that in this dreadful situation he can still act as he would desire to act, animates and transports him with joy, and enables him to support that triumphant gaiety which seems to exult in the victory he thus gains over his misfortunes.

On the contrary, he always appears, in some measure, mean and despicable, who is sunk in sorrow and dejection upon account of any calamity of his own. We cannot bring ourselves to feel for him what he feels for himself, and what, perhaps, we should feel for ourselves if in his situation: we, therefore, despise him; unjustly, perhaps, if any sentiment could be regarded as unjust, to which we are by nature irresistibly determined. The weakness of sorrow never appears in any respect agreeable, except when it arises from what we feel for others more than from what we feel for ourselves. A son, upon the death of an indulgent and respectable father, may give way to it without much blame. His sorrow is chiefly founded upon a sort of sympathy with his departed parent; and we readily enter into this humane emotion. But if he should indulge the same weakness upon account of any misfortune which affected himself only, he would no longer meet with any such indulgence. If he should be reduced to beggary and ruin, if he should be exposed to the most dreadful dangers, if he should even be led out to a public execution, and there shed one single tear upon the scaffold, he would disgrace himself for ever in the opinion of all the gallant and generous part of mankind. Their compassion for him, however, would be very strong, and very sincere; but as it would still fall short of this excessive weakness, they would have no pardon for the man who could thus expose himself in the eyes of the world. His behaviour would affect them with shame rather than with sorrow; and the dishonour which he had thus brought upon himself would appear to them the most lamentable circumstance in his misfortune. How did it disgrace the memory of the intrepid Duke of Biron, who had so often braved death in the field, that he wept upon the scaffold, when he beheld the state to which he was fallen, and remembered the favour and the glory from which his own rashness had so unfortunately thrown him!

CHAP. II.
Of the origin of ambition, and of the distinction of ranks.

It is because mankind are disposed to sympathize more entirely with our joy than with our sorrow, that we make parade of our riches, and conceal our poverty. Nothing is so mortifying as to be obliged to expose our distress to the view of the public, and to feel, that though our situation is open to the eyes of all mankind, no mortal conceives for us the half of what we suffer. Nay, it is chiefly from this regard to the sentiments of mankind, that we pursue riches and avoid poverty. For to what purpose is all the toil and bustle of this world? what is the end of avarice and ambition, of the pursuit of wealth, of power, and pre-eminence? Is it to supply the necessities of nature? The wages of the meanest labourer can supply them. We see that they afford him food and clothing, the comfort of a house, and of a family. If we examine his œconomy with rigor, we should find that he spends a great part of them upon conveniences, which may be regarded as superfluities, and that, upon extraordinary occasions, he can give something even to vanity and distinction. What then is the cause of our aversion to his situation, and why should those who have been educated in the higher ranks of life, regard it as worse than death, to be reduced to live, even without labour, upon the same simple fare with him, to dwell under the same lowly roof, and to be clothed in the same humble attire? Do they imagine that their stomach is better, or their sleep sounder in a palace than in a cottage? the contrary has been so often observed, and, indeed, is so very obvious, though it had never been observed, that there is no body ignorant of it. From whence, then, arises that emulation which runs through all the different ranks of men, and what are the advantages which we propose by that great purpose of human life which we call bettering our condition? To be observed, to be attended to, to be taken notice of with sympathy, complacency, and approbation, are all the advantages which we can propose to derive from it. It is the vanity, not the ease, or the pleasure, which interests us. But vanity is always founded upon the belief of our being the object of attention and approbation. The rich man glories in his riches, because he feels that they naturally draw upon him the attention of the world, and that mankind are disposed to go along with him in all those agreeable emotions with which the advantages of his situation so readily inspire him. At the thought of this, his heart seems to swell and dilate itself within him, and he is fonder of his wealth upon this account, than for all the other advantages it procures him. The poor man, on the contrary, is ashamed of his poverty. He feels that it either places him out of the sight of mankind, or, that, if they take any notice of him, they have, however, scarce any fellow-feeling with the misery and distress which he suffers. He is mortified upon both accounts; for though to be overlooked, and to be disapproved of, are things entirely different, yet as obscurity covers us from the daylight of honour and approbation, to feel that we are taken no notice of necessarily damps the most agreeable hope, and disappoints the most ardent desire, of human nature. The poor man goes out and comes in unheeded, and when in the midst of a croud is in the same obscurity as if shut up in his own hovel. Those humble cares and painful attentions which occupy those in his situation, afford no amusement to the dissipated and the gay. They turn away their eyes from him, or if the extremity of his distress forces them to look at him, it is only to spurn so disagreeable an object from among them. The fortunate and the proud wonder at the insolence of human wretchedness, that it should dare to present itself before them, and with the loathsome aspect of its misery, presume to disturb the serenity of their happiness. The man of rank and distinction, on the contrary, is observed by all the world. Every body is eager to look at him, and to conceive, at least by sympathy, that joy and exultation with which his circumstances naturally inspire him. His actions are the objects of the public care. Scarce a word, scarce a gesture, can fall from him that is altogether neglected. In a great assembly he is the person upon whom all direct their eyes; it is upon him that their passions seem all to wait with expectation, in order to receive that movement and direction which he shall impress upon them; and if his behaviour is not altogether absurd, he has, every moment, an opportunity of interesting mankind, and of rendering himself the object of the observation and fellow-feeling of every body about him. It is this, which notwithstanding the restraint it imposes, notwithstanding the loss of liberty with which it is attended, renders greatness the object of envy, and compensates in the opinion of mankind, all that toil, all that anxiety, all those mortifications which must be undergone in the pursuit of it; and what is of yet more consequence, all that leisure, all that ease, all that careless security, which are forfeited for ever by the acquisition.

When we consider the condition of the great, in those delusive colours in which the imagination is apt to paint it, it seems to be almost the abstract idea of a perfect and happy state. It is the very state which, in all our waking dreams and idle reveries, we had sketched out to ourselves as the final object of all our desires. We feel, therefore, a peculiar sympathy with the satisfaction of those who are in it. We favour all their inclinations, and forward all their wishes. What pity, we think, that any thing should spoil and corrupt so agreeable a situation! We could even wish them immortal; and it seems hard to us, that death should at last put an end to such perfect enjoyment. It is cruel, we think, in Nature, to compel them from their exalted stations to that humble, but hospitable home, which she has provided for all her children. Great King, live for ever! is the compliment, which after the manner of eastern adulation, we should readily make them, if experience did not teach us its absurdity. Every calamity that befalls them, every injury that is done them, excites in the breast of the spectator ten times more compassion and resentment than he would have felt, had the same things happened to other men. It is the misfortunes of Kings only which afford the proper subjects for tragedy. They resemble, in this respect, the misfortunes of lovers. Those two situations are the chief which interest us upon the theatre; because, in spite of all that reason and experience can tell us to the contrary, the prejudices of the imagination attach to these two states a happiness superior to any other. To disturb, or to put an end to such perfect enjoyment, seems to be the most atrocious of all injuries. The traitor who conspires against the life of his monarch, is thought a greater monster than [79] any other murderer. All the innocent blood that was shed in the civil wars, provoked less indignation than the death of Charles I. A stranger to human nature, who saw the indifference of men about the misery of their inferiors, and the regret and indignation which they feel for the misfortunes and sufferings of those above them, would be apt to imagine, that pain must be more agonizing, and the convulsions of death more terrible to persons of higher rank, than to those of meaner stations.

Upon this disposition of mankind, to go along with all the passions of the rich and the powerful, is founded the distinction of ranks, and the order of society. Our obsequiousness to our superiors more frequently arises from our admiration for the advantages of their situation, than from any private expectations of benefit from their good-will. Their benefits can extend but to a few; but their fortunes interest almost every body. We are eager to assist them in compleating a system of happiness that approaches so near to perfection; and we desire to serve them for their own sake, without any other recompense but the vanity or the honour of obliging them. Neither is our deference to their inclinations founded chiefly, or altogether, upon a regard to the utility of such submission, and to the order of society, which is best supported by it. Even when the order of society seems to require that we should oppose them, we can hardly bring ourselves to do it. That kings are the servants of the people, to be obeyed, resisted, deposed, or punished, as the public conveniency may require, is the doctrine of reason and philosophy; but it is not the doctrine of [80] Nature. Nature would teach us to submit to them, for their own sake, to tremble and bow down before their exalted station, to regard their smile as a reward sufficient to compensate any services, and to dread their displeasure, though no other evil was to follow from it, as the severest of all mortifications. To treat them in any respect as men, to reason and dispute with them upon ordinary occasions, requires such resolution, that there are few men whose magnanimity can support them in it, unless they are likewise assisted by familiarity and acquaintance. The strongest motives, the most furious passions, fear, hatred, and resentment, are scarce sufficient to balance this natural disposition to respect them: and their conduct must, either justly or unjustly, have excited the highest degree of all those passions, before the bulk of the people can be brought to oppose them with violence, or to desire to see them either punished or deposed. Even when the people have been brought this length, they are apt to relent every moment, and easily relapse into their habitual state of deference to those whom they have been accustomed to look upon as their natural superiors. They cannot stand the mortification of their monarch. Compassion soon takes the place of resentment, they forget all past provocations, their old principles of loyalty revive, and they run to re-establish the ruined authority of their old master, with the same violence with which they had opposed it. The death of Charles I. brought about the Restoration of the royal family. Compassion for James II. when he was seized by the populace in making his escape on ship-board, had almost prevented the Revolution, [81] and made it go on more heavily than before.

Do the great seem insensible of the easy price at which they may acquire the public admiration; or do they seem to imagine that to them, as to other men, it must be the purchase either of sweat or of blood? By what important accomplishments is the young nobleman instructed to support the dignity of his rank, and to render himself worthy of that superiority over his fellow-citizens, to which the virtue of his ancestors had raised them? Is it by knowledge, by industry, by patience, by self-denial, or by virtue of any kind? As all his words, as all his motions are attended to, he learns an habitual regard to every circumstance of ordinary behaviour, and studies to perform all those small duties with the most exact propriety. As he is conscious how much he is observed, and how much mankind are disposed to favour all his inclinations, he acts, upon the most indifferent occasions, with that freedom and elevation which the thought of this naturally inspires. His air, his manner, his deportment, all mark that elegant and graceful sense of his own superiority, which those who are born to inferior stations can hardly ever arrive at: these are the arts by which he proposes to make mankind more easily submit to his authority, and to govern their inclinations according to his own pleasure: and in this he is seldom disappointed. These arts, supported by rank and pre-eminence, are, upon ordinary occasions, sufficient to govern the world. Lewis XIV. during the greater part of his reign, was regarded, not only in France, but over all [82] Europe, as the most perfect model of a great prince. But what were the talents and virtues by which he acquired this great reputation? Was it by the scrupulous and inflexible justice of all his undertakings, by the immense dangers and difficulties with which they were attended, or by the unwearied and unrelenting application with which he pursued them? Was it by his extensive knowledge, by his exquisite judgment, or by his heroic valour? It was by none of these qualities. But he was, first of all, the most powerful prince in Europe, and consequently held the highest rank among kings; and then, says his historian, "he surpassed all his courtiers in the gracefulness of his shape, and the majestic beauty of his features. The sound of his voice, noble and affecting, gained those hearts which his presence intimidated. He had a step and deportment which could suit only him and his rank, and which would have been ridiculous in any other person. The embarrassment which he occasioned to those who spoke to him, flattered that secret satisfaction with which he felt his own superiority. The old officer, who was confounded and faultered in asking him a favour, and not being able to conclude his discourse, said to him, Sir, your majesty, I hope, will believe that I do not tremble thus before your enemies: had no difficulty to obtain what he demanded." These frivolous accomplishments, supported by his rank, and, no doubt, too, by a degree of other talents and virtues, which seems, however, not to have been much above mediocrity, established this prince in the esteem of his own age, and have drawn, even from posterity, a good deal of [83] respect for his memory. Compared with those of his own times, and in his own presence, no other virtue, it seems, appeared to have any merit. Knowledge, industry, valour, and beneficence, trembled, were abashed, and lost all dignity before them.

But it is not by accomplishments of this kind, that the man of inferior rank must hope to distinguish himself. Politeness is so much the virtue of the great, that it will do little honour to any body but themselves. The coxcomb, who imitates their manner, and affects to be eminent by the superior propriety of his ordinary behaviour, is rewarded with a double share of contempt for his folly and presumption. Why should the man, whom nobody thinks it worth while to look at, be very anxious about the manner in which he holds up his head, or disposes of his arms while he walks through a room? He is occupied surely with a very superfluous attention, and with an attention too that marks a sense of his own importance, which no other mortal can go along with. The most perfect modesty and plainness, joined to as much negligence as is consistent with the respect due to the company, ought to be the chief characteristics of the behaviour of a private man. If ever he hopes to distinguish himself, it must be by more important virtues. He must acquire dependants to balance the dependants of the great, and he has no other fund to pay them from, but the labour of his body, and the activity of his mind. He must cultivate these therefore: he must acquire superior knowledge in his profession, and superior industry in the exercise of it. He 84 must be patient in labour, resolute in danger, and firm in distress. These talents he must bring into public view, by the difficulty, importance, and, at the same time, good judgment of his undertakings, and by the severe and unrelenting application with which he pursues them. Probity and prudence, generosity and frankness, must characterize his behaviour upon all ordinary occasions; and he must, at the same time, be forward to engage in all those situations in which it requires the greatest talents and virtues to act with propriety, but in which the greatest applause is to be acquired by those who can acquit themselves with honour. With what impatience does the man of spirit and ambition, who is depressed by his situation, look round for some great opportunity to distinguish himself? No circumstances, which can afford this, appear to him undesirable. He even looks forward with satisfaction to the prospect of foreign war, or civil dissension; and, with secret transport and delight, sees through all the confusion and bloodshed which attend them, the probability of those wished for occasions presenting themselves, in which he may draw upon himself the attention and admiration of mankind. The man of rank and distinction, on the contrary, whose whole glory consists in the propriety of his ordinary behaviour, who is contented with the humble renown which this can afford him, and has no talents to acquire any other, is unwilling to embarrass himself with what can be attended either with difficulty or distress. To figure at a ball is his great triumph, and to succeed in an intrigue of gallantry, his highest exploit. He has an aversion to all public confusions, not from 85 the love of mankind, for the great never look upon their inferiors as their fellow-creatures; nor yet from want of courage, for in that he is seldom defective; but from a consciousness that he possesses none of the virtues which are required in such situations, and that the public attention will certainly be drawn away from him by others. He may be willing to expose himself to some little danger, and to make a campaign when it happens to be the fashion. But he shudders with horror at the thought of any situation which demands the continual and long exertion of patience, industry, fortitude, and application of thought. These virtues are hardly ever to be met with in men who are born to those high stations. In all governments accordingly, even in monarchies, the highest offices are generally possessed, and the whole detail of the administration conducted by men who were educated in the middle and inferior ranks of life, who have been carried forward by their own industry and abilities, though loaded with the jealousy, and opposed by the resentment of all those who were born their superiors, and to whom the great, after having regarded them first with contempt, and afterwards with envy, are at last contented to truckle with the same abject meanness with which they desire that the rest of mankind should behave to themselves.

It is the loss of this easy empire over the affections of mankind which renders the fall from greatness so insupportable. When the family of the King of Macedon was led in triumph by Paulus Æmilius, their misfortunes, it is said, made them divide with their conqueror the attention 86 of the Roman people. The sight of the royal children, whose tender age rendered them insensible of their situation, struck the spectators, amidst the public rejoicings and prosperity, with the tenderest sorrow and compassion. The King appeared next in the procession; and seemed like one confounded and astonished, and bereft of all sentiment, by the greatness of his calamities. His friends and ministers followed after him. As they moved along, they often cast their eye upon their fallen sovereign, and always burst into tears at the sight; their whole behaviour demonstrating that they thought not of their misfortunes, but were occupied entirely by the superior greatness of his. The generous Romans, on the contrary, beheld him with disdain and indignation, and regarded as unworthy of all compassion the man who could be so mean-spirited as to bear to live under such calamities. Yet what did those calamities amount to? According to the greater part of historians, he was to spend the remainder of his days under the protection of a powerful and humane people, in a state which in itself should seem worthy of envy, a state of plenty, ease, leisure, and security, from which it was impossible for him even by his own folly to fall. But he was no longer to be surrounded by that admiring mob of fools, flatterers, and dependants, who had formerly been accustomed to attend upon all his motions. He was no longer to be gazed upon by multitudes, nor to have it in his power to render himself the object of their respect, their gratitude, their love, their admiration. The passions of nations were no longer to mould themselves 87 upon his inclinations. This was that insupportable calamity which bereaved the King of all sentiment; which made his friends forget their own misfortunes; and which the Roman magnanimity could scarce conceive how any man could be so mean-spirited as to bear to survive.

"Love, says my Lord Rochefoucault, is commonly succeeded by ambition; but ambition is hardly ever succeeded by love." That passion when once it has got entire possession of the breast, will admit neither a rival nor a successor. To those who have been accustomed to the possession, or even to the hope of public admiration, all other pleasures sicken and decay. Of all the discarded statesmen who for their own ease have studied to get the better of ambition, and to despise those honours which they could no longer arrive at, how few have been able to succeed? The greater part have spent their time in the most listless and insipid indolence, chagrined at the thoughts of their own insignificancy, incapable of being interested in the occupations of private life, without enjoyment except when they talked of their former greatness, and without satisfaction except when they were employed in some vain project to recover it. Are you in earnest resolved never to barter your liberty for the lordly servitude of a Court, but to live free, fearless, and independent? There seems to be one way to continue in that virtuous resolution; and perhaps but one. Never enter the place from whence so few have been able to return; never come within the circle of ambition; nor even bring yourself into comparison with those masters of the 88 earth who have already engrossed the attention of half mankind before you.

Of such mighty importance does it appear to be, in the imaginations of men, to stand in that situation which sets them most in the view of general sympathy and attention. And thus, place, that great object which divides the wives of aldermen, is the end of half the labours of life; and is the cause of all the tumult and bustle, all the rapine and injustice, which avarice and ambition have introduced into this world. People of sense, it is said, indeed despise place; that is, they despise sitting at the head of the table, and are indifferent who it is that is pointed out to the company by that frivolous circumstance, which the smallest advantage is capable of overbalancing. But rank, distinction, pre-eminence, no man despises, unless he is either raised very much above, or sunk very much below, the ordinary standard of human nature; unless he is either so confirmed in wisdom and real philosophy, as to be satisfied that, while the propriety of his conduct renders him the just object of approbation, it is of little consequence though he be neither attended to, nor approved of; or so habituated to the idea of his own meanness, so sunk in slothful and sottish indifference, as entirely to have forgot the desire, and almost the very wish, for superiority.

CHAP. III.
Of the stoical philosophy.

When we examine in this manner into the ground of the different degrees of estimation which mankind are apt to bestow upon the different conditions of life, we shall find, that the excessive preference, which they generally give to some of them above others, is in a great measure without any foundation. If to be able to act with propriety, and to render ourselves the proper objects of the approbation of mankind, be, as we have been endeavouring to show, what chiefly recommends to us one condition above another, this may equally be attained in them all. The noblest propriety of conduct may be supported in adversity, as well as in prosperity; and though it is somewhat more difficult in the first, it is upon that very account more admirable. Perils and misfortunes are not only the proper school of heroism, they are the only proper theatre which can exhibit its virtue to advantage, and draw upon it the full applause of the world. The man, whose whole life has been one even and uninterrupted course of prosperity, who never braved any danger, who never encountered any difficulty, who never surmounted any distress, can excite but an inferior degree of admiration. When poets and romance-writers endeavour to invent a train of adventures, which shall give the greatest lustre to those 90 characters for whom they mean to interest us, they are all of a different kind. They are rapid and sudden changes of fortune, situations the most apt to drive those who are in them to frenzy and distraction, or to abject despair; but in which their heroes act with so much propriety, or at least with so much spirit and undaunted resolution, as still to command our esteem. Is not the unfortunate magnanimity of Cato, Brutus, and Leonidas, as much the object of admiration, as that of the successful Cæsar or Alexander? To a generous mind, therefore, ought it not to be as much the object of envy? If a more dazzling splendor seems to attend the fortunes of successful conquerors, it is because they join together the advantages of both situations, the lustre of prosperity to the high admiration which is excited by dangers encountered, and difficulties surmounted, with intrepidity and valour.

It was upon this account that, according to the stoical philosophy, to a wise man all the different conditions of life were equal. Nature, they said, had recommended some objects to our choice, and others to our disapprobation. Our primary appetites directed us to the pursuit of health, strength, ease, and perfection, in all the qualities of mind and body; and of whatever could promote or secure these, riches, power, authority: and the same original principle taught us to avoid the contrary. But in chusing or rejecting, in preferring or postponing, those first objects of original appetite and aversion, Nature had likewise taught us, that there was a certain order, propriety, and grace, to be observed, of infinitely greater consequence to happiness and perfection, than the attainment of those objects themselves. The objects of our primary appetites or aversions were to be pursued or avoided, chiefly because a regard to this grace and propriety required such conduct. In directing all our actions according to these, consisted the happiness and glory of human nature. In departing from those rules which they prescribed to us, its greatest wretchedness and most complete depravity. The outward appearance of this order and propriety was indeed more easily maintained in some circumstances than in others. To a fool, however, to one whose passions were subjected to no proper controul, to act with real grace and propriety, was equally impossible in every situation. Though the giddy multitude might admire him, though his vanity might sometimes be elevated by their ignorant praises into something that resembled self-approbation, yet still when he turned his view to what passed within his own breast, he was secretly conscious to himself of the absurdity and meanness of all his motives, and inwardly blushed and trembled at the thoughts of the contempt which he knew he deserved, and which mankind would certainly bestow upon him if they saw his conduct in the light in which in his own heart he was obliged to regard it. To a wise man, on the contrary, to one whose passions were all brought under perfect subjection to the ruling principles of his nature, to reason and the love of propriety, to act so as to deserve approbation was equally easy upon all occasions. Was he in prosperity, he returned thanks to Jupiter for having joined him with circumstances which were easily mastered, and in which there was little temptation to do wrong. Was he in adversity, he equally, returned thanks to the director of this spectacle of human life, for having opposed to him a vigorous athlete, over whom, though the contest was likely to be more violent, the victory was more glorious, and equally certain. Can there be any shame in that distress which is brought upon us without any fault of our own, and in which we behave with perfect propriety? There can therefore, be no evil, but, on the contrary, the greatest good and advantage. A brave man exults in those dangers, in which, from no rashness of his own, his fortune has involved him. They afford an opportunity of exercising that heroic intrepidity, whose exertion gives the exalted delight which flows from the consciousness of superior propriety and deserved admiration. One who is master of all his exercises has no aversion to measure his strength and activity with the strongest. And in the same manner, one who is master of all his passions, does not dread any circumstances in which the superintendant of the universe may think proper to place him. The bounty of that Divine Being has provided him with virtues which render him superior to every situation. If it is pleasure, he has temperance to refrain from it; if it is pain, he has constancy to bear it; if it is danger or death, he has magnanimity and fortitude to despise it. He never complains of the destiny of providence, nor thinks the universe in confusion when he is out of order. He does not look upon himself, according to what self-love would suggest, as a whole, separated and detached from every other part of nature, to be taken care of by itself, and for itself. He regards himself in the light in which he imagines the great Genius of human nature, and of the world, regards him. He enters, if I may say so, into the [93] sentiments of that Divine Being, and considers himself as an atom, a particle, of an immense and infinite system, which must, and ought to be disposed of, according to the conveniency of the whole. Assured of the wisdom which directs all the events of human life, whatever lot befalls him, he accepts it with joy, satisfied that, if he had known all the connexions and dependencies of the different parts of the universe, it is the very lot which he himself would have wished for. If it is life, he is contented to live: and if it is death, as Nature must have no further occasion for his presence here, he willingly goes where he is appointed. I accept, said a stoical philosopher, with equal joy and satisfaction, whatever fortune can befal me. Riches or poverty, pleasure or pain, health or sickness, all is alike: nor would I desire that the gods should in any respect change my destination. If I was to ask of them any thing, beyond what their bounty has already bestowed, it should be that they would inform me beforehand what it was their pleasure should be done with me, that I might of my own accord place myself in this situation, and demonstrate the chearfulness with which I embraced their allotment. If I am going to fail, says Epictetus, I chuse the best ship, and the best pilot, and I wait for the fairest weather that my circumstances and duty will allow. Prudence and propriety, the principles which the gods have given me for the direction of my conduct, require this of me; but they require no more: and if, notwithstanding, a storm arises, which neither the strength of the vessel, nor the skill of the pilot are likely to withstand, I give myself no trouble about the consequence. All that I had to do, is done already. The directors of my conduct never command me [94] to be miserable, to be anxious, desponding, or afraid. Whether we are to be drowned, or to come to a harbour, is the business of Jupiter, not mine. I leave it entirely to his determination, nor ever break my rest with considering which way he is likely to decide it, but receive whatever comes with equal indifference and security.

Such was the philosophy of the stoics, a philosophy which affords the noblest lessons of magnanimity, is the best school of heroes and patriots, and to the greater part of whose precepts there can be no objection, except that honourable one, that they teach us to aim at a perfection altogether beyond the reach of human nature. I shall not at present stop to examine it. I shall only observe, in confirmation of what has formerly been said, that the most dreadful calamities are not always those which it is most difficult to support. It is often more mortifying to appear in public, under small disasters, than under great misfortunes. The first excite no sympathy; but the second, though they may excite none that approaches to the anguish of the sufferer, call forth, however, a very lively compassion. The sentiments of the spectators are, in this last case, therefore, less wide of those of the sufferer, and their imperfect fellow-feeling lends him some assistance in supporting his misery. Before a gay assembly, a gentleman would be more mortified to appear covered with filth and rags than with blood and wounds. This last situation would interest their pity; the other would provoke their laughter. The judge who orders a criminal to be set in the pillory, dishonours him more than if he had condemned him to the scaffold. The great prince, [95] who, some years ago, caned a general officer at the head of his army, disgraced him irrecoverably. The punishment would have been much less had he shot him through the body. By the laws of honour, to strike with a cane dishonours, to strike with a sword does not, for an obvious reason. Those slighter punishments when inflicted on a gentleman, to whom dishonour is the greatest of all evils, come to be regarded among a humane and generous people, as the most dreadful of any. With regard to persons of that rank, therefore, they are universally laid aside, and the law, while it takes their life upon many occasions, respects their honour upon almost all. To scourge a person of quality, or to set him in the pillory, upon account of any crime whatever, is a brutality of which no European government, except that of Russia, is capable.

A brave man is not rendered contemptible by being brought to the scaffold; he is, by being set in the pillory. His behaviour in the one situation may gain him universal esteem and admiration. No behaviour in the other can render him agreeable. The sympathy of the spectators supports him in the one case, and saves him from that shame, that consciousness that his misery is felt by himself only, which is of all sentiments the most unsupportable. There is no sympathy in the other; or, if there is any, it is not with his pain, which is a trifle, but with his consciousness of the want of sympathy with which this pain is attended. It is with his shame, not with his sorrow. Those who pity him, blush and hang down their heads for him. He droops in the same manner, and feels himself irrecoverably degraded by the punishment, though not by the crime. The good man, on the contrary, who dies with resolution, as he is naturally regarded with the erect aspect of esteem and approbation, so he wears himself the same undaunted countenance; and, if the crime does not deprive him of the respect of others, the punishment never will. He has no suspicion that his situation is the object of contempt or derision to any body, and he can, with propriety, assume the air, not only of perfect serenity, but of triumph and exaltation.

"Great dangers," says the Cardinal de Retz, "have their charms, because there is some glory to be got, even when we miscarry. But moderate dangers have nothing but what is horrible, because the loss of reputation always attends the want of success." His maxim has the same foundation with what we have been just now observing with regard to punishments.

Human virtue is superior to pain, to poverty, to danger, and to death; nor does it even require its utmost efforts to despise them. But to have its misery exposed to insult and derision, to be led in triumph, to be set up for the hand of scorn to point at, is a situation in which its constancy is much more apt to fail. Compared with the contempt of mankind, all other evils are easily supported.

PART II.
Of MERIT and DEMERIT; or, of the Objects of REWARD and PUNISHMENT.

CONSISTING OF THREE SECTIONS.

SECTION I.
Of the sense of merit and demerit.

INTRODUCTION.

There is another set of qualities ascribed to the actions and conduct of mankind, distinct from their propriety or impropriety, their decency or ungracefulness, and which are the objects of a distinct species of approbation and disapprobation. These are merit and demerit, the qualities of deserving reward, and of deserving punishment.

It has already been observed, that the sentiment or affection of the heart, from which any action proceeds, and upon which its whole virtue or vice depends, may be considered under two different aspects, or in two different relations: first, in relation to the cause or object which excites it; and, secondly, in relation to the end which it proposes, |98| or to the effect which it tends to produce: that upon the suitableness or unsuitableness, upon the proportion or disproportion, which the affection seems to bear to the cause or object which excites it, depends the propriety or impropriety, the decency or ungracefulness of the consequent action; and that upon the beneficial or hurtful effects which the affection proposes or tends to produce, depends the merit or demerit, the good or ill desert of the action to which it gives occasion. Wherein consists our sense of the propriety or impropriety of actions, has been explained in the former part of this discourse. We come now to consider, wherein consists that of their good or ill desert.

CHAP. I.
That whatever appears to be the proper object of gratitude, appears to deserve reward; and that, in the same manner, whatever appears to be the proper object of resentment, appears to deserve punishment.

To us, therefore, that action must appear to deserve reward, which appears to be the proper and approved object of that sentiment, which most immediately and directly prompts us to reward, or to do good to another. And in the same manner, that action must appear to deserve punishment, which appears to be the proper and approved object of that sentiment which most immediately and directly prompts us to publish, or inflict evil upon another.

|99| The sentiment which most immediately and directly prompts us to reward, is gratitude; that which most immediately and directly prompts us to punish, is resentment.

To us, therefore, that action must appear to deserve reward, which appears to be the proper and approved object of gratitude; as, on the other hand, that action must appear to deserve punishment, which appears to be the proper and approved object of resentment.

To reward, is to recompense, to remunerate, to return good for good received. To punish, too, is to recompense, to remunerate, though in a different manner; it is to return evil for evil that has been done.

There are some other passions, besides gratitude and resentment, which interest us in the happiness or misery of others; but there are none which so directly excite us to be the instruments of either. The love and esteem which grow upon acquaintance and habitual approbation, necessarily lead us to be pleased with the good fortune of the man who is the object of such agreeable emotions, and consequently, to be willing to lend a hand to promote it. Our love, however, is fully satisfied, though his good fortune should be brought about without our assistance. All that this passion desires is to see him happy, without regarding who was the author of his prosperity. But gratitude is not to be satisfied in this manner. If the person to whom we owe many obligations, is made happy without our assistance, though it pleases our love, it does not content our gratitude. Till we 100 have recompensed him, till we ourselves have been instrumental in promoting his happiness, we feel ourselves still loaded with that debt which his past services have laid upon us.

The hatred and dislike, in the same manner, which grow upon habitual disapprobation, would often lead us to take a malicious pleasure in the misfortune of the man whose conduct and character excite so painful a passion. But though dislike and hatred harden us against all sympathy, and sometimes dispose us even to rejoice at the distress of another, yet, if there is no resentment in the case, if neither we nor our friends have received any great personal provocation, these passions would not naturally lead us to wish to be instrumental in bringing it about. Tho' we could fear no punishment in consequence of our having had some hand it, we would rather that it should happen by other means. To one under the dominion of violent hatred it would be agreeable, perhaps, to hear, that the person whom he abhorred and detested was killed by some accident. But if he had the least spark of justice, which, though this passion is not very favourable to virtue, he might still have, it would hurt him excessively to have been himself, even without design, the occasion of this misfortune. Much more would the very thought of voluntarily contributing to it shock him beyond all measure. He would reject with horror even the imagination of so execrable a design; and if he could imagine himself capable of such an enormity, he would begin to regard himself in the same odious light in which he had considered the person who was the object of his dislike. But it is quite otherwise with resentment: 101 if the person who had done us some great injury, who had murdered our father or our brother, for example, should soon afterwards die of a fever, or even be brought to the scaffold upon account of some other crime, though it might sooth our hatred, it would not fully gratify our resentment. Resentment would prompt us to desire, not only that he should be punished, but that he should be punished by our means, and upon account of that particular injury which he had done to us. Resentment cannot be fully gratified, unless the offender is not only made to grieve in his turn, but to grieve for that particular wrong which we have suffered from him. He must be made to repent and be sorry for this very action, that others, through fear of the like punishment, may be terrified from being guilty of the like offence. The natural gratification of this passion tends, of its own accord, to produce all the political ends of punishment; the correction of the criminal, and the example to the public.

Gratitude and resentment, therefore, are the sentiments which most immediately and directly prompt to reward and to punish. To us, therefore, he must appear to deserve reward, who appears to be the proper and approved object of gratitude; and he to deserve punishment, who appears to be that of resentment.

CHAP. II.
Of the proper objects of gratitude and resentment.

To be the proper and approved object either of gratitude or resentment, can mean nothing but to be the object of that gratitude, and of that resentment, which naturally seems proper, and is approved of.

But these, as well as all the other passions of human nature, seem proper and are approved of, when the heart of every impartial spectator entirely sympathizes with them, when every indifferent by-stander entirely enters into, and goes along with them.

He, therefore, appears to deserve reward, who, to some person or persons, is the natural object of a gratitude which every human heart is disposed to beat time to, and thereby applaud: and he, on the other hand, appears to deserve punishment, who in the same manner is to some person or persons the natural object of a resentment which the breast of every reasonable man is ready to adopt and sympathize with. To us, surely, that action must appear to deserve reward, which every body who knows of it would wish to reward, and therefore 103 delights to see rewarded: and that action must as surely appear to deserve punishment, which every body who hears of it is angry with, and upon that account rejoices to see punished.

1. As we sympathize with the joy of our companions when in prosperity, so we join with them in the complacency and satisfaction with which they naturally regard whatever is the cause of their good fortune. We enter into the love and affection which they conceive for it, and begin to love it too. We should be sorry for their sakes if it was destroyed, or even if it was placed at too great a distance from them, and out of the reach of their care and protection, though they should lose nothing by its absence except the pleasure of seeing it. If it is man who has thus been the fortunate instrument of the happiness of his brethren, this is still more peculiarly the case. When we see one man assisted, protected, relieved by another, our sympathy with the joy of the person who receives the benefit serves only to animate our fellow-feeling with his gratitude towards him who bestows it. When we look upon the person who is the cause of his pleasure with the eyes with which we imagine he must look upon him, his benefactor seems to stand before us in the most engaging and amiable light. We readily therefore sympathize with the grateful affection which he conceives for a person to whom he has been so much obliged; and consequently applaud the returns which he is disposed to make for the good offices conferred upon him. As we entirely enter into the affection from which these returns proceed, they necessarily seem every way proper and suitable to their object.

104 2. In the same manner, as we sympathize with the sorrow of our fellow-creature whenever we see his distress, so we likewise enter into his abhorrence and aversion for whatever has given occasion to it. Our heart, as it adopts and beats time to his grief, so is it likewise animated with that spirit by which he endeavours to drive away or destroy the cause of it. The indolent and passive fellow-feeling, by which we accompany him in his sufferings, readily gives way to that more vigorous and active sentiment by which we go along with him in the effort he makes, either to repel them, or to gratify his aversion to what has given occasion to them. This is still more peculiarly the case, when it is man who has caused them. When we see one man oppressed or injured by another, the sympathy which we feel with the distress of the sufferer seems to serve only to animate our fellow-

feeling with his resentment against the offender. We are rejoiced to see him attack his adversary in his turn, and are eager and ready to assist him whenever he exerts himself for defence, or even for vengeance within a certain degree. If the injured should perish in the quarrel, we not only sympathize with the real resentment of his friends and relations, but with the imaginary resentment which in fancy we lend to the dead, who is no longer capable of feeling that or any other human sentiment. But as we put ourselves in his situation, as we enter, as it were, into his body, and in our imaginations, in some measure, animate anew the deformed and mangled carcass of the slain, when we bring home in this manner his case to our own bosoms, we feel upon this, as upon many other occasions, an emotion which the person principally concerned is incapable of feeling, and which yet we feel by an illusive sympathy with him. The sympathetic tears which we shed for that immense and irretrievable loss, which in our fancy he appears to have sustained, seem to be but a small part of the duty which we owe him. The injury which he has suffered demands, we think, a principal part of our attention. We feel that resentment which we imagine he ought to feel, and which he would feel, if in his cold and lifeless body there remained any consciousness of what passes upon earth. His blood, we think, calls aloud for vengeance. The very ashes of the dead seem to be disturbed at the thought that his injuries are to pass unrevenged. The horrors which are supposed to haunt the bed of the murderer, the ghosts which, superstition imagines, rise from their graves to demand vengeance upon those who brought them to an untimely end, all take their origin from this natural sympathy with the imaginary resentment of the slain. And with regard, at least, to this most dreadful of all crimes, Nature, antecedent to all reflections upon the utility of punishment, has in this manner stamped upon the human heart, in the strongest and most indelible characters, an immediate and instinctive approbation of the sacred and necessary law of retaliation.

106

CHAP. III.
That where there is no approbation of the conduct of the person who confers the benefit, there is little sympathy with the gratitude of him who receives it: and that, on the contrary, where there is no disapprobation of the motives of the person who does the mischief, there is no sort of sympathy with the resentment of him who suffers it.

It is to be observed, however, that, how beneficial soever on the one hand, or how hurtful soever on the other, the actions or intentions of the person who acts may have been to the person who is, if I may say so, acted upon, yet if in the one case there appears to have been no propriety in the motives of the agent, if we cannot enter into the affections which influenced his conduct, we have little sympathy with the gratitude of the person who receives the benefit: or if, in the other case, there appears to have been no impropriety in the motives of the agent, if, on the contrary, the affections which influenced his conduct are such as we must necessarily enter into, we can have no sort of sympathy with the resentment of the person who suffers. Little gratitude seems due in the one case, and all sort of resentment seems unjust in the other. The one action seems to merit little reward, the other to deserve no punishment.

1071. First, I say, that wherever we cannot sympathize with the affections of the agent, wherever there seems to be no propriety in the motives which influenced his conduct, we are less disposed to enter into the gratitude of the person who received the benefit of his actions. A very small return seems due to that foolish and profuse generosity which confers the greatest benefits from the most trivial motives, and gives an estate to a man merely because his name and surname happen to be the same with those of the giver. Such services do not seem to demand any proportionable recompense. Our contempt for the folly of the agent hinders us from thoroughly entering into the gratitude of the person to whom the good office has been done. His benefactor seems unworthy of it. As when we place ourselves in the situation of the person obliged, we feel that we could conceive no great reverence for such a benefactor, we easily absolve him from a great deal of that submissive veneration and esteem which we should think due to a more respectable character; and provided he always treats his weak friend with kindness and humanity, we are willing to excuse him from many attentions and regards which we should demand to a worthier patron. Those Princes, who have heaped, with the greatest profusion, wealth, power, and honours, upon their favourites, have seldom excited that degree of attachment to their persons which has often been experienced by those who were more frugal of their favours. The well-natured, but injudicious prodigality of James the First of Great Britain seems to have attached no body to his person; and that Prince, notwithstanding his social and harmless disposition, appears to have lived and died without 108a friend. The whole gentry and nobility of England exposed their lives and fortunes in the cause of his more frugal and distinguishing son, notwithstanding the coldness and distant severity of his ordinary deportment.

2. Secondly, I say, That wherever the conduct of the agent appears to have been entirely directed by motives and affections which we thoroughly enter into and approve of, we can have no sort of sympathy with the resentment of the sufferer, how great soever the mischief which may have been done to him. When two people quarrel, if we take part with, and entirely adopt the resentment of one of them, it is impossible that we should enter into that of the other. Our sympathy with the person whose motives we go along with, and whom therefore we look upon as in the right, cannot but harden us against all fellow-feeling with the other, whom we necessarily regard as in the wrong. Whatever this last, therefore, may have suffered, while it is no more than what we ourselves should have wished him to suffer, while it is no more than what our own sympathetic indignation would have prompted us to inflict upon him, it cannot either displease or provoke us. When an inhuman murderer is brought to the scaffold, though we have some compassion for his misery, we can have no sort of fellow-feeling with his resentment, if he should be so absurd as to express any against either his prosecutor or his judge. The natural tendency of their just indignation against so vile a criminal is indeed the most fatal and ruinous to him. But it is impossible that we should be displeased 109with the tendency of a sentiment, which, when we bring the case home to ourselves, we feel that we cannot avoid adopting.

CHAP. IV.
Recapitulation of the foregoing Chapters.

We do not, therefore, thoroughly and heartily sympathize with the gratitude of one man towards another, merely because this other has been the cause of his good fortune, unless he has been the cause of it from motives which we entirely go along with. Our heart must adopt the principles of the agent, and go along with all the affections which influenced his conduct, before it can entirely sympathize with, and beat time to, the gratitude of the person who has been benefited by his actions. If in the conduct of the benefactor there appears to have been no propriety, how beneficial soever its effects, it does not seem to demand, or necessarily to require, any proportionable recompense.

But when to the beneficent tendency of the action is joined the propriety of the affection from which it proceeds, when we entirely sympathize and go along with the motives of the agent, the love which we conceive for him upon his own account, enhances and enlivens our fellow-feeling 110 with the gratitude of those who owe their prosperity to his good conduct. His actions seem then to demand, and, if I may say so, to call aloud for a proportionable recompense. We then entirely enter into that gratitude which prompts to bestow it. The benefactor seems then to be the proper object of reward, when we thus entirely sympathize with, and approve of, that sentiment which prompts to reward him. When we approve of, and go along with, the affection from which the action proceeds, we must necessarily approve of the action, and regard the person towards whom it is directed as its proper and suitable object.

2. In the same manner, we cannot at all sympathize with the resentment of one man against another, merely because this other has been the cause of his misfortune, unless he has been the cause of it from motives which we cannot enter into. Before we can adopt the resentment of the sufferer, we must disapprove of the motives of the agent, and feel that our heart renounces all sympathy with the affections which influenced his conduct. If there appears to have been no impropriety in these, how fatal soever the tendency of the action which proceeds from them to those against whom it is directed, it does not seem to deserve any punishment, or to be the proper object of any resentment.

But when to the hurtfulness of the action is joined the impropriety of the affection from whence it proceeds, when our heart rejects with abhorrence all fellow-feeling with the motives of the agent, 111 we then heartily and entirely sympathize with the resentment of the sufferer. Such actions seem then to deserve, and, if I may say so, to call aloud for, a proportionable punishment; and we entirely enter into, and thereby approve of, that resentment which prompts to inflict it. The offender necessarily seems then to be the proper object of punishment, when we thus entirely sympathize with, and thereby approve of, that sentiment which prompts to punish. In this case too, when we approve, and go along with, the affection from which the action proceeds, we must necessarily approve of the action, and regard the person against whom it is directed, as its proper and suitable object.

112

CHAP. V.
The analysis of the sense of merit and demerit.

1.As our sense, therefore, of the propriety of conduct arises from what I shall call a direct sympathy with the affections and motives of the person who acts, so our sense of its merit arises from what I shall call an indirect sympathy with the gratitude of the person who is, if I may say so, acted upon.

As we cannot indeed enter thoroughly into the gratitude of the person who receives the benefit, unless we beforehand approve of the motives of the benefactor, so, upon this account, the sense of merit seems to be a compounded sentiment, and to be made up of two distinct emotions; a direct sympathy with the sentiments of the agent, and an indirect sympathy with the gratitude of those who receive the benefit of his actions.

We may, upon many different occasions, plainly distinguish those two different emotions combining and uniting together in our sense of the good desert of a particular character or action. When we read in history concerning actions of proper and beneficent greatness of mind, how eagerly do we enter into such designs? How much are we animated by that [113] high-spirited generosity which directs them? How keen are we for their success? How grieved at their disappointment? In imagination we become the very person whose actions are represented to us: we transport ourselves in fancy to the scenes of those distant and forgotten adventures, and imagine ourselves acting the part of a Scipio or a Camillus, a Timoleon or an Aristides. So far our sentiments are founded upon the direct sympathy with the person who acts. Nor is the indirect sympathy with those who receive the benefit of such actions less sensibly felt. Whenever we place ourselves in the situation of these last, with what warm and affectionate fellow-feeling do we enter into their gratitude towards those who served them so essentially? We embrace, as it were, their benefactor along with them. Our heart readily sympathizes with the highest transports of their grateful affection. No honours, no rewards, we think, can be too great for them to bestow upon him. When they make this proper return for his services, we heartily applaud and go along with them; but are shocked beyond all measure, if by their conduct they appear to have little sense of the obligations conferred upon them. Our whole sense, in short, of the merit and good desert of such actions, of the propriety and fitness of recompensing them, and making the person who performed them rejoice in his turn, arises from the sympathetic emotions of gratitude and love, with which, when we bring home to our own breast the situation of those principally concerned, we feel ourselves naturally transported towards the man who could act with such proper and noble beneficence.

[114] 2. In the same manner as our sense of the impropriety of conduct arises from a want of sympathy, or from a direct antipathy to the affections and motives of the agent, so our sense of its demerit arises from what I shall here too call an indirect sympathy with the resentment of the sufferer.

As we cannot indeed enter into the resentment of the sufferer, unless our heart beforehand disapproves the motives of the agent, and renounces all fellow-feeling with them; so upon this account the sense of demerit, as well as that of merit, seems to be a compounded sentiment, and to be made up of two distinct emotions; a direct antipathy to the sentiments of the agent, and an indirect sympathy with the resentment of the sufferer.

We may here too, upon many different occasions, plainly distinguish those two different emotions combining and uniting together in our sense of the ill desert of a particular character or action. When we read in history concerning the perfidy and cruelty of a Borgia or a Nero, our heart rises up against the detestable sentiments which influenced their conduct, and renounces with horror and abomination all fellow-feeling with such execrable motives. So far our sentiments are founded upon the direct antipathy to the affections of the agent: and the indirect sympathy with the resentment of the sufferers is still more sensibly felt. When we bring home to ourselves the situation of the persons whom those scourges of mankind insulted, murdered, or betrayed, what indignation do we not feel against such insolent and inhuman oppressors of the earth? Our [115] sympathy with the unavoidable distress of the innocent sufferers is not more real nor more lively, than our fellow-feeling with their just and natural resentment. The former sentiment only heightens the latter, and the idea of their distress serves only to inflame and blow up our animosity against those who occasioned it. When we think of the anguish of the sufferers, we take part with them more earnestly against their oppressors; we enter with more eagerness into all their schemes of vengeance, and feel ourselves every moment wreaking, in imagination, upon such violators of the laws of society, that punishment which our sympathetic indignation tells us is due to their crimes. Our sense of the horror and dreadful atrocity of such conduct, the delight which we take in hearing that it was properly punished, the indignation which we feel when it escapes this due retaliation, our whole sense and feeling, in short, of its ill desert, of the propriety and fitness of inflicting evil upon the person who is guilty of it, and of making him grieve in his turn, arises from the sympathetic indignation which naturally boils up in the breast of the spectator, whenever he thoroughly brings home to himself the case of the sufferer[a].

2. To ascribe in this manner our natural sense of the ill desert of human actions to a sympathy with the resentment of the sufferer, may seem, to the greater part of people, to be a degradation of that sentiment. Resentment is commonly regarded as so odious a passion, that they will be apt to think it impossible that so laudable a principle, as the sense of the ill desert of vice, should in any respect be founded upon it. They will be more willing, perhaps, to admit that our sense of the merit of good actions is founded upon a sympathy with the gratitude of the persons who receive the benefit of them; because gratitude, as well as all the other benevolent passions, is regarded as an amiable principle, which can take nothing from the worth of whatever is founded [116] upon it. Gratitude and resentment, however, are in every respect, it is evident, counterparts to one another; and if our sense of merit arises from a sympathy with the one, our sense of demerit can scarce miss to proceed from a fellow-feeling with the other.

Let it be considered too that resentment, though, in the degrees in which we too often see it, the most odious, perhaps, of all the passions, is not disapproved of when properly humbled and entirely brought down to the level of the sympathetic indignation of the spectator. When we, who are the bystanders, feel that our own animosity entirely corresponds with that of the sufferer, when the resentment of this last does not in any respect go beyond our own, when no word, no gesture, escapes him that denotes an emotion more violent than what we can keep time to, and when he never aims at inflicting any punishment beyond what we should rejoice to see inflicted, or what we ourselves would upon this account even desire to be the instruments of inflicting, it is impossible that we should not entirely approve of his sentiments. Our own emotion in this case must, in our eyes, undoubtedly justify his. And as experience teaches us how much the greater part of mankind are incapable of this moderation, and how great an effort must be made in order to bring down the rude and undisciplined impulse of resentment to this suitable temper, we cannot avoid conceiving a considerable degree of esteem and admiration for one who appears capable of exerting so much self-command over one of the most ungovernable passions of his nature. When indeed the animosity of the sufferer exceeds, as it almost always does, what we can go along with, as we cannot enter into it, we necessarily disapprove of it. We even disapprove of it more than we should of an equal excess of almost any other passion derived from the imagination. And this too violent resentment, instead of carrying us along with it, becomes itself the object of our resentment and indignation. We enter into the opposite resentment of the person who is the object of this unjust emotion, and who is in danger of suffering from it. Revenge, therefore, the excess of resentment, appears to be the most detestable of all the passions, and is the object of the horror and indignation of every body. And as in the way in which this passion commonly discovers itself among mankind, it is excessive a hundred times for once that it is moderate, we are very apt to consider it as altogether odious and detestable, because in its most ordinary appearances it is so. Nature, however, even in the present depraved state of mankind, does not seem to have dealt so unkindly 117 with us, as to have endowed us with any principle which is wholly in every respect evil, or which, in no degree and in no direction, can be the proper object of praise and approbation. Upon some occasions we are sensible that this passion, which is generally too strong, may likewise be too weak. We sometimes complain that a particular person shows too little spirit, and has too little sense of the injuries that have been done to him; and we are as ready to despise him for the defect, as to hate him for the excess of this passion.

The inspired writers would not surely have talked so frequently or so strongly of the wrath and anger of God, if they had regarded every degree of those passions as vicious and evil, even in so weak and imperfect a creature as man.

Let it be considered too, that the present inquiry is not concerning a matter of right, if I may say so, but concerning a matter of fact. We are not at present examining upon what principles a perfect being would approve of the punishment of bad actions; but upon what principles so weak and imperfect a creature as man actually and in fact approves of it. The principles which I have just now mentioned, it is evident, have a very great effect upon his sentiments; and it seems wisely ordered that it should be so. The very existence of society requires that unmerited and unprovoked malice should be restrained by proper punishments; and consequently, that to inflict those punishments should be regarded as a proper and laudable action. Though man, therefore, be naturally endowed with a desire of the welfare and preservation of society, yet the Author of nature has not entrusted it to his reason to find out that a certain application of punishments is the proper means of attaining this end; but has endowed him with an immediate and instinctive approbation of that very application which is most proper to attain it. The œconomy of nature is in this respect exactly of a piece with what it is upon many other occasions. With regard to all those ends which, upon account of their peculiar importance, may be regarded, if such an expression is allowable, as the favourite ends of nature, she has constantly in this manner not only endowed mankind with an appetite for the end which she proposes, but likewise with an appetite for the means by which alone this end can be brought about, for their own sakes, and independent of their tendency to produce it. Thus self-preservation, and the propagation of the species, are the great ends which Nature seems to have proposed in the formation of all animals. Mankind are 118 endowed with a desire of those ends, and an aversion to the contrary; with a love of life, and a dread of dissolution; with a desire of the continuance and perpetuity of the species, and with an aversion to the thoughts of its entire extinction. But though we are in this manner endowed with a very strong desire of those ends, it has not been entrusted to the slow and uncertain determinations of our reason, to find out the proper means of bringing them about. Nature has directed us to the greater part of these by original and immediate instincts. Hunger, thirst, the passion which unites the two sexes, the love of pleasure, and the dread of pain, prompt us to apply those means for their own sakes, and without any consideration of their tendency to those beneficent ends which the great Director of nature intended to produce by them.

Before I conclude this note, I must take notice of a difference between the approbation of propriety and that of merit or beneficence. Before we approve of the sentiments of any person as proper and suitable to their objects, we must not only be affected in the same manner as he is, but we must perceive this harmony and correspondence of sentiments between him and ourselves. Thus, though upon hearing of a misfortune that had befallen my friend, I should conceive precisely that degree of concern which he gives way to; yet till I am informed of the manner in which he behaves, till I perceive the harmony between his emotions and mine, I cannot be said to approve of the sentiments which influence his behaviour. The approbation of propriety therefore requires, not only that we should intirely sympathize with the person who acts, but that we should perceive this perfect concord between his sentiments and our own. On the contrary, when I hear of a benefit that has been bestowed upon another person, let him who has received it be affected in what manner he pleases, if, by bringing his case home to myself, I feel gratitude arise in my own breast, I necessarily approve of the conduct of his benefactor, and regard it as meritorious, and the proper object of reward. Whether the person who has received the benefit conceives gratitude or not, cannot, it is evident, in any degree alter our sentiments with regard to the merit of him who has bestowed it. No actual correspondence of sentiments, therefore, is here required. It is sufficient that if he was grateful, they would correspond; and our sense of merit is often founded upon one of those illusive sympathies, by which, when we bring home to ourselves the case of another, we are often affected in a manner in which the person principally concerned is incapable of being affected. There is a similar difference between our disapprobation of demerit, and that of impropriety.

SECTION II.
Of justice and beneficence.

CHAP. I.
Comparison of those two virtues.

Actions of a beneficent tendency, which proceed from proper motives, seem alone to require reward; because such alone are the approved objects of gratitude, or excite the sympathetic gratitude of the spectator.

Actions of a hurtful tendency, which proceed from improper motives, seem alone to deserve punishment; because such alone are the approved objects of resentment, or excite the sympathetic resentment of the spectator.

Beneficence is always free, it cannot be extorted by force, the mere want of it exposes to no punishment; because the mere want of beneficence tends to do no real positive evil. It may disappoint of the good which might reasonably have been expected, and upon that account it may justly excite dislike and disapprobation: it cannot, however, provoke 120 any resentment which mankind will go along with. The man who does not recompense his benefactor, when he has it in his power, and when his benefactor needs his assistance, is, no doubt, guilty of the blackest ingratitude. The heart of every impartial spectator rejects all fellow-feeling with the selfishness of his motives, and he is the proper object of the highest disapprobation. But still he does no positive hurt to any body. He only does not do that good which in propriety he ought to have done. He is the object of hatred, a passion which is naturally excited by impropriety of sentiment and behaviour; not of resentment, a passion which is never properly called forth but by actions which tend to do real and positive hurt to some particular persons. His want of gratitude, therefore, cannot be punished. To oblige him by force to perform what in gratitude he ought to perform, and what every impartial spectator would approve of him for performing, would if possible, be still more improper than his neglecting to perform it. His benefactor would dishonour himself if he attempted by violence to constrain him to gratitude, and it would be impertinent for any third person, who was not the superior of either, to intermeddle. But of all the duties of beneficence, those which gratitude recommends to us approach nearest to what is called a perfect and complete obligation. What friendship, what generosity, what charity, would prompt us to do with universal approbation, is still more free, and can still less be extorted by force than the duties of gratitude. We talk of the debt of gratitude, not of charity, or generosity, nor even of friendship, when friendship is mere esteem, and has not been enhanced and complicated with gratitude for good offices.

[121] Resentment seems to have been given us by nature for defence, and for defence only. It is the safeguard of justice and the security of innocence. It prompts us to beat off the mischief which is attempted to be done to us, and to retaliate that which is already done; that the offender may be made to repent of his injustice, and that others, through fear of the like punishment, may be terrified from being guilty of the like offence. It must be reserved therefore for these purposes, nor can the spectator ever go along with it when it is exerted for any other. But the mere want of the beneficent virtues, though it may disappoint us of the good which might reasonably be expected, neither does, nor attempts to do, any mischief from which we can have occasion to defend ourselves.

There is however another virtue, of which the observance is not left to the freedom of our own wills, which may be extorted by force, and of which the violation exposes to resentment, and consequently to punishment. This virtue is justice: the violation of justice is injury: it does real and positive hurt to some particular persons, from motives which are naturally disapproved of. It is, therefore, the proper object of resentment, and of punishment, which is the natural consequence of resentment. As mankind go along with, and approve of, the violence employed to avenge the hurt which is done by injustice, so they much more go along with, and approve of, that which is employed to prevent and beat off the injury, and to restrain the offender from hurting his neighbours. The person himself who meditates an injustice is sensible of this, and feels that force may, with the utmost propriety, be [122] made use of, both by the person whom he is about to injure, and by others, either to obstruct the execution of his crime, or to punish him when he has executed it. And upon this is founded that remarkable distinction between justice and all the other social virtues, which has of late been particularly insisted upon by an author of very great and original genius, that we feel ourselves to be under a stricter obligation to act according to justice, than agreeably to friendship, charity, or generosity; that the practice of these last mentioned virtues seems to be left in some measure to our own choice, but that, somehow or other, we feel ourselves to be in a peculiar manner tied, bound, and obliged to the observation of justice. We feel, that is to say, that force may, with the utmost propriety and with the approbation of all mankind, be made use of to constrain us to observe the rules of the one, but not to follow the precepts of the other.

We must always, however, carefully distinguish what is only blamable, or the proper object of disapprobation, from what force may be employed either to punish or to prevent. That seems blamable which falls short of that ordinary degree of proper beneficence which experience teaches us to expect of every body; and on the contrary, that seems praise-worthy which goes beyond it. The ordinary degree itself, seems neither blamable nor praise-worthy. A father, a son, a brother, who behaves to the correspondent relation, neither better nor worse than the greater part of men commonly do, seems properly to deserve neither praise nor blame. He who surprises us by extraordinary and unexpected, [123] though still proper and suitable kindness, or on the contrary, by extraordinary and unexpected, as well as unsuitable unkindness, seems praise-worthy in the one case, and blamable in the other.

Even the most ordinary degree of kindness or beneficence, however, cannot, among equals, be extorted by force. Among equals each individual is naturally, and antecedent to the institution of civil government, regarded as having a right both to defend himself from injuries, and to exact a certain degree of punishment for those which have been done to him. Every generous spectator not only approves of his conduct when he does this, but enters so far into his sentiments as often to be willing to assist him. When one man attacks, or robs, or attempts to murder another, all the neighbours take the alarm, and think that they do right when they run, either to revenge the person who has been injured, or to defend him who is in danger of being so. But when a father fails in the ordinary degree of parental affection towards a son, when a son seems to want that filial reverence which might be expected to his father; when brothers are without the usual degree of brotherly affection; when a man shuts his breast against compassion, and refuses to relieve the misery of his fellow-creatures, when he can with the greatest ease; in all these cases, though every body blames the conduct, nobody imagines that those who might have reason, perhaps, to expect more kindness, have any right to extort it by force. The sufferer can only complain, and the spectator can intermeddle no other way than by advice and persuasion. Upon all such occasions, for equals to use force 124 against one another, would be thought the highest degree of insolence and presumption.

A superior may, indeed, sometimes, with universal approbation, oblige those under his jurisdiction to behave, in this respect, with a certain degree of propriety to one another. The laws of all civilized nations oblige parents to maintain their children, and children to maintain their parents, and impose upon men many other duties of beneficence. The civil magistrate is entrusted with the power not only of preserving the public peace by retraining injustice, but of promoting the prosperity of the commonwealth, by establishing good discipline, and by discouraging every sort of vice and impropriety; he may prescribe rules, therefore, which not only prohibit mutual injuries among fellow-citizens, but command mutual good offices to a certain degree. When the sovereign commands what is merely indifferent, and what, antecedent to his orders, might have been omitted without any blame, it becomes not only blamable but punishable to disobey him. When he commands, therefore, what, antecedent to any such order, could not have been omitted without the greatest blame, it surely becomes much more punishable to be wanting in obedience. Of all the duties of a law-giver, however, this, perhaps, is that which it requires the greatest delicacy and reserve to execute with propriety and judgment. To neglect it altogether exposes the commonwealth to many gross disorders and shocking enormities, and to push it too far is destructive of all liberty, security, and justice.

125 Though the mere want of beneficence seems to merit no punishment from equals, the greater exertions of that virtue appear to deserve the highest reward. By being productive of the greatest good, they are the natural and approved objects of the liveliest gratitude. Though the breach of justice, on the contrary, exposes to punishment, the observance of the rules of that virtue seems scarce to deserve any reward. There is, no doubt, a propriety in the practice of justice, and it merits, upon that account, all the approbation which is due to propriety. But as it does no real positive good, it is entitled to very little gratitude. Mere justice is, upon most occasions, but a negative virtue, and only hinders us from hurting our neighbour. The man who barely abstains from violating either the person, or the estate, or the reputation of his neighbours, has surely very little positive merit. He fulfils, however, all the rules of what is peculiarly called justice, and does everything which

his equals can with propriety force him to do, or which they can punish him for not doing. We may often fulfil all the rules of justice by sitting still and doing nothing.

As every man doth, so shall it be done to him, and retaliation seems to be the great law which is dictated to us by Nature. Beneficence and generosity we think due to the generous and beneficent. Those whose hearts never open to the feelings of humanity, should, we think, be shut out in the same manner, from the affections of all their fellow-creatures, and be allowed to live in the midst of society, as in a great desert where there is nobody to care for them, or to inquire after them. The violator 126 of the laws of justice ought to be made to feel himself that evil which he has done to another; and since no regard to the sufferings of his brethren are capable of restraining him, he ought to be over-awed by the fear of his own. The man who is barely innocent, who only observes the law of justice with regard to others, and merely abstains from hurting his neighbours, can merit only that his neighbours in their turn should respect his innocence, and that the same laws should be religiously observed with regard to him.

CHAP. II.
Of the sense of justice, of remorse, and of the consciousness of merit.

There can be no proper motive for hurting our neighbour, there can be no incitement to do evil to another, which mankind will go along with, except just indignation for evil which that other has done to us. To disturb his happiness merely because it stands in the way of our own, to take from him what is of real use to him merely because it may be of equal or more use to us, or to indulge, in this manner, at the expence of other people, the natural preference which every man has for his own happiness above that of other people, is what no impartial spectator can go along with. Every man is, no doubt, by nature, first and principally recommended to his own care; and as he is fitter to take care 127 of himself than of any other person, it is fit and right that it should be so. Every man, therefore, is much more deeply interested in whatever immediately concerns himself, than in what concerns any other man: and to hear, perhaps, of the death of another person, with whom we have no particular connexion, will give us less concern, will spoil our stomach, or break our rest much less than a very insignificant disaster which has befallen ourselves. But though the ruin of our neighbour may affect us much less than a very small misfortune of our own, we must not ruin him to prevent that small misfortune, nor even to prevent our own ruin. We must, here, as in all other cases, view ourselves not so much according to that light in which we may naturally appear to ourselves, as according to that in which we naturally appear to others. Though every man may, according to the proverb, be the whole world to himself, to the rest of mankind he is a most insignificant part of it. Though his own happiness may be of more importance to him than that of all the world besides, to every other person it is of no more consequence than that of any other man. Though it may be true, therefore, that every individual, in his own breast, naturally prefers himself to all mankind, yet he dares not look mankind in the face, and avow that he acts according to this principle. He feels that in this preference they can never go along with him, and that how natural soever it may be to him, it must always appear excessive and extravagant to them. When he views himself in the light in which he is conscious that others will view him, he sees that to them he is but one of the multitude in no respect better than any other in it. If he would act so as that the impartial spectator may [128] enter into the principles of his conduct, which is what of all things he has the greatest desire to do, he must, upon this, as upon all other occasions, humble the arrogance of his self-love, and bring it down to something which other men can go along with. They will indulge it so far as to allow him to be more anxious about, and to pursue with more earnest assiduity, his own happiness than that of any other person. Thus far, whenever they place themselves in his situation, they will readily go along with him. In the race for wealth and honours, and preferments, he may run as hard as he can, and strain every nerve and every muscle, in order to outstrip all his competitors. But if he should justle, or throw down any of them, the indulgence of the spectators is entirely at an end. It is a violation of fair play, which they cannot admit of. This man is to them, in every respect, as good as he: they do not enter into that self-love by which he prefers himself so much to this other, and cannot go along with the motive from which he hurt him. They readily, therefore, sympathize with the natural resentment of the injured, and the offender becomes the object of their hatred and indignation. He is sensible that he becomes so, and feels that those sentiments are ready to burst out from all sides against him.

As the greater and more irreparable the evil that is done, the resentment of the sufferer runs naturally the higher, so does likewise the sympathetic indignation of the spectator, as well as the sense of guilt in the agent. Death is the greatest evil which one man can inflict upon another, and excites the highest degree of resentment in those who are immediately connected with the slain. Murder, therefore, [129] is the most atrocious of all crimes which affect individuals only, in the sight both of mankind, and of the person who has committed it. To be deprived of that which we are possessed of, is a greater evil than to be disappointed of what we have only the expectation. Breach of property, therefore, theft and robbery, which take from us what we are possessed of, are greater crimes than breach of contract, which only disappoints us of what we expected. The most sacred laws of justice, therefore, those whose violation seems to call the loudest for vengeance and punishment, are the laws which guard the life and person of our neighbour; the next are those which guard his property and possessions; and last of all come those which guard what are called his personal rights, or what is due to him from the promises of others.

The violator of the more sacred laws of justice can never reflect on the sentiments which mankind must entertain with regard to him, without feeling all the agonies of shame, and horror, and consternation. When his passion is gratified, and he begins coolly to reflect upon his conduct, he can enter into none of the motives which influenced it. They appear now as detestable to him as they did always to other people. By sympathizing with the hatred and abhorrence which other men must entertain for him, he becomes in some measure the object of his own hatred and abhorrence. The situation of the person, who suffered by his injustice, now calls upon his pity. He is grieved at the thought of it; regrets the unhappy effects of his own conduct, and feels at the same time that they have rendered him the proper object of the resentment and indignation [130] of mankind, and of what is the natural consequence of resentment, vengeance and punishment. The thought of this perpetually haunts him, and fills him with terror and amazement. He dares no longer look society in the face, but imagines himself as it were rejected, and thrown out from the affections of all mankind. He cannot hope for the consolation of sympathy in this his greatest, and most dreadful distress. The remembrance of his crimes has shut out all fellow-feelings with him from the hearts of his fellow-creatures. The sentiments which they entertain with regard to him, are the very thing which he is most afraid of. Every thing seems hostile, and he would be glad to fly to some inhospitable desert, where he might never more behold the face of a human creature, nor read in the countenance of mankind the condemnation of his crimes. But solitude is still more dreadful than society. His own thoughts can present him with nothing but what is black, unfortunate, and disastrous, the melancholy forebodings of incomprehensible misery and ruin. The horror of solitude drives him back into society, and he comes again into the presence of mankind, astonished to appear before them, loaded with shame and distracted with fear, in order to supplicate some little protection from the countenance of those very judges, who he knows have already all unanimously condemned him. Such is the nature of that sentiment, which is properly called remorse; of all the sentiments which can enter the human breast the most dreadful. It is made up of shame from the sense of the impropriety of past conduct; of grief for the effects of it; of pity for those who suffer by it; and of the dread and terror of punishment from the consciousness of the justly provoked resentment of all rational creatures.

[131]The opposite behaviour naturally inspires the opposite sentiment. The man who, not from frivolous fancy, but from proper motives, has performed a generous action, when he looks forward to those whom he has served, feels himself to be the natural object of their love and gratitude, and, by sympathy with them, of the esteem and approbation of all mankind. And when he looks backward to the motive from which he acted, and surveys it in the light in which the indifferent spectator will survey it, he still continues to enter into it, and applauds himself by sympathy with the approbation of this supposed impartial judge. In both these points of view his own conduct appears to him every way agreeable. His mind, at the thought of it, is filled with chearfulness, serenity, and composure. He is in friendship and harmony with all mankind, and looks upon his fellow-creatures with confidence and benevolent satisfaction, secure that he has rendered himself worthy of their most favourable regards. In the combination of all these sentiments consists the consciousness of merit, or of deserved reward.

[132]

CHAP. III.
Of the utility of this constitution of nature.

It is thus that man, who can subsist only in society, was fitted by nature to that situation for which he was made. All the members of human society stand in need of each others assistance, and are likewise exposed to mutual injuries. Where the necessary assistance is reciprocally afforded from love, from gratitude, from friendship and esteem, the society flourishes and is happy. All the different members of it are bound together by the agreeable bands of love and affection, and are, as it were, drawn to one common centre of mutual good offices.

But though the necessary assistance should not be afforded from such generous and disinterested motives, though among the different members of the society there should be no mutual love and affection, the society, though less happy and agreeable, will not necessarily be dissolved. Society may subsist among different men, as among different merchants, from a sense of its utility, without any mutual love or affection; and though no man in it should owe any obligation, or be bound in gratitude to any other, it may still be upheld by a mercenary exchange of good offices according to an agreed valuation.

Society, however, cannot subsist among those who are at all times ready to hurt and injure one another. The moment that injury begins, the moment that mutual resentment and animosity take place, all the bands of it are broke asunder, and the different members of which it consisted are, as it were, dissipated and scattered abroad by the violence and opposition of their discordant affections. If there is any society among robbers and murderers, they must at least, according to the trite observation, abstain from robbing and murdering one another. Beneficence, therefore, is less essential to the exigence of society than justice. Society may subsist, though not in the most comfortable state, without beneficence; but the prevalence of injustice must utterly destroy it.

Though Nature, therefore, exhorts mankind to acts of beneficence, by the pleasing consciousness of deserved reward, she has not thought it necessary to guard and enforce the practice of it by the terrors of merited punishment in case it should be neglected. It is the ornament which embellishes, not the foundation which supports the building, and which it was, therefore, sufficient to recommend, but by no means necessary to impose. Justice, on the contrary, is the main pillar that upholds the whole edifice. If it is removed, the great, the immense fabric of human society, that fabric which to raise and support seems in this world, if I may say so, to have been the peculiar and darling care of Nature, must in a moment crumble into atoms. In order to enforce the observation of justice, therefore, Nature has implanted in the human breast that consciousness of ill desert, those terrors of merited punishment which attend upon its violation, as the great safeguards of the association of mankind, to protect the weak, to curb the violent, and to chastise the guilty. Men, though naturally sympathetic, feel so little for another, with whom they have no particular connexion, in comparison for what they feel for themselves; the misery of one, who is merely their fellow-creature, is of so little importance to them in comparison even of a small conveniency of their own; they have it so much in their power to hurt him, and may have so many temptations to do so, that if this principle did not stand up within them in his defence, and overawe them into a respect for his innocence, they would, like wild beasts, be at all times ready to fly upon him; and a man would enter an assembly of men as he enters a den of lions.

In every part of the universe we observe means adjusted with the nicest artifice to the ends which they are intended to produce; and in the mechanism of a plant, or animal body, admire how every thing is contrived for advancing the two great purposes of nature, the support of the individual, and the propagation of the species. But in these, and in all such objects, we still distinguish the efficient from the final cause of their several motions and organizations. The digestion of the food, the circulation of the blood, and the secretion of the several juices which are drawn from it, are operations all of them necessary for the great purposes of animal life. Yet we never endeavour to account for them from those purposes as from their efficient causes, nor imagine that the blood circulates, or that the food digests of its own accord, and with a view or intention to the purposes of circulation or digestion. The wheels of the watch are all admirably adjusted to the end for which it was made, the pointing of the hour. All their various motions conspire in the nicest manner to produce this effect. If they were endowed with a desire and intention to produce it, they could not do it better. Yet we never ascribe any such desire or intention to them, but to the watch-maker, and we know that they are put in motion by a spring, which intends the effect it produces as little as they do. But though, in accounting for the operations of bodies, we never fail to distinguish in this manner the efficient from the final cause, in accounting for those of the mind, we are very apt to confound those two different things with one another. When by natural principles we are led to advance those ends, which a refined and enlightened reason should recommend to us, we are very apt to impute to that reason, as to their efficient cause, the sentiments and actions by which we advance those ends, and to imagine that to be the wisdom of man, which in reality is the wisdom of God. Upon a superficial view this cause seems sufficient to produce the effects which are ascribed to it; and the system of human nature seems to be more simple and agreeable when all its different operations are in this manner deduced from a single principle.

As society cannot subsist unless the laws of justice are totally observed, as no social intercourse can take place among men who do not generally abstain from injuring one another; the consideration of this necessity, it has been thought, was the ground upon which we approved of the enforcement of the laws of justice by the punishment of those who violated 136 them. Man, it has been said, has a natural love for society, and desires that the union of mankind should be preserved for its own sake, and though he himself was to derive no benefit from it. The orderly and flourishing state of society is agreeable to him, and he takes delight in contemplating it. Its disorder and confusion, on the contrary, is the object of his aversion, and he is chagrined at whatever tends to produce it. He is sensible too that his own interest is connected with the prosperity of society, and that the happiness, perhaps the preservation of his existence, depends upon its preservation. Upon every account, therefore, he has an abhorrence at whatever can tend to destroy society, and is willing to make use of every means, which can hinder so hated and so dreadful an event. Injustice necessarily tends to destroy it. Every appearance of injustice, therefore, alarms him, and he runs, if I may say so, to stop the progress of what, if allowed to go on, would quickly put an end to every thing that is dear to him. If he cannot restrain it by gentle and fair means, he must bear it down by force and violence, and at any rate must put a stop to its further progress. Hence it is, they say, that he often approves of the enforcement of the law of justice even by the capital punishment of those who violate them. The disturber of the public peace is hereby removed out of the world, and others are terrified by his fate from imitating his example.

Such is the account commonly given of our approbation of the punishment of injustice. And so far this account is undoubtedly true, that we frequently have occasion to confirm our natural sense of the propriety and fitness of punishment, by reflecting 137 how necessary it is for preserving the order of society. When the guilty is about to suffer that just retaliation, which the natural indignation of mankind tells them is due to his crimes; when the insolence of his injustice is broken and humbled by the terror of his approaching punishment; when he ceases to be an object of fear, with the generous and humane he begins to be an object of pity. The thought of what he is about to suffer extinguishes their resentment for the sufferings of others to which he has given occasion. They are disposed to pardon and forgive him, and to save him from that punishment, which in all their cool hours they had considered as the retribution due to such crimes. Here, therefore, they have occasion to call to their assistance the consideration of the general interest of society. They counterbalance the impulse of this weak and partial humanity by the dictates of a humanity that is more generous and comprehensive. They reflect that mercy to the guilty is cruelty to the innocent, and oppose to the emotions of compassion which they feel for a particular person, a more enlarged compassion which they feel for mankind.

Sometimes too we have occasion to defend the propriety of observing the general rules of justice by the consideration of their necessity to the support of society. We frequently hear the young and the licentious ridiculing the most sacred rules of morality, and professing, sometimes from the corruption, but more frequently from the vanity of their hearts, the most abominable maxims of conduct. Our indignation rouses, and we are eager to refute and expose such detestable principles. But though it is 138 their intrinsic hatefulness and detestableness, which originally inflames us against them, we are unwilling to assign this as the sole reason why we condemn them, or to pretend that it is merely because we ourselves hate and detest them. The reason, we think, would not appear to be conclusive. Yet why should it not; if we hate and detest them because they are the natural and proper objects of hatred and detestation? But when we are asked why we should not act in such or such a manner, the very question seems to suppose that, to those who ask it, this manner of acting does not appear to be for its own sake the natural and proper object of those sentiments. We must show them, therefore, that it ought to be so for the sake of something else. Upon this account we generally cast about for other arguments, and the consideration which first occurs to us is the disorder and confusion of society which would result from the universal prevalence of such practices. We seldom fail, therefore, to insist upon this topic.

But though it commonly requires no great discernment to see the destructive tendency of all licentious practices to the welfare of society, it is seldom this consideration which first animates us against them. All men, even the most stupid and unthinking, abhor fraud, perfidy, and injustice, and delight to see them punished. But few men have reflected upon the necessity of justice to the existence of society, how obvious soever that necessity may appear to be.

That it is not a regard to the preservation of society, which originally interests us in the punishment 139 of crimes committed against individuals, may be demonstrated by many obvious considerations. The concern which we take in the fortune and happiness of individuals does not, in common cases, arise from that which we take in the fortune and happiness of society. We are no more concerned for the destruction or loss of a single man, because this man is a member or part of society, and because we should be concerned for the destruction of society, than we are concerned for the loss of a single guinea, because this guinea is a part of a thousand guineas, and because we should be concerned for the loss of the whole sum. In neither case does our regard for the individuals arise from our regard for the multitude: but in both cases our regard for the multitude is compounded and made up of the particular regards which we feel for the different individuals of which it is composed. As when a small sum is unjustly taken from us we do not so much prosecute the injury from a regard to the preservation of our whole fortune, as from a regard to that particular sum which we have lost; so when a single man is injured or destroyed, we demand the punishment of the wrong that has been done to him, not so much from a concern for the general interest of society, as from a concern for that very individual who has been injured. It is to be observed, however, that this concern does not necessarily include in it any degree of those exquisite sentiments which are commonly called love, esteem, and affection, and by which we distinguish our particular friends and acquaintance. The concern which is requisite for this is no more than the general fellow-feeling which we have with every man merely because he is our fellow-creature. We enter into the resentment even of an odious person, [140] when he is injured by those to whom he has given no provocation. Our disapprobation of his ordinary character and conduct, does not in this case altogether prevent our fellow-feeling with his natural indignation; though with those who are not either extremely candid, or who have not been accustomed to correct and regulate their natural sentiments by general rules, it is very apt to damp it.

Upon some occasions, indeed, we both punish and approve of punishment, merely from a view to the general interest of society, which, we imagine, cannot otherwise be secured. Of this kind are all the punishments inflicted for breaches of what is called either civil police, or military discipline. Such crimes do not immediately or directly hurt any particular person; but their remote consequences, it is supposed, do produce, or might produce, either a considerable inconveniency, or a great disorder in the society. A centinel, for example, who falls asleep upon his watch, suffers death by the law of war, because such carelessness might endanger the whole army. This severity may, upon many occasions, appear necessary, and, for that reason, just and proper. When the preservation of an individual is inconsistent with the safety of a multitude, nothing can be more just than that the many should be preferred to the one. Yet this punishment, how necessary soever, always appears to be excessively severe. The natural atrocity of the crime seems to be so little, and the punishment so great, that it is with great difficulty that our hearts can reconcile itself to it. Though such carelessness appears very blamable, yet the thought of this crime does not naturally excite any such resentment, as would prompt us to [141] take such dreadful revenge. A man of humanity must recollect himself, must make an effort, and exert his whole firmness and resolution, before he can bring himself either to inflict it, or to go along with it when it is inflicted by others. It is not, however, in this manner, that he looks upon the just punishment of an ungrateful murderer or parricide. His heart, in this case, applauds with ardour, and even with transport, the just retaliation which seems due to such detestable crimes, and which, if, by any accident, they should happen to escape, he would be highly enraged and disappointed. The very different sentiment with which the spectator views those different punishments, is a proof that his approbation of the one is far from being founded upon the same principles with that of the other. He looks upon the centinel as an unfortunate victim, who, indeed, must, and ought to be, devoted to the safety of numbers, but whom still, in his heart, he would be glad to save; and he is only sorry, that the interest of the many should oppose it. But if the murderer should escape from punishment, it would excite his highest indignation, and he would call upon God to avenge, in another world, that crime which the injustice of mankind had neglected to chastise upon earth.

For it well deserves to be taken notice of, that we are so far from imagining that injustice ought to be punished in this life, merely on account of the order of society, which cannot otherwise be maintained, that Nature teaches us to hope, and religion, we suppose, authorizes us to expect, that it will be punished, even in a life to come. Our sense of its ill desert pursues it, if I may say so, even beyond the [142] grave, though the example of its punishment there cannot serve to deter the rest of mankind, who see it not, who know it not, from being guilty of the like practices here. The justice of God, however, we think, still requires, that he should hereafter avenge the injuries of the widow and the fatherless, who are here so often insulted with impunity.

That the Deity loves virtue and hates vice, as a voluptuous man loves riches and hates poverty, not for their own sakes, but for the effects which they tend to produce; that he loves the one, only because it promotes the happiness of society, which his benevolence prompts him to desire; and that he hates the other, only because it occasions the misery of mankind, which the same divine quality renders the object of his aversion; is not the doctrine of untaught nature, but of an artificial refinement of reason and philosophy. Our untaught, natural sentiments, all prompt us to believe, that as perfect virtue is supposed necessarily to appear to the Deity, as it does to us, for its own sake, and without any further view, the natural and proper object of love and reward, so must vice, of hatred and punishment. That the gods neither resent nor hurt, was the general maxim of all the different sects of the ancient philosophy: and if, by resenting, be understood, that violent and disorderly perturbation, which often distracts and confounds the human breast; or if, by hurting, be understood, the doing mischief wantonly, and without regard to propriety or justice, such weakness is undoubtedly unworthy of the divine perfection. But if it be meant, that vice does not appear to the Deity to be, for its own sake, the object of abhorrence and aversion, and what, for its 143 own sake, it is fit and right should be punished, the truth of this maxim seems repugnant to some very natural feelings. If we consult our natural sentiments, we are even apt to fear, lest, before the holiness of God, vice should appear to be more worthy of punishment than the weakness and imperfection of human virtue can ever seem to be of reward. Man, when about to appear before a Being of infinite perfection, can feel but little confidence in his own merit, or in the imperfect propriety of his own conduct. In the presence of his fellow-creatures, he may even justly elevate himself, and may often have reason to think highly of his own character and conduct, compared to the still greater imperfection of theirs. But the case is quite different when about to appear before his infinite Creator. To such a Being, he fears, that his littleness and weakness can scarce ever appear the proper object, either of esteem or of reward. But he can easily conceive, how the numberless violations of duty, of which he has been guilty, should render him the proper object of aversion and punishment; and he thinks he can see no reason why the divine indignation should not be let loose without any restraint, upon so vile an insect, as he imagines that he himself must appear to be. If he would still hope for happiness, he suspects that he cannot demand it from the justice, but that he must entreat it from the mercy of God. Repentance, sorrow, humility, contrition at the thought of his past conduct, seem, upon this account, the sentiments which become him, and to be the only means which he has left for appeasing that wrath which, he knows, he has justly provoked. He even distrusts the efficacy of all these, and naturally fears, lest the wisdom of God should not, like the 144 weakness of man, be prevailed upon to spare the crime by the most importunate lamentations of the criminal. Some other intercession, some other sacrifice, some other atonement, he imagines must be made for him, beyond what he himself is capable of making, before the purity of the divine justice can be reconciled to his manifold offences. The doctrines of revelation coincide, in every respect, with those original anticipations of nature; and as they teach us how little we can depend upon the imperfection of our own virtue, so they show us, at the same time, that the most powerful intercession has been made, and that the most dreadful atonement has been paid for our manifold transgressions and iniquities.

145

SECTION III.
Of the influence of fortune upon the sentiments of mankind, with regard to the merit or demerit of actions.

INTRODUCTION.

Whatever praise or blame can be due to any action, must belong either, first, to the intention or affection of the heart, from which it proceeds; or, secondly, to the external action or movement of the body, which this affection gives occasion to; or, last, to all the good or bad consequences, which actually, and in fact, proceed from it. These three different things constitute the whole nature and circumstances of the action, and must be the foundation of whatever quality can belong to it.

That the two last of these three circumstances cannot be the foundation of any praise or blame, is abundantly evident; nor has the contrary ever been asserted by any body. The external action or movement of the body is often the same in the most innocent and in the most blamable actions. He who shoots a bird, and he who shoots a man, both of them 146 perform the same external movement: each of them draws the tricker of a gun. The consequences which actually, and in fact, happen to proceed from any action, are, if possible, still more indifferent either to praise or blame, than even the external movement of the body. As they depend, not upon the agent, but upon fortune, they cannot be the proper foundation for any sentiment, of which his character and conduct are the objects.

The only consequences for which he can be answerable, or by which he can deserve either approbation or disapprobation of any kind, are those which were some way or other intended, or those which, at least, show some agreeable or disagreeable quality in the intention of the heart, from which he acted. To the intention or affection of the heart, therefore, to the propriety or impropriety, to the beneficence or hurtfulness of the design, all praise or blame, all approbation or disapprobation, of any kind, which can justly be bestowed upon any action, must ultimately belong.

When this maxim is thus proposed in abstract and general terms, there is no body who does not agree to it. Its self-evident justice is acknowledged by all the world, and there is not a dissenting voice among all mankind. Every body allows, that how different soever the accidental, the unintended and unforeseen consequences of different actions, yet, if the intentions or affections from which they arose were, on the one hand, equally proper and equally beneficent, or, on the other, equally improper and equally malevolent, the merit or demerit of the actions is still the same, and the agent is equally the suitable object either of gratitude or of resentment.

But how well soever we may seem to be persuaded of the truth of this equitable maxim, when we consider it after this manner, in abstract, yet when we come to particular cases, the actual consequences which happen to proceed from any action, have a very great effect upon our sentiments concerning its merit or demerit, and almost always either enhance or diminish our sense of both. Scarce, in any one instance, perhaps, will our sentiments be found, after examination, to be entirely regulated by this rule, which we all acknowledge ought entirely to regulate them.

This irregularity of sentiment, which every body feels, which scarce any body is sufficiently aware of, and which no body is willing to acknowledge, I proceed now to explain; and I shall consider, first, the cause which gives occasion to it, or the mechanism by which nature produces it; secondly, the extent of its influence; and, last of all, the end which it answers, or the purpose which the Author of nature seems to have intended by it.

CHAP. I.
Of the causes of this influence of fortune.

The causes of pain and pleasure, whatever they are, or however they operate, seem to be the objects, which, in all animals, immediately excite those two passions of gratitude and resentment. They are excited by inanimated, as well as by animated objects. We are angry, for a moment, even at the stone that hurts us. A child beats it, a dog barks at it, a choleric man is apt to curse it. The least reflection, indeed, corrects this sentiment, and we soon become sensible, that what has no feeling is a very improper object of revenge. When the mischief, however, is very great, the object which caused it becomes disagreeable to us ever after, and we take pleasure to burn or destroy it. We should treat, in this manner, the instrument which had accidentally been the cause of the death of a friend, and we should often think ourselves guilty of a sort of inhumanity, if we neglected to vent this absurd sort of vengeance upon it.

We conceive, in the same manner, a sort of gratitude for those inanimated objects, which have been the causes of great, or frequent pleasure to us. The sailor, who, as soon as he got ashore, should mend his fire with the plank upon which he had just escaped from a shipwreck, would seem to be guilty of an unnatural action. We should expect that he would rather preserve it with care and affection, as a monument that was, in some measure, dear to him. A man grows fond of a snuff-box, of a pen-knife, of a staff which he has long made use of, and conceives something like a real love and affection for them. If he breaks or loses them, he is vexed out of all proportion to the value of the damage. The house which we have long lived in, the tree, whose verdure and shade we have long enjoyed, are both looked upon with a sort of respect that seems due to such benefactors. The decay of the one, or the ruin of the other, affects us with a kind of melancholy, though we should sustain no loss by it. The Dryads and the Lares of the ancients, a sort of genii of trees and houses, were probably first suggested by this sort of affection, which the authors of those superstitions felt for such objects, and which seemed unreasonable, if there was nothing animated about them.

But, before any thing can be the proper object of gratitude or resentment, it must not only be the cause of pleasure or pain, it must likewise be capable of feeling them. Without this other quality, those passions cannot vent themselves with any sort of satisfaction upon it. As they are excited by the causes of pleasure and pain, so their gratification consists in retaliating those sensations upon what gave occasion to them; which it is to no purpose to attempt upon what has no sensibility. Animals, therefore, are less improper objects of gratitude and resentment than inanimated objects. The dog that bites, the ox that gores, are both of them punished. [150] If they have been the causes of the death of any person, neither the public, nor the relations of the slain, can be satisfied, unless they are put to death in their turn: nor is this merely for the security of the living, but in some measure, to revenge the injury of the dead. Those animals, on the contrary, that have been remarkably serviceable to their masters, become the objects of a very lively gratitude. We are shocked at the brutality of that officer, mentioned in the Turkish Spy, who stabbed the horse that had carried him a-cross an arm of the sea, lest that animal should afterwards distinguish some other person by a similar adventure.

But, though animals are not only the causes of pleasure and pain, but are also capable of feeling those sensations, they are still far from being complete and perfect objects, either of gratitude or resentment; and those passions still feel, that there is something wanting to their entire gratification. What gratitude chiefly desires, is not only to make the benefactor feel pleasure in his turn, but to make him conscious that he meets with this reward on account of his past conduct, to make him pleased with that conduct, and to satisfy him that the person upon whom he bestowed his good offices was not unworthy of them. What most of all charms us in our benefactor, is the concord between his sentiments and our own, with regard to what interests us so nearly as the worth of our own character, and the esteem that is due to us. We are delighted to find a person who values us as well as we value ourselves, and distinguishes us from the rest of mankind, with an attention not unlike that with which we distinguish ourselves. To maintain in him these agreeable and flattering [151] sentiments, is one of the chief ends proposed by the returns we are disposed to make to him. A generous mind often disdains the interested thought of extorting new favours from its benefactor, by what may be called the importunities of its gratitude. But to preserve and to increase his esteem, is an interest which the greatest mind does not think unworthy of its attention. And this is the foundation of what I formerly observed, that when we cannot enter into the motives of our benefactor, when his conduct and character appear unworthy of our approbation, let his services have been ever so great, our gratitude is always sensibly diminished. We are less flattered by the distinction; and to preserve the esteem of so weak, or so worthless a patron, seems to be an object which does not deserve to be pursued for its own sake.

The object, on the contrary, which resentment is chiefly intent upon, is not so much to make our enemy feel pain in his turn, as to make him conscious that he feels it upon account of his past conduct, to make him repent of that conduct, and to make him sensible, that the person whom he injured did not deserve to be treated in that manner. What chiefly enrages us against the man who injures or insults us, is the little account which he seems to make of us, the unreasonable preference which he gives to himself above us, and that absurd self-love, by which he seems to imagine, that other people may be sacrificed at any time, to his conveniency or his humour. The glaring impropriety of this conduct, the gross insolence and injustice which it seems to involve in it, often shock and exasperate us more than all the mischief which we have suffered. To bring him back to a more just sense of what is due to other people, to make him sensible of what he owes us, and of the wrong that he has done to us, is frequently the principal end proposed in our revenge, which is always imperfect when it cannot accomplish this. When our enemy appears to have done us no injury, when we are sensible that he acted quite properly, that, in his situation, we should have done the same thing, and that we deserved from him all the mischief we met with; in that case, if we have the least spark either of candour or justice, we can entertain no sort of resentment.

Before any thing, therefore, can be the complete and proper object, either of gratitude or resentment, it must possess three different qualifications. First, it must be the cause of pleasure in the one case, and of pain in the other. Secondly, it must be capable of feeling those sensations. And, thirdly, it must not only have produced those sensations, but it must have produced them from design, and from a design that is approved of in the one case, and disapproved of in the other. It is by the first qualification, that any object is capable of exciting those passions: it is by the second, that it is in any respect capable of gratifying them: the third qualification is both necessary for their complete satisfaction, and as it gives a pleasure or pain that is both exquisite and peculiar, it is likewise an additional exciting cause of those passions.

As what gives pleasure or pain, therefore, either in one way or another, is the sole exciting cause of gratitude and resentment; though the intentions of any person should be ever so proper and beneficent, on the one hand, or ever so improper and malevolent on the other; yet, if he has failed in producing either the good or evil which he intended, as one of the exciting causes is wanting in both cases, less gratitude seems due to him in the one, and less resentment in the other. And, on the contrary, though in the intentions of any person, there was either no laudable degree of benevolence on the one hand, or no blamable degree of malice on the other; yet, if his actions should produce either great good or great evil, as one of the exciting causes takes place upon both these occasions, some gratitude is apt to arise towards him in the one, and some resentment in the other. A shadow of merit seems to fall upon him in the first, a shadow of demerit in the second. And, as the consequences of actions are altogether under the empire of Fortune, hence arises her influence upon the sentiments of mankind, with regard to merit and demerit.

CHAP. II.
Of the extent of this influence of fortune.

The effect of this influence of fortune is, first, to diminish our sense of the merit or demerit of those actions which arose from the most laudable or blamable intentions, when they fail of producing their proposed effects: and, secondly, to increase our sense of the merit or demerit of actions, beyond what is due to the motives or affections from which they proceed, when they accidentally give occasion either to extraordinary pleasure or pain.

1. First, I say, though the intentions of any person should be ever so proper and beneficent, on the one hand, or ever so improper and malevolent, on the other, yet, if they fail in producing their effects, his merit seems imperfect in the one case, and his demerit incomplete in the other. Nor is this irregularity of sentiment felt only by those who are immediately affected by the consequences of any action. It is felt, in some measure, even by the impartial spectator. The man who solicits an office for another, without obtaining it, is regarded as his friend, and seems to deserve his love and affection. But the man who not only solicits, but procures it, is more peculiarly considered as his patron and benefactor, and is entitled to his respect and gratitude. The person obliged, we are apt to think, may with some 155 justice, imagine himself on a level with the first: but we cannot enter into his sentiments, if he does not feel himself inferior to the second. It is common indeed to say, that we are equally obliged to the man who has endeavoured to serve us, as to him who actually did so. It is the speech which we constantly make upon every unsuccessful attempt of this kind; but which, like all other fine speeches, must be understood with a grain of allowance. The sentiments which a man of generosity entertains for the friend who fails, may often indeed be nearly the same with those which he conceives for him who succeeds: and the more generous he is, the more nearly will those sentiments approach to an exact level. With the truly generous, to be beloved, to be esteemed by those whom they themselves think worthy of esteem, gives more pleasure, and thereby excites more gratitude, than all the advantages which they can ever expect from those sentiments. When they lose those advantages therefore, they seem to lose but a trifle, which is scarce worth regarding. They still however lose something. Their pleasure therefore, and consequently their gratitude, is not perfectly complete: and accordingly if, between the friend who fails and the friend who succeeds, all other circumstances are equal, there will, even in the noblest and the best mind, be some little difference of affection in favour of him who succeeds. Nay, so unjust are mankind in this respect, that though the intended benefit should be procured, yet if it is not procured by the means of a particular benefactor, they are apt to think that less gratitude is due to the man, who with the best intentions in the world could do no more than help it a little forward. As their gratitude is in this case divided 156 among the different persons who contributed to their pleasure, a smaller share of it seems due to any one. Such a person, we hear men commonly say, intended no doubt to serve us; and we really believe exerted himself to the utmost of his abilities for that purpose. We are not, however, obliged to him for this benefit; since had it not been for the concurrence of others, all that he could have done would never have brought it about. This consideration, they imagine, should, even in the eyes of the impartial spectator, diminish the debt which they owe to him. The person himself who has unsuccessfully endeavoured to confer a benefit, has by no means the same dependency upon the gratitude of the man whom he meant to oblige, nor the same sense of his own merit towards him, which he would have had in the case of success.

Even the merit of talents and abilities which some accident has hindered from producing their effects, seems in some measure imperfect, even to those who are fully convinced of their capacity to produce them. The general who has been hindered by the envy of ministers from gaining some great advantage over the enemies of his country, regrets the loss of the opportunity for ever after. Nor is it only upon account of the public that he regrets it. He laments that he was hindered from performing an action which would have added a new lustre to his character in his own eyes, as well as in those of every other person. It satisfies neither himself nor others to reflect that the plan or design was all that depended on him, that no greater capacity was required to execute it than what was necessary to concert it: that he was allowed to be every way capable [157] of executing it, and that had he been permitted to go on, success was infallible. He still did not execute it; and though he might deserve all the approbation which is due to a magnanimous and great design, he still wanted the actual merit of having performed a great action. To take the management of any affair of public concern from the man who has almost brought it to a conclusion, is regarded as the most invidious injustice. As he had done so much, he should, we think, have been allowed to acquire the complete merit of putting an end to it. It was objected to Pompey, that he came in upon the victories of Lucullus, and gathered those laurels which were due to the fortune and valour of another. The glory of Lucullus, it seems, was less complete even in the opinion of his own friends, when he was not permitted to finish that conquest which his conduct and courage had put in the power of almost any man to finish. It mortifies an architect when his plans are either not executed at all, or when they are so far altered as to spoil the effect of the building. The plan, however, is all that depends upon the architect. The whole of his genius is, to good judges, as completely discovered in that as in the actual execution. But a plan does not, even to the most intelligent, give the same pleasure as a noble and magnificent building. They may discover as much both of taste and genius in the one as in the other. But their effects are still vastly different, and the amusement derived from the first, never approaches to the wonder and admiration which are sometimes excited by the second. We may believe of many men, that their talents are superior to those of Cæsar and Alexander; and that in the same situations they would perform still greater actions. In the mean time, however, [158] we do not behold them with that astonishment and admiration with which those two heroes have been regarded in all ages and nations. The calm judgments of the mind may approve of them more, but they want the splendor of great actions to dazzle and transport it. The superiority of virtues and talents have not, even upon those who acknowledge that superiority, the same effect with the superiority of atchievements.

As the merit of an unsuccessful attempt to do good seems thus, in the eyes of ungrateful mankind, to be diminished by the miscarriage, so does likewise the demerit of an unsuccessful attempt to do evil. The design to commit a crime, how clearly soever it may be proved, is scarce ever punished with the same severity as the actual commission of it. The case of treason is perhaps the only exception. That crime immediately affecting the being of the government itself, the government is naturally more jealous of it than of any other. In the punishment of treason, the sovereign resents the injuries which are immediately done to himself: in the punishment of other crimes, he resents those which are done to other men. It is his own resentment which he indulges in the one case: it is that of his subjects which by sympathy he enters into it in the other. In the first case, therefore, as he judges in his own cause, he is very apt to be more violent and sanguinary in his punishments than the impartial spectator can approve of. His resentment too rises here upon smaller occasions, and does not always, as in other cases, wait for the perpetration of the crime, or even for the attempt to commit it. A treasonable concert, though nothing has been done, or even attempted in consequence of it, nay, a treasonable conversation, [159] is in many countries punished in the same manner as the actual commission of treason. With regard to all other crimes, the mere design, upon which no attempt has followed, is seldom punished at all, and is never punished severely. A criminal design, and a criminal action, it may be said indeed, do not necessarily suppose the same degree of depravity, and ought not therefore to be subjected to the same punishment. We are capable, it may be said, of resolving, and even of taking measures to execute, many things which, when it comes to the point, we feel ourselves altogether incapable of executing. But this reason can have no place when the design has been carried the length of the last attempt. The man, however, who fires a pistol at his enemy, but misses him, is punished with death by the laws of scarce any country. By the old law of Scotland, though he should wound him, yet, unless death ensues within a certain time, the assassin is not liable to the last punishment. The resentment of mankind, however, runs so high against this crime, their terror for the man who shows himself capable of committing it, is so great, that the mere attempt to commit it ought in all countries to be capital. The attempt to commit smaller crimes is almost always punished very lightly, and sometimes is not punished at all. The thief, whose hand has been caught in his neighbour's pocket before he had taken any thing out of it, is punished with ignominy only. If he had got time to take away an handkerchief, he would have been put to death. The house-breaker, who has been found setting a ladder to his neighbour's window, but had not got into it, is not exposed to the capital punishment. The attempt to ravish is not punished as a rape. The attempt to seduce a married 160 woman is not punished at all, though seduction is punished severely. Our resentment against the person who only attempted to do a mischief, is seldom so strong as to bear us out in inflicting the same punishment upon him, which we should have thought due if he had actually done it. In the one case, the joy of our deliverance alleviates our sense of the atrocity of his conduct; in the other, the grief of our misfortune increases it. His real demerit, however, is undoubtedly the same in both cases, since his intentions were equally criminal: and there is in this respect, therefore, an irregularity in the sentiments of all men, and a consequent relaxation of discipline in the laws of, I believe, all nations, of the most civilized, as well as of the most barbarous. The humanity of a civilized people disposes them either to dispense with, or to mitigate punishments wherever their natural indignation is not goaded on by the consequences of the crime. Barbarians, on the other hand, when no actual consequence has happened from any action, are not apt to be very delicate or inquisitive about the motives.

The person himself who either from passion, or from the influence of bad company, has resolved, and perhaps taken measures to perpetrate some crime, but who has fortunately been prevented by an accident which put it out of his power, is sure, if he has any remains of conscience, to regard this event all his life after as a great and signal deliverance. He can never think of it without returning thanks to Heaven for having been thus graciously pleased to save him from the guilt in which he was just ready to plunge himself, and to hinder him from rendering all the rest of his life a scene of horror, remorse, and repentance. But though his hands are 161 innocent, he is conscious that his heart is equally guilty as if he had actually executed what he was so fully resolved upon. It gives great ease to his conscience, however, to consider that the crime was not executed, though he knows that the failure arose from no virtue in him. He still considers himself as less deserving of punishment and resentment; and this good fortune either diminishes, or takes away altogether, all sense of guilt. To remember how much he was resolved upon it, has no other effect than to make him regard his escape as the greater and more miraculous: for he still fancies that he has escaped, and he looks back upon the danger to which his peace of mind was exposed, with that terror, with which one who is in safety may sometimes remember the hazard he was in of falling over a precipice, and shudder with horror at the thought.

2. The second effect of this influence of fortune, is to increase our sense of the merit or demerit of actions beyond what is due to the motives or affection from which they proceed, when they happen to give occasion to extraordinary pleasure or pain. The agreeable or disagreeable effects of the action often throw a shadow of merit or demerit upon the agent, though in his intention there was nothing that deserved either praise or blame, or at least that deserved them in the degree in which we are apt to bestow them. Thus, even the messenger of bad news is disagreeable to us, and, on the contrary, we feel a sort of gratitude for the man who brings us good tidings. For a moment we look upon them both as the authors, the one of our good, the other of our bad fortune, and regard them in some measure as if they had really brought about the events which they only give an account of. The first author of our joy is naturally the object of a transitory gratitude: we embrace him with warmth and affection, and should be glad, during the instant of our prosperity, to reward him as for some signal service. By the custom of all courts, the officer who brings the news of a victory, is entitled to considerable preferments, and the general always chuses one of his principal favourites to go upon so agreeable an errand. The first author of our sorrow is, on the contrary, just as naturally the object of a transitory resentment. We can scarce avoid looking upon him with chagrin and uneasiness; and the rude and brutal are apt to vent upon him that spleen which his intelligence gives occasion to. Tigranes, King of Armenia, struck off the head of the man who brought him the first account of the approach of a formidable enemy. To punish in this manner the author of bad tidings, seems barbarous and inhuman: yet, to reward the messenger of good news, is not disagreeable to us; we think it suitable to the bounty of kings. But why do we make this difference, since, if there is no fault in the one, neither is there any merit in the other? It is because any sort of reason seems sufficient to authorize the exertion of the social and benevolent affections; but it requires the most solid and substantial to make us enter into that of the unsocial and malevolent.

But though in general we are averse to enter into the unsocial and malevolent affections, though we lay it down for a rule that we ought never to approve of their gratification, unless so far as the malicious and unjust intention of the person, against whom they are directed renders him their proper object; yet, upon some occasions, we relax of this severity. When the negligence of one man has occasioned some unintended damage to another, we generally enter so far into the resentment of the sufferer, as to approve of his inflicting a punishment upon the offender much beyond what the offence will have appeared to deserve, had no such unlucky consequence followed from it.

There is a degree of negligence, which would appear to deserve some chastisement though it should occasion no damage to any body. Thus, if a person should throw a large stone over a wall into a public street without giving warning to those who might be passing by, and without regarding where it was likely to fall, he would undoubtedly deserve some chastisement. A very accurate police would punish so absurd an action, even though it had done no mischief. The person who has been guilty of it, shows an insolent contempt of the happiness and safety of others. There is real injustice in his conduct. He wantonly exposes his neighbour to what no man in his senses would chuse to expose himself, and evidently wants that sense of what is due to his fellow-creatures which is the basis of justice and of society. Gross negligence therefore is, in the law, said to be almost equal to malicious design[a]. When any unlucky consequences happen from such carelessness, the person who has been guilty of it is often punished as if he had really intended those consequences; and his conduct, which was only thoughtless and insolent, and what deserved some chastisement, is considered as atrocious, and as liable to the severest [164] punishment. Thus if, by the imprudent action above-mentioned, he should accidentally kill a man, he is, by the laws of many countries, particularly by the old law of Scotland, liable to the last punishment. And though this is no doubt excessively severe, it is not altogether inconsistent with our natural sentiments. Our just indignation against the folly and inhumanity of his conduct is exasperated by our sympathy with the unfortunate sufferer. Nothing however would appear more shocking to our natural sense of equity, than to bring a man to the scaffold merely for having thrown a stone carelessly into the street without hurting any body. The folly and inhumanity of his conduct, however, would in this case be the same; but still our sentiments would be very different. The consideration of this difference may satisfy us how much the indignation, even of the spectator, is apt to be animated by the actual consequences of the action. In cases of this kind there will, if I am not mistaken, be found a great degree of severity in the laws of almost all nations; as I have already observed that in those of an opposite kind there was a very general relaxation of discipline.

3. Lata culpa prope dolum est.

There is another degree of negligence which does not involve in it any sort of injustice. The person who is guilty of it treats his neighbour as he treats himself, means no harm to any body, and is far from entertaining any insolent contempt for the safety and happiness of others. He is not, however, so careful and circumspect in his conduct as he ought to be, and deserves upon this account some degree of blame and censure, but no sort of punishment. Yet if by a negligence[a] of this kind he should occasion [165] some damage to another person, he is by the laws of, I believe, all countries, obliged to compensate it. And though this is no doubt a real punishment, and what no mortal would have thought of inflicting upon him, had it not been for the unlucky accident which his conduct gave occasion to; yet this decision of the law is approved of by the natural sentiments of all mankind. Nothing, we think, can be more just than that one man should not suffer by the carelessness of another; and that the damage occasioned by blamable negligence should be made up by the person who was guilty of it.

4. Culpa levis.

There is another species of negligence[a], which consists merely in a want of the most anxious timidity and circumspection, with regard to all the possible consequences of our actions. The want of this painful attention, when no bad consequences follow from it, is so far from being regarded as blamable, that the contrary quality is rather considered as such. That timid circumspection which is afraid of every thing, is never regarded as a virtue, but as a quality which more than any other incapacitates for action and business. Yet when, from a want of this excessive care, a person happens to occasion some damage to another, he is often by the law obliged to compensate it. Thus, by the Aquilian law, the man, who not being able to manage a horse that had accidentally taken fright, should happen to ride down his neighbour's slave, is obliged to compensate the damage. When an accident of this kind happens, we are apt to think that he ought not to have rode such a horse, and to regard his attempting it as an unpardonable [166] levity; though without this accident we should not only have made no such reflection, but should have regarded his refusing it as the effect of timid weakness, and of an anxiety about merely possible events, which it is to no purpose to be aware of. The person himself, who by an accident even of this kind has involuntarily hurt another, seems to have some sense of his own ill desert, with regard to him. He naturally runs up to the sufferer to express his concern for what has happened, and to make every acknowledgment in his power. If he has any sensibility, he necessarily desires to compensate the damage, and to do every thing he can to appease that animal resentment, which he is sensible will be apt to arise in the breast of the sufferer. To make no apology, to offer no atonement, is regarded as the highest brutality. Yet why should he make an apology more than any other person? Why should he, since he was equally innocent with any other by-stander, be thus singled out from among all mankind, to make up for the bad fortune of another? This task would surely never be imposed upon him, did not even the impartial spectator feel some indulgence for what may be regarded as the unjust resentment of that other.

5. Culpa levissima.

107

CHAP. III.
Of the final cause of this irregularity of sentiments.

Such is the effect of the good or bad consequence of actions upon the sentiments both of the person who performs them, and of others; and thus, Fortune, which governs the world, has some influence where we should be least willing to allow her any, and directs in some measure the sentiments of mankind, with regard to the character and conduct both of themselves and others. That the world judges by the event, and not by the design, has been in all ages the complaint, and is the great discouragement of virtue. Every body agrees to the general maxim, that as the event does not depend on the agent, it ought to have no influence upon your sentiments, with regard to the merit or propriety of his conduct. But when we come to particulars, we find that our sentiments are scarce in any one instance exactly conformable to what this equitable maxim would direct. The happy or unprosperous event of any action, is not only apt to give us a good or bad opinion of the prudence with which it was conducted, but almost always too animates our gratitude or resentment, our sense of the merit or demerit of the design.

168 Nature, however, when the implanted the seeds of this irregularity in the human breast, seems, as upon all other occasions, to have intended the happiness and perfection of the species. If the hurtfulness of the design, if the malevolence of the affection, were alone the causes which excited our resentment, we should feel all the furies of that passion against any person in whose breast we suspected or believed such designs or affections were harboured, though they had never broke out into any actions. Sentiments, thoughts, intentions, would become the objects of punishment; and if the indignation of mankind ran as high against them as against actions; if the baseness of the thought which had given birth to no action, seemed in the eyes of the world as much to call aloud for vengeance as the baseness of the action, every court of judicature would become a real inquisition.

There would be no safety for the most innocent and circumspect conduct. Bad wishes, bad views, bad designs, might still be suspected; and while these excited the same indignation with bad conduct, while bad intentions were as much resented as bad actions, they would equally expose the person to punishment and resentment. Actions therefore which either produce actual evil, or attempt to produce it, and thereby put us in the immediate fear of it, are by the Author of nature rendered the only proper and approved objects of human punishment and resentment. Sentiments, designs, affections, though it is from these that according to cool reason human actions derive their whole merit or demerit, are placed by the great Judge of hearts beyond the limits of every human jurisdiction, and are reserved for the cognizance of his own unerring tribunal. [169] That necessary rule of justice, therefore, that men in this life are liable to punishment for their actions only, not for their designs and intentions, is founded upon this salutary and useful irregularity in human sentiments concerning merit or demerit, which at first sight appears so absurd and unaccountable. But every part of nature, when attentively surveyed, equally demonstrates the providential care of its Author, and we may admire the wisdom and goodness of God even in the weakness and folly of men.

Nor is that irregularity of sentiments altogether without its utility, by which the merit of an unsuccessful attempt to serve, and much more that of mere good inclinations and kind wishes, appears to be imperfect. Man was made for action, and to promote by the exertion of his faculties such changes in the external circumstances both of himself and others, as may seem most favourable to the happiness of all. He must not be satisfied with indolent benevolence, nor fancy himself the friend of mankind, because in his heart he wishes well to the prosperity of the world. That he may call forth the whole vigour of his soul, and strain every nerve, in order to produce those ends which it is the purpose of his being to advance, Nature has taught him, that neither himself nor mankind can be fully satisfied with his conduct, nor bestow upon it the full measure of applause, unless he has actually produced them. He is made to know, that the praise of good intentions, without the merit of good offices, will be but of little avail to excite either the loudest acclamations of the world, or even the highest degree of self-applause. The man who has performed no single action of importance, but whose whole conversation [170] and deportment express the justest, the noblest, and most generous sentiments, can be entitled to demand no very high reward, even though his inutility should be owing to nothing but the want of an opportunity to serve. We can still refuse it him without blame. We can still ask him, what have you done? What actual service can you produce, to entitle you to so great a recompense? We esteem you, and love you; but we owe you nothing. To reward indeed that latent virtue which has been useless only for want of an opportunity to serve, to bestow upon it those honours and preferments, which, though in some measure it may be said to deserve them, it could not with propriety have insisted upon, is the effect of the most divine benevolence. To punish, on the contrary, for the affections of the heart only, where no crime has been committed, is the most insolent and barbarous tyranny. The benevolent affections seem to deserve most praise, when they do not wait till it becomes almost a crime for them not to exert themselves. The malevolent, on the contrary, can scarce be too tardy, too slow, or deliberate.

It is even of use that the evil which is done without design should be regarded as a misfortune to the doer as well as to the sufferer. Man is thereby taught to reverence the happiness of his brethren, to tremble lest he should, even unknowingly, do any thing that can hurt them, and to dread that animal resentment which he feels is ready to burst out against him, if he should without design be the unhappy instrument of their calamity.

Notwithstanding, however, all these seeming irregularities of sentiment, if man should unfortunately 171 either give occasion to those evils which he did not intend, or fail in producing that good which he intended, nature has not left his innocence altogether without consolation, nor his virtue altogether without reward. He then calls to his assistance that just and equitable maxim, that those events which did not depend upon our conduct ought not to diminish the esteem that is due to us. He summons up his whole magnanimity and firmness of soul, and strives to regard himself, not in the light in which he at present appears, but in that in which he ought to appear, in which he would have appeared had his generous designs been crowned with success, and in which he would still appear, notwithstanding their miscarriage, if the sentiments of mankind were either altogether candid and equitable, or even perfectly consistent with themselves. The more candid and humane part of mankind entirely go along with the efforts which he thus makes to support himself in his own opinion. They exert their whole generosity and greatness of mind, to correct in themselves this irregularity of human nature, and endeavour to regard his unfortunate magnanimity in the same light in which, had it been successful, they would, without any such generous exertion, have naturally been disposed to consider it.

173

PART III.
Of the foundation of our judgments concerning our own sentiments and conduct, and of the sense of duty.

CONSISTING OF ONE SECTION.

CHAP. I.
Of the consciousness of merited praise or blame.

In the two foregoing parts of this discourse, I have chiefly considered the origin and foundation of our judgments concerning the sentiments and conduct of others. I come now to consider the origin of those concerning our own.

The desire of the approbation and esteem of those we live with, which is of such importance to our happiness, cannot be fully and entirely contented but by rendering ourselves the just and proper objects of those sentiments, and by adjusting our own character and conduct according to those measures and rules by which esteem and approbation are naturally bestowed. It is not sufficient, that from ignorance 174 or mistake, esteem and approbation should some way or other be bestowed upon us. If we are conscious that we do not deserve to be so favourably thought of, and that if the truth was known, we should be regarded with very opposite sentiments, our satisfaction is far from being complete. The man who applauds us either for actions which we did not perform, or for motives which had no sort of influence upon our conduct, applauds not us, but another person. We can derive no sort of satisfaction from his praises. To us they should be more mortifying than any censure, and should perpetually call to our minds, the most humbling of all reflections, the reflection upon what we ought to be, but what we are not. A woman who paints to conceal her ugliness, could derive, one should imagine, but little vanity from the compliments that are paid to her beauty. These, we should expect, ought rather to put her in mind of the sentiments which her real complexion would excite, and mortify her more by the contrast. To be pleased with such groundless applause is a proof of the most superficial levity and weakness. It is what is properly called vanity, and is the foundation of the most ridiculous and contemptible vices, the vices of affectation and common lying; follies which, if experience did not teach us how common they are, one should imagine the least spark of common sense would save us from. The foolish liar, who endeavours to excite the admiration of the company by the relation of adventures which never had any existence, the important coxcomb who gives himself airs of rank and distinction which he well knows he has no just pretensions to, are both of them, no doubt, pleased with the applause which they fancy 175 they meet with. But their vanity arises from so gross an illusion of the imagination, that it is difficult to conceive how any rational creature should be imposed upon by it. When they place themselves in the situation of those whom they fancy they have deceived, they are struck with the highest admiration for their own persons. They look upon themselves, not in that light in which, they know, they ought to appear to their companions, but in that in which they believe their companions actually look upon them. Their superficial weakness and trivial folly hinder them from ever turning their eyes inwards, or from seeing themselves in that despicable point of view in which their own consciences should tell them that they would appear to every body, if the real truth should ever come to be known.

As ignorant and groundless praise can give no solid joy, no satisfaction that will bear any serious examination, so, on the contrary, it often gives real comfort to reflect, that though no praise should actually be bestowed upon us, our conduct, however, has been such as to deserve it, and has been in every respect suitable to those measures and rules by which praise and approbation are naturally and commonly bestowed. We are pleased not only with praise, but with having done what is praise-worthy. We are pleased to think that we have rendered ourselves the natural objects of approbation, though no approbation, should ever actually be bestowed upon us: and we are mortified to reflect that we have justly incurred the blame of those we live with, though that sentiment should never actually be exerted against us. 176 The man who is conscious to himself that he has exactly observed those measures of conduct which experience informs him are generally agreeable, reflects with satisfaction on the propriety of his own behaviour; when he views it in the light in which the impartial spectator would view it, he thoroughly enters into all the motives which influenced it; he looks back upon every part of it with pleasure and approbation, and though mankind should never be acquainted with what he has done, he regards himself not so much according to the light in which they actually regard him, as according to that, in which they would regard him if they were better informed. He anticipates the applause and admiration which in this case would be bestowed upon him and he applauds and admires himself by sympathy with sentiments which do not indeed actually take place, but which the ignorance of the public alone hinders from taking place, which he knows are the natural and ordinary effects of such conduct, which his imagination strongly connects with it, and which he has acquired a habit of conceiving as something that naturally and in propriety ought to flow from it. Men have often voluntarily thrown away life to acquire after death a renown which they could no longer enjoy. Their imagination, in the mean time, anticipated that fame which was thereafter to be bestowed upon them. Those applauses which they were never to hear rung in their ears; the thoughts of that admiration, whose effects they were never to feel, played about their hearts, banished from their breasts the strongest of all natural fears, and transported them to perform actions which seem aimed beyond the reach of human nature. But in 177 point of reality there is surely no great difference between that approbation which is not to be bestowed till we can no longer enjoy it, and that which indeed is never to be bestowed, but which would be bestowed if the world was ever made to understand properly the real circumstances of our behaviour. If the one often produces such violent effects, we cannot wonder that the other should always be highly regarded.

On the contrary, the man who has broke through all those measures of conduct, which can alone render him agreeable to mankind, tho' he should have the most perfect assurance that what he had done was for ever to be concealed from every human eye, it is all to no purpose. When he looks back upon it, and views it in the light in which the impartial spectator would view it, he finds that he can enter into none of the motives which influenced it. He is abashed and confounded at the thoughts of it, and necessarily feels a very high degree of that shame which he would be exposed to, if his actions should ever come to be generally known. His imagination, in this case too, anticipates the contempt and derision from which nothing saves him but the ignorance of those he lives with. He still feels that he is the natural object of these sentiments, and still trembles at the thought of what he would suffer if they were ever actually exerted against him. But if what he had been guilty of was not merely one of those improprieties which are the objects of simple disapprobation, but one of those enormous crimes which excite detestation and resentment, he could never think of it, as long as he had any sensibility left, without feeling all 178 the agony of horror and remorse; and though he could be assured that no man was ever to know it, and could even bring himself to believe that there was no God to revenge it, he would still feel enough of both these sentiments to embitter the whole of his life: He would still regard himself as the natural object of the hatred and indignation of all his fellow-creatures; and if his heart was not grown callous by the habit of crimes, he could not think without terror and astonishment even of the manner in which mankind would look upon him, of what would be the expression of their countenance and of their eyes, if the dreadful truth should ever come to be known. These natural pangs of an affrighted conscience are the dæmons, the avenging furies which in this life haunt the guilty, which allow them neither quiet nor repose, which often drive them to despair and distraction, from which no assurance of secrecy can protect them, from which no principles of irreligion can entirely deliver them, and from which nothing can free them but the vilest and most abject of all states, a complete insensibility of honour and infamy, to vice and virtue. Men of the most detestable characters, who, in the execution of the most dreadful crimes, had taken their measures so coolly as to avoid even the suspicion of guilt, have sometimes been driven, by the horror of their situation, to discover of their own accord, what no human sagacity could ever have investigated. By acknowledging their guilt, by submitting themselves to the resentment of their offended citizens, and by thus satiating that vengeance of which they were sensible that they were become the proper objects, they hoped by their death 179 to reconcile themselves, at least in their own imagination, to the natural sentiments of mankind, to be able to consider themselves as less worthy of hatred and resentment, to atone in some measure for their crimes, and, if possible, to die in peace and with the forgiveness of all their fellow-creatures. Compared to what they felt before the discovery, even the thought of this, it seems, was happiness.

180

CHAP. II.
In what manner our own judgments refer to what ought to be the judgments of others: and of the origin of general rules.

Agreat part, perhaps the greatest part, of human happiness and misery arises from the view of our past conduct, and from the degree of approbation or disapprobation which we feel from the consideration of it. But in whatever manner it may affect us, our sentiments of this kind have always some secret reference either to what are, or to what upon a certain condition would be, or to what we imagine ought to be the sentiments of others. We examine it as we imagine an impartial spectator would examine it. If upon placing ourselves in his situation we thoroughly enter into all the passions and motives which influenced it, we approve of it by sympathy with the approbation of this supposed equitable judge. If otherwise, we enter into his disapprobation and condemn it.

Was it possible that a human creature could grow up to manhood in some solitary place without any communication with his own species, he could no more think of his own character, of the propriety or demerit of his own sentiments and conduct, of the beauty or deformity of his own mind, than of the beauty or deformity of his own face. All these are objects which he cannot easily see, which naturally he does not look at; and with regard to which he 181 is provided with no mirror which can present them to his view. Bring him into society, and he is immediately provided with the mirror which he wanted before. It is placed in the countenance and behaviour of those he lives with, which always mark when they enter into, and when they disapprove of his sentiments; and it is here that he first views the propriety and impropriety of his own passions, the beauty and deformity of his own mind. To a man who from his birth was a stranger to society, the objects of his passions, the external bodies which either pleased or hurt him, would occupy his whole attention. The passions themselves, the desires or aversions, the joys or sorrows, which those objects excited, though of all things the most immediately present to him, could scarce ever be the objects of his thoughts. The idea of them could never interest him so much as to call upon his attentive consideration. The consideration of his joy could in him excite no new joy, nor that of his sorrow any new sorrow, though the consideration of the causes of those passions might often excite both. Bring him into society, and all his own passions will immediately become the causes of new passions. He will observe that mankind approve of some of them, and are disgusted by others. He will be elevated in the one case, and cast down in the other; his desires and aversions, his joys and sorrows will now often become the causes of new desires and new aversions, new joys and new sorrows: they will now therefore interest him deeply, and often call upon his most attentive consideration.

Our first ideas of personal beauty and deformity, are drawn from the shape and appearance of others, not from our own. We soon become sensible, however, that others exercise the same criticism upon us. We are pleased when they approve of our figure, and are disobliged when they seem to be disgusted. We become anxious to know how far our appearance deserves either their blame or approbation. We examine our own persons limb by limb, and by placing ourselves before a looking-glass, or by some such expedient, endeavour, as much as possible, to view ourselves at the distance and with the eyes of other people. If after this examination we are satisfied with our own appearance, we can more easily support the most disadvantageous judgments of others: if, on the contrary, we are sensible that we are the natural objects of distaste, every appearance of their disapprobation mortifies us beyond all measure. A man who is tolerably handsome, will allow you to laugh at any little irregularity in his person; but all such jokes are commonly insupportable to one who is really deformed. It is evident, however, that we are anxious about our own beauty and deformity only on account of its effect upon others. If we had no connexion with society, we should be altogether indifferent about either.

In the same manner our first moral criticisms are exercised upon the characters and conduct of other people; and we are all very forward to observe how each of these affects us. But we soon learn, that others are equally frank with regard to our own. We become anxious to know how far we deserve their censure or applause, and whether to them we must necessarily appear those agreeable or disagreeable creatures which they represent us. We begin upon this account to examine our own passions and conduct, and to consider how these must appear to them, by considering how they would appear to us if in their situation. We suppose ourselves the spectators of our own behaviour, and endeavour to imagine what effect it would, in this light, produce upon us. This is the only looking-glass by which we can, in some measure, with the eyes of others, scrutinize the propriety of our own conduct. If in this view it pleases us, we are tolerably satisfied. We can be more indifferent about the applause, and, in some measure, despise the censure of others; secure that, however misunderstood or misrepresented, we are the natural and proper objects of approbation. On the contrary, if we are displeased with it, we are often upon that very account more anxious to gain their approbation, and, provided we have not already, as they say, shaken hands with infamy, we are altogether distracted at the thoughts of their censure, which then strikes us with double severity.

When I endeavour to examine my own conduct, when I endeavour to pass sentence upon it, and either to approve or condemn it, it is evident that, in all such cases, I divide myself, as it were, into two persons, and that I, the examiner and judge, represent a different character from that other I, the person whose conduct is examined into and judged of. The first is the spectator, whose sentiments with regard to my own conduct I endeavour to enter into, by placing myself in his situation, and by considering how it would appear to me when seen from that particular point of view. The second is the agent, the person whom I properly call myself, and of whose conduct, under the character of a spectator, I was endeavouring to form some opinion. The first is the judge; the second the pannel. But that the judge should, in every respect, be the same ⌊184⌋ with the pannel, is as impossible, as that the cause should, in every respect, be the same with the effect.

To be amiable and to be meritorious, that is, to deserve love and to deserve reward, are the great characters of virtue, and to be odious and punishable, of vice. But all these characters have an immediate reference to the sentiments of others. Virtue is not said to be amiable or to be meritorious, because it is the object of its own love, or of its own gratitude; but because it excites those sentiments in other men. The consciousness that it is the object of such favourable regards is the source of that inward tranquillity and self-satisfaction with which it is naturally attended, as the suspicion of the contrary gives occasion to the torments of vice. What so great happiness as to be beloved, and to know that we deserve to be beloved? What so great misery as to be hated, and to know that we deserve to be hated?

Man is considered as a moral, because he is regarded as an accountable being. But an accountable being, as the word expresses, is a being that must give an account of its actions to some other, and that consequently must regulate them according to the good liking of this other. Man is accountable to God and his fellow-creatures. But though he is, no doubt, principally accountable to God; in the order of time, he must necessarily conceive himself as accountable to his fellow-creatures, before he can form any idea of the Deity, or of the rules by which that divine being will judge of his conduct. A child surely conceives itself as accountable to its parents, and is elevated or cast down by ⌊185⌋ the thought of their merited approbation or disapprobation, long before it forms any idea of its accountableness to the Deity, or of the rules by which that divine being will judge of its conduct.

The great judge of the world, has, for the wisest reasons, thought proper to interpose, between the weak eye of human reason, and the throne of his eternal justice, a degree of obscurity and darkness, which though it does not entirely cover that great tribunal from the view of mankind, yet renders the impression of it faint and feeble in comparison of what might be expected from the grandeur and importance of so mighty an object. If those infinite rewards and punishments which the Almighty has prepared for those who obey or transgress his will, were perceived as distinctly as we foresee the frivolous and temporary retaliations which we may expect from one another, the weakness of human nature, astonished at the immensity of objects so little fitted to its comprehension, could no longer attend to the little affairs of this world; and it is absolutely impossible that the business of society could have been carried on, if, in this respect, there had been a fuller revelation of the intentions of Providence than that which has already been made. That men, however, might never be without a rule to direct their conduct by, nor without a judge whose authority should enforce its observation, the Author of nature has made man the immediate judge of mankind, and has, in this respect, as in many others, created him after his own image, and appointed him his vicegerent upon earth, to superintend the behaviour of his brethren. They are taught by nature to acknowledge that power and ⌊186⌋ jurisdiction which has thus been conferred upon him, and to tremble and exult according as they imagine that they have either merited his censure, or deserved his applause.

But whatever may be the authority of this inferior tribunal which is continually before their eyes, if at any time it should decide contrary to those principles and rules, which Nature has established for regulating its judgments, men feel that they may appeal from this unjust decision, and call upon a superior tribunal, the tribunal established in their own breasts, to redress the injustice of this weak or partial judgment.

There are certain principles established by Nature for governing our judgment concerning the conduct of those we live with. As long as we decide according to those principles, and neither applaud nor condemn any thing which Nature has not rendered the proper object of applause or condemnation, nor any further than she has rendered it such, as our sentence is, in this case, if I may say so, quite agreeable to law, it is liable neither to repeal nor to correction of any kind. The person concerning whom we form these judgments, must himself necessarily approve of them. When he puts himself into our situation, he cannot avoid viewing his own conduct in the very same light in which we appear to view it. He is sensible, that to us, and to every impartial spectator, he must necessarily appear the natural and proper object of those sentiments which we express with regard to him. Those sentiments, therefore, must necessarily produce their full effect upon him, and he cannot fail to conceive all the triumph of self-approbation 187 from, what appears to him, such merited applause, as well as all the horrors of shame from, what, he is sensible, is such deserved condemnation.

But it is otherwise, if we have either applauded or condemned him, contrary to those principles and rules which Nature has established for the direction of our judgments concerning every thing of this kind. If we have either applauded or condemned him for what, when he put himself into our situation, does not appear to him to be the object either of applause or condemnation; as in this case he cannot enter into our sentiments, provided he has any constancy or firmness, he is but little affected by them, and can neither be much elevated by the favourable, nor greatly mortified by the unfavourable decision. The applause of the whole world will avail but little, if our own conscience condemn us; and the disapprobation of all mankind is not capable of oppressing us, when we are absolved by the tribunal within our own breast, and when our own mind tells us that mankind are in the wrong.

But though this tribunal within the breast be thus the supreme arbiter of all our actions, though it can reverse the decisions of all mankind with regard to our character and conduct, and mortify us amidst the applause, or support us under the censure of the world; yet, if we inquire into the origin of its institution, its jurisdiction we shall find is in a great measure derived from the authority of that very tribunal, whose decisions it so often and so justly reverses.

When we first come into the world, from the natural desire to please, we accustom ourselves to consider 188 what behaviour is likely to be agreeable to every person we converse with, to our parents, to our masters, to our companions. We address ourselves to individuals, and for some time fondly pursue the impossible and absurd project of gaining the good-will and approbation of every body. We are soon taught by experience, however, that this universal approbation is altogether unattainable. As soon as we come to have more important interests to manage, we find, that by pleasing one man, we almost certainly disoblige another, and that by humouring an individual, we may often irritate a whole people. The fairest and most equitable conduct must frequently obstruct the interests, or thwart the inclinations of particular persons, who will seldom have candour enough to enter into the propriety of our motives, or to see that this conduct, how disagreeable soever to them, is perfectly suitable to our situation. In order to defend ourselves from such partial judgments, we soon learn to set up in our own minds a judge between ourselves and those we live with. We conceive ourselves as acting in the presence of a person quite candid and equitable, of one who has no particular relation either to ourselves, or to those whose interests are affected by our conduct, who is neither father, nor brother, nor friend either to them or to us, but is merely a man in general, an impartial spectator who considers our conduct with the same indifference with which we regard that of other people. If, when we place ourselves in the situation of such a person, our own actions appear to us under an agreeable aspect, if we feel that such a spectator cannot avoid entering into all the motives which 189 influenced us, whatever may be the judgments of the world, we must still be pleased with our own behaviour, and regard ourselves, in spite of the censure of our companions, as the just and proper objects of approbation.

On the contrary, if the man within condemns us, the loudest acclamations of mankind appear but as the noise of ignorance and folly, and whenever we assume the character of this impartial judge, we cannot avoid viewing our own actions with this distaste and dissatisfaction. The weak, the vain, and the frivolous, indeed, may be mortified by the most groundless censure, or elated by the most absurd applause. Such persons are not accustomed to consult the judge within concerning the opinion which they ought to form of their own conduct. This inmate of the breast, this abstract man, the representative of mankind, and substitute of the Deity, whom Nature has constituted the supreme judge of all their actions, is seldom appealed to by them. They are contented with the decision of the inferior tribunal. The approbation of their companions, of the particular persons whom they have lived and conversed with, has generally been the ultimate object of all their wishes. If they obtain this, their joy is complete; and if they fail, they are entirely disappointed. They never think of appealing to the superior court. They have seldom inquired after its decisions, and are altogether unacquainted with the rules and forms of its procedure. When the world injures them, therefore, they are incapable of doing themselves justice, and are, in consequence, necessarily the slaves of the 190 world. But it is otherwise with the man who has, upon all occasions, been accustomed to have recourse to the judge within, and to consider, not what the world approves or disapproves of, but what appears to this impartial spectator, the natural and proper object of approbation or disapprobation. The judgment of this supreme arbiter of his conduct, is the applause, which he has been accustomed principally to court, is the censure which he has been accustomed principally to fear. Compared with this final decision, the sentiments of all mankind, though not altogether indifferent, appear to be but of small moment; and he is incapable of being either much elevated by their favourable, or greatly depressed by their most disadvantageous judgment.

It is only by consulting this judge within, that we can see whatever relates to ourselves in its proper shape and dimensions, or that we can make any proper comparison between our own interests and those of other men.

As to the eye of the body, objects appear great or small, not so much according to their real dimensions, as according to the nearness or distance of their situation; so do they likewise to what may be called the natural eye of the mind: and we remedy the defects of both these organs pretty much in the same manner. In my present situation an immense landscape of lawns, and woods, and distant mountains, seems to do no more than cover the little window which I write by, and to be out of all proportion less than the chamber in which I am sitting. I can form a just comparison between those great objects and the little objects around me, in no other way, than by transporting myself, at least in fancy, to a different station, from whence I can survey both at nearly equal distances, and thereby form some judgment of their real proportions. Habit and experience have taught me to do this so easily and so readily, that I am scarce sensible that I do it; and a man must be, in some measure, acquainted with the philosophy of vision, before he can be thoroughly convinced, how little those distant objects would appear to the eye, if the imagination, from a knowledge of their real magnitudes, did not swell and dilate them.

In the same manner, to the selfish and original passions of human nature, the loss or gain of a very small interest of our own, appears to be of vastly more importance, excites a much more passionate joy or sorrow, a much more ardent desire or aversion, than the greatest concern of another with whom we have no particular connexion. His interests, as long as they are surveyed from this station, can never be put into the balance with our own, can never restrain us from doing whatever may tend to promote our own, how ruinous soever to him. Before we can make any proper comparison of those opposite interests, we must change our position. We must view them, neither from our own place, nor yet from his, neither with our own eyes nor yet with his, but from the place, and with the eyes of a third person, who has no particular connexion with either, and who judges with impartiality between us. Here too, habit and experience have taught us to do this so easily and so readily, that we are scarce sensible that we do it; and it requires, in this case too, some degree of reflection, and even of philosophy to convince us, how little interest we should take in the greatest concerns of our neighbour, how little we should be affected by whatever relates to him, if the sense of propriety and justice did not correct the otherwise natural inequality of our sentiments.

Let us suppose that the great empire of China, with all its myriads of inhabitants, was suddenly swallowed up by an earthquake, and let us consider how a man of humanity in Europe, who had no sort of connexion with that part of the world, would be affected upon receiving intelligence of this dreadful calamity. He would, I imagine, first of all, express very strongly his sorrow for the misfortune of that unhappy people, he would make many melancholy reflections upon the precariousness of human life, and the vanity of all the labours of man, which could thus be annihilated in a moment. He would too, perhaps, if he was a man of speculation, enter into many reasonings concerning the effects which this disaster might produce upon the commerce of Europe, and the trade and business of the world in general. And when all this fine philosophy was over, when all these humane sentiments had been once fairly expressed, he would pursue his business or his pleasure, take his repose or his diversion, with the same ease and tranquility, as if no such accident had happened. The most frivolous disaster which could befal himself would occasion a more real disturbance. If he was to lose his little finger to-morrow, he would not sleep to-night; but provided he never saw them, he will snore with the most profound security over the ruin of a hundred millions of his brethren, and the destruction of that immense multitude seems plainly an object less interesting to him, than this paltry misfortune of his own. To prevent therefore, this paltry misfortune to himself would a man of humanity be willing to sacrifice the lives of a hundred millions of his brethren, provided he had never seen them? Human nature startles with horror at the thought, and the world, in its greatest depravity and corruption, never produced such a villain as could be capable of entertaining it. But what makes this difference? When our passive feelings are almost always so sordid and so selfish, how comes it that our active principles should often be so generous and so noble? When we are always so much more deeply affected by whatever concerns ourselves, than by whatever concerns other men; what is it which prompts the generous, upon all occasions, and the mean upon many, to sacrifice their own interests to the greater interests of others? It is not the soft power of humanity, it is not that feeble spark of benevolence which Nature has lighted up in the human heart, that is thus capable of counteracting the strongest impulses of self-love. It is a stronger power, a more forcible motive, which exerts itself upon such occasions. It is reason, principle, conscience, the inhabitant of the breast, the man within, the great judge and arbiter of our conduct. It is he, who, whenever we are about to act so as to affect the happiness of others, calls to us with a voice capable of astonishing the most presumptuous of our passions, that we are but one of the multitude, in no respect better than any other in it; and that when we prefer ourselves so shamefully and so blindly to others, we become the proper objects of resentment, abhorrence, and execration. It is from him only that we learn the real littleness of ourselves, and of whatever relates to ourselves, and the natural misrepresentations of self-love can be corrected only by the eye of 194 this impartial spectator. It is he who shows us the propriety of generality and the deformity of injustice; the propriety of resigning the greatest interests of our own, for the yet greater interests of others, and the deformity of doing the smallest injury to another, in order to obtain the greatest benefit to ourselves. It is not the love of our neighbour, it is not the love of mankind, which upon many occasions prompts us to the practice of those divine virtues. It is a stronger love, a more powerful affection which generally takes place upon such occasions, the love of what is honourable and noble, of the grandeur, and dignity, and superiority of our own characters.

When the happiness or misery of others depends in any respect upon our conduct, we dare not, as self-love would suggest to us, prefer any little interest of our own, to the yet greater interest of our neighbour. We feel that we should become the proper objects of the resentment and indignation of our brethren, and the sense of the impropriety of this affection is supported and enlivened by the yet stronger sense of the demerit of the action, which it would in this case give occasion to. But when the happiness or misery of others in no respect depends upon our conduct, when our own interests are altogether separated and detached from theirs, so that there is neither connexion nor competition between them, as the sense of demerit does not in this case interpose, the mere sense of impropriety is seldom able to restrain us from abandoning ourselves to our natural anxiety about our own affairs, and to our natural indifference about those of other men. The most vulgar education teaches us to act, upon all important occasions, with some sort of impartiality between 195 ourselves and others, and even the ordinary commerce of the world is capable of adjusting our active principles to some degree of propriety. But it is the most artificial and refined education only, which pretends to correct the inequalities of our passive feelings, and we must for this purpose have recourse to the severest, as well as to the profoundest philosophy.

Two different sets of philosophers have attempted to teach us this hardest of all the lessons of morality. One set have laboured to increase our sensibility to the interests of others; another to diminish that to our own. The first would have us feel for others as we naturally feel for ourselves. The second would have us feel for ourselves, as we naturally feel for others.

The first are those melancholy moralists, who are perpetually reproaching us with our happiness, while so many of our brethren are in misery,[6] who regard as impious the natural joy of prosperity, which does not think of the many wretches that are at every instant labouring under all sorts of calamities, in the languor of poverty, in the agony of disease, in the horrors of death, under the insults and oppression of their enemies. Commiseration for those miseries which we never saw, which we never heard of, but which we may be assured are at all times infecting such numbers of our fellow-creatures, ought, they think, to damp the pleasures of the fortunate, and to render a certain melancholy dejection habitual to all men. But first of all, this extreme sympathy with 196 misfortunes, which we know nothing about, seems altogether absurd and unreasonable. Take the whole earth at an average, for one man who suffers pain or misery, you will find twenty in prosperity and joy, or at least in tolerable circumstances. No reason, surely, can be assigned why we should rather weep with the one than rejoice with the twenty. This artificial commiseration, besides, is not only absurd, but seems altogether unattainable; and those who affect this character have commonly nothing but a certain hypocritical sadness, which, without reaching the heart, serves only to render the countenance and convocation impertinently dismal and disagreeable. And last of all, this disposition of mind, though it could be attained, would be perfectly useless, and could serve no other purpose than to render miserable the person who was possessed of it. Whatever interest we take in the fortune of those with whom we have no acquaintance or connexion, and who are placed altogether out of the sphere of our activity, can produce only anxiety to ourselves, without any manner of advantage to them. To what purpose should we trouble ourselves about the world in the moon? All men, even those at the greatest distance, are no doubt entitled to our good wishes, and our good wishes we naturally give them. But if, notwithstanding, they should be unfortunate, to give ourselves any anxiety upon that account, seems to be no part of our duty. That we should be but little interested, therefore, in the fortune of those whom we can neither serve nor hurt, and who are in every respect so very remote from us, seems wisely ordered by nature; and if it were possible to alter in this respect the original constitution of our frame, we could yet gain nothing by the change.

6. See Thomson's Seasons, Winter:

"Ah! little think the gay licentious proud," &c.

See also Pascal.

197 Among the moralists who endeavour to correct the natural inequality of our passive feelings by diminishing our sensibility to what peculiarly concerns ourselves, we may count all the ancient sects of philosophers, but particularly the ancient stoics. Man, according to the stoics, ought to regard himself, not as something separated and detached, but as a citizen of the world, a member of the vast commonwealth of nature. To the interest of this great community, he ought at all times to be willing that his own little interest should be sacrificed. Whatever concerns himself, ought to affect him no more than whatever concerns any other equally important part of this immense system. We should view ourselves, not in the light in which our own selfish passions are apt to place us, but in the light in which any other citizen of the world would view us. What befalls ourselves we should regard as what befalls our neighbour, or, what comes to the same thing, as our neighbour regards what befalls us. "When our neighbour," says Epictetus,

"loses his wife or his son, there is nobody who is not sensible that this is a human calamity, a natural event altogether, according to the ordinary course of things: but when the same thing happens to ourselves, then we cry out, as if we had suffered the most dreadful misfortune. We ought, however, to remember how we were affected when this accident happened to another, and such as we were in his case, such ought we to be in our own." How difficult soever it may be to attain this supreme degree of magnanimity and firmness, it is by no means either absurd or useless to attempt it. Though few men have the stoical idea of what this perfect propriety requires, yet all men endeavour in some measure 198 to command themselves, and to bring down their selfish passions to something which their neighbour can go along with. But this can never be done so effectually as by viewing whatever befalls themselves in the light in which their neighbours are apt to view it. The stoical philosophy, in this respect, does little more than unfold our natural ideas of perfection. There is nothing absurd or improper, therefore, in aiming at this perfect self-command. Neither would the attainment of it be useless, but, on the contrary, the most advantageous of all things, as establishing our happiness upon the most solid and secure foundation, a firm confidence in that wisdom and justice which governs the world, and an entire resignation of ourselves, and of whatever relates to ourselves to the all-wise disposal of this ruling principle in nature.

It scarce ever happens, however, that we are capable of adjusting our passive feelings to this perfect propriety. We indulge ourselves, and even the world indulges us, in some degree of irregularity in this respect. Though we should be too much affected by what concerns ourselves, and too little by what concerns other men, yet, if we always act with impartiality between ourselves and others, if we never actually sacrifice any great interest of others, to any little interest of our own, we are easily pardoned: and it were well, if, upon all occasions, those who desire to do their duty were capable of maintaining even this degree of impartiality between themselves and others. But this is very far from being the case. Even in good men, the judge within is often in danger of being corrupted by the violence and injustice of their selfish passions, and is 199 often induced to make a report very different from what the real circumstances of the case are capable of authorizing.

There are two different occasions, upon which we examine our own conduct, and endeavour to view it in the light in which the impartial spectator would view it. First, when we are about to act; and, secondly, after we have acted. Our views are very partial in both cases, but they are most so, when it is of most importance that they should be otherwise.

When we are about to act, the eagerness of passion will seldom allow us to consider what we are doing with the candour of an indifferent person. The violent emotions which at that time agitate us, discolour our views of things, even when we are endeavouring to place ourselves in the situation of another, and to regard the objects that interest us, in the light in which they will naturally appear to him. The fury of our own passions constantly calls us back to our own place, where every thing appears magnified and misrepresented by self-love. Of the manner in which those objects would appear to another, of the view which he would take of them, we can obtain, if I may say so, but instantaneous glimpses, which vanish in a moment, and which even while they last are not altogether just. We cannot even for that moment divest ourselves entirely of the heat and keenness with which our peculiar situation inspires us, nor consider what we are about to do with the complete impartiality of an equitable judge. The passions, upon this account, as father Malebranche says, all justify themselves, and seem 200 reasonable, and proportioned to their objects, as long as we continue to feel them.

When the action is over, indeed, and the passions which prompted it have subsided, we can enter more coolly into sentiments of the indifferent spectator. What before interested us, is now become almost as indifferent to us as it always was to him, and we can now examine our own conduct with his candour and impartiality. But our judgments now are of little importance, compared to what they were before; and when they are most severely impartial, can commonly produce nothing but vain regret, and unavailing repentance, without securing us from the like errors for the future. It is seldom, however, that they are quite candid even in this case. The opinion which we entertain of our own character, depends entirely on our judgment concerning our past conduct. It is so disagreeable to think ill of ourselves, that we often purposely turn away our view from those circumstances which might render that judgment unfavourable. He is a bold surgeon, they say, whose hand does not tremble when he performs an operation upon his own person; and he is often equally bold who does not hesitate to pull off the mysterious veil of self-delusion, which covers from his view the deformities of his own conduct. Rather than see our own behaviour under so disagreeable an aspect, we too often, foolishly and weakly, endeavour to exasperate anew those unjust passions which had formerly misled us; we endeavour by artifice to awaken our old hatreds, and irritate afresh our almost forgotten resentments: we even exert ourselves for this miserable purpose, and thus persevere in injustice, merely because we once were unjust, 201 and because we are ashamed and afraid to see that we were so.

So partial are the views of mankind with regard to the propriety of their own conduct, both at the time of action and after it; and so difficult is it for them to view it in the light in which any indifferent spectator would consider it. But if it was by a peculiar faculty, such as the moral sense is supposed to be, that they judged of their own conduct, if they were endued with a particular power of perception, which distinguished the beauty or deformity of passions and affections; as their own passions would be more immediately exposed to the view of this faculty, it would judge with more accuracy concerning them, than concerning those of other men, of which it had only a more distant prospect.

This self-deceit, this fatal weakness of mankind, is the source of half the disorders of human life. If we saw ourselves in the light in which others see us, or in which they would see us if they knew all, a reformation would generally be unavoidable. We could not otherwise endure the sight.

Nature, however, has not left this weakness, which is of so much importance, altogether without a remedy; nor has she abandoned us entirely to the delusions of self-love. Our continual observations upon the conduct of others, insensibly lead us to form to ourselves certain general rules concerning what is fit and proper either to be done or to be avoided. Some of their actions shock all our natural sentiments. We hear every body about us express the like detestation against them. This still further confirms, and even exasperates our natural sense of 202 their deformity. It satisfies us that we view them in the proper light, when we see other people view them in the same light. We resolve never to be guilty of the like, nor ever, upon any account, to render ourselves in this manner the objects of universal disapprobation. We thus naturally lay down to ourselves a general rule, that all such actions are to be avoided, as tending to render us odious, contemptible, or punishable, the objects of all those sentiments for which we have the greatest dread and aversion. Other actions, on the contrary, call forth our approbation, and we hear every body around us express the same favourable opinion concerning them. Every body is eager to honour and reward them. They excite all those sentiments for which we have by nature the strongest desire; the love, the gratitude, the admiration of mankind. We become ambitious of performing the like; and thus naturally lay down to ourselves a rule of another kind, that every opportunity of acting in this manner is carefully to be sought after.

It is thus that the general rules of morality are formed. They are ultimately founded upon experience of what, in particular instances, our moral faculties, our natural sense of merit and propriety, approve, or disapprove of. We do not originally approve or condemn particular actions; because, upon examination, they appear to be agreeable or inconsistent with a certain general rule. The general rule, on the contrary, is formed by finding from experience, that all actions of a certain kind, or circumstanced in a certain manner, are approved or disapproved of. To the man who first saw an inhuman murder, committed from avarice, envy, or 203 unjust resentment, and upon one too that loved and trusted the murderer, who beheld the last agonies of the dying person, who heard him, with his expiring breath, complain more of the perfidy and ingratitude of his false friend, than of the violence which had been done to him, there could be no occasion, in order to conceive how horrible such an action was, that he should reflect, that one of the most sacred rules of conduct was what prohibited the taking away the life of an innocent person, that this was a plain violation of that rule, and consequently a very blamable action. His detestation of this crime, it is evident, would arise instantaneously and antecedent to his having formed to himself any such general rule. The general rule, on the contrary, which he might afterwards form, would be founded upon the detestation which he felt necessarily arise in his own breast, at the thought of this, and every other particular action of the same kind.

When we read in history or romance, the account of actions either of generosity or of baseness, the admiration which we conceive for the one, and the contempt which we feel for the other, neither of them arise from reflecting that there are certain general rules which declare all actions of the one kind admirable, and all actions of the other contemptible. Those general rules, on the contrary, are all formed from the experience we have had of the effects which actions of all different kinds naturally produce upon us.

An amiable action, a respectable action, an horrid action, are all of them actions which naturally excite the love, the respect, or the horror of the 204 spectator, for the person who performs them. The general rules which determine what actions are, and what are not, the objects of each of those sentiments, can be formed no other way than by observing what actions actually and in fact excite them.

When these general rules, indeed, have been formed, when they are universally acknowledged and established, by the concurring sentiments of mankind, we frequently appeal to them as to the standards of judgment, in debating concerning the degree of praise or blame that is due to certain actions of a complicated and dubious nature. They are upon these occasions commonly cited as the ultimate foundations of what is just and unjust in human conduct; and this circumstance seems to have misled several very eminent authors, to draw up their systems in such a manner, as if they had supposed that the original judgments of mankind with regard to right and wrong, were formed like the decisions of a court of judicatory, by considering first the general rule, and then, secondly, whether the particular action under consideration fell properly within its comprehension.

Those general rules of conduct, when they have been fixed in our mind by habitual reflection, are of great use in correcting misrepresentations of self-love concerning what is fit and proper to be done in our particular situation. The man of furious resentment, if he was to listen to the dictates of that passion, would perhaps regard the death of his enemy, as but a small compensation for the wrong, he imagines, he has received; which, however, may be no more than a very slight provocation. But his observations 205 upon the conduct of others, have taught him how horrible all such sanguinary revenges appear. Unless his education has been very singular, he has laid it down to himself as an inviolable rule, to abstain from them upon all occasions. This rule preserves its authority with him, and renders him incapable of being guilty of such a violence. Yet the fury of his own temper may be such, that had this been the first time in which he considered such an action, he would undoubtedly have determined it to be quite just and proper, and what every impartial spectator would approve of. But that reverence for the rule which past experience has impressed upon him, checks the impetuosity of his passion, and helps him to correct the too partial views which self-love might otherwise suggest, of what was proper to be done in his situation. If he should allow himself to be so far transported by passion as to violate this rule, yet even in this case, he cannot throw off altogether the awe and respect with which he has been accustomed to regard it. At the very time of acting, at the moment in which passion mounts the highest, he hesitates and trembles at the thought of what he is about to do: he is secretly conscious to himself that he is breaking through those measures of conduct, which, in all his cool hours, he had resolved never to infringe, which he had never seen infringed by others without the highest disapprobation, and of which the infringement, his own mind forebodes, must soon render him the object of the same disagreeable sentiments. Before he can take the last fatal resolution, he is tormented with all the agonies of doubt and uncertainty; he is terrified at the thought of violating so sacred a rule, and at the same time is urged and goaded on by the fury of his desires 206 to violate it. He changes his purpose every moment; sometimes he resolves to adhere to his principle, and not indulge a passion which may corrupt the remaining part of his life with the horrors of shame and repentance; and a momentary calm takes possession of his breast, from the prospect of that security and tranquillity which he will enjoy when he thus determines not to expose himself to the hazard of a contrary conduct. But immediately the passion rouses anew, and with fresh fury drives him on to commit what he had the instant before resolved to abstain from. Wearied and distracted with those continual irresolutions, he at length, from a sort of despair, makes the last fatal and irrecoverable step; but with that terror and amazement with which one flying from an enemy, throws himself over a precipice, where he is sure of meeting with more certain destruction than from any thing that pursues him from behind. Such are his sentiments even at the time of acting; though he is then, no doubt, less sensible of the impropriety of his own conduct than afterwards, when his passion being gratified and palled, he begins to view what he has done in the light in which others are apt to view it; and actually feels, what he had only foreseen very imperfectly before, the stings of remorse and repentance begin to agitate and torment him.

CHAP. III.
Of the influence and authority of the general rules of morality, and that they are justly regarded as the laws of the Deity.

The regard to those general rules of conduct, is what is properly called a sense of duty, a principle of the greatest consequence in human life, and the only principle by which the bulk of mankind are capable of directing their actions. Many men behave very decently, and through the whole of their lives avoid any considerable degree of blame, who yet, perhaps, never felt the sentiment upon the propriety of which we found our approbation of their conduct, but acted merely from a regard to what they saw were the established rules of behaviour. The man who has received great benefits from another person, may, by the natural coldness of his temper, feel but a very small degree of the sentiment of gratitude. If he has been virtuously educated, however, he will often have been made to observe how odious those actions appear which denote a want of this sentiment, and how amiable the contrary. Tho' his heart therefore is not warmed with any grateful affection, he will strive to act as if it was, and will endeavour to pay all those regards and attentions to his patron which the liveliest gratitude 208 could suggest. He will visit him regularly; he will behave to him respectfully; he will never talk of him but with expressions of the highest esteem, and of the many obligations which he owes to him. And what is more, he will carefully embrace every opportunity of making a proper return for past services. He may do all this too without any hypocrisy or blamable dissimulation, without any selfish intention of obtaining new favours, and without any design of imposing either upon his benefactor or the public. The motive of his actions may be no other than a reverence for the established rule of duty, a serious and earnest desire of acting, in every respect, according to the law of gratitude. A wife, in the same manner, may sometimes not feel that tender regard for her husband which is suitable to the relation that subsists between them. If she has been virtuously educated, however, she will endeavour to act as if she felt it, to be careful, officious, faithful, and sincere, and to be deficient in none of those attentions which the sentiment of conjugal affection could have prompted her to perform. Such a friend, and such a wife, are neither of them, undoubtedly, the very best of their kinds; and though both of them may have the most serious and earnest desire to fulfil every part of their duty, yet they will fail in many nice and delicate regards, they will miss many opportunities of obliging, which they could never have overlooked if they had possessed the sentiment that is proper to their situation. Though not the very first of their kinds, however, they are perhaps the second; and if the regard to the general rules of conduct has been very strongly impressed upon them, neither of them will fail in any essential part of their duty. None but those of 209 the happiest mould are capable of suiting, with exact justness, their sentiments and behaviour to the smallest difference of situation, and of acting upon all occasions with the most delicate and accurate propriety. The coarse clay of which the bulk of mankind are formed, cannot be wrought up to such perfection. There is scarce any man, however, who by discipline, education, and example, may not be impressed with a regard to general rules, as to act upon almost every occasion with tolerable decency, and through the whole of his life avoid any considerable degree of blame.

Without this sacred regard to general rules, there is no man whose conduct can be much depended upon. It is this which constitutes the most essential difference between a man of principle and honour and a worthless fellow. The one adheres, on all occasions, steadily and resolutely to his maxims, and preserves through the whole of his life one even tenour of conduct. The other, acts variously and accidentally, as humour, inclination, or interest chance to be uppermost. Nay, such are the inequalities of humour to which all men are subject, that without this principle, the man who, in his cool hours, had the most delicate sensibility to the propriety of conduct, might often be led to act absurdly upon the most frivolous occasions, and when it was scarce possible to assign any serious motive for his behaviour in this manner. Your friend makes you a visit when you happen to be in a humour which makes it disagreeable to receive him: in your present mood this civility is very apt to appear an impertinent intrusion; and if you were to give way to the views of things which at this time occur, [210] though civil in your temper, you would behave to him with coldness and contempt. What renders you incapable of such a rudeness, is nothing but a regard to the general rules of civility and hospitality, which prohibit it. That habitual reverence which your former experience has taught you for these, enables you to act, upon all such occasions, with nearly equal propriety, and hinders those inequalities of temper, to which all men are subject, from influencing your conduct in any very sensible degree. But if without regard to these general rules, even the duties of politeness, which are so easily observed, and which can scarce have any serious motive to violate, would yet be so frequently violated, what would become of the duties of justice, of truth, of chastity, of fidelity, which it is often so difficult to observe, and which there may be so many strong motives to violate? But upon the tolerable observance of these duties, depends the very existence of human society, which would crumble into nothing if mankind were not generally impressed with a reverence for those important rules of conduct.

This reverence is still further enhanced by an opinion which is first impressed by nature, and afterwards confirmed by reasoning and philosophy, that those important rules of morality, are the commands and laws of the Deity, who will finally reward the obedient, and punish the transgressors of their duty.

This opinion or apprehension, I say, seems first to be impressed by nature. Men are naturally led to ascribe to those mysterious beings, whatever they are, which happen, in any country, to be the objects [211] of religious fear, all their own sentiments and passions. They have no other, they can conceive no other to ascribe to them. Those unknown intelligences which they imagine but see not, must necessarily be formed with some sort of resemblance to those intelligences of which they have experience. During the ignorance and darkness of pagan superstition, mankind seem to have formed the ideas of their divinities with so little delicacy, that they ascribed to them, indiscriminately, all the passions of human nature, those not excepted which do the least honour to our species, such as lust, hunger, avarice, envy, revenge. They could not fail therefore, to ascribe to those beings, for the excellence of whose nature they still conceived the highest admiration, those sentiments and qualities which are the great ornaments of humanity, and which seem to raise it to a resemblance of divine perfection, the love of virtue and beneficence, and the abhorrence of vice and injustice. The man who was injured, called upon Jupiter to be witness of the wrong that was done to him, and could not doubt, but that divine being would behold it with the same indignation which would animate the meanest of mankind, who looked on when injustice was committed. The man who did the injury, felt himself to be the proper object of detestation and resentment of mankind; and his natural fears led him to impute the same sentiments to those awful beings, whose presence he could not avoid, and whose power he could not resist. These natural hopes and fears, and suspicions, were propagated by sympathy, and confirmed by education; and the gods were universally represented and believed to be the rewarders of humanity and mercy, and the avengers of perfidy 212 and injustice. And thus religion, even in its rudest form, gave a sanction to the rules of morality, long before the age of artificial reasoning and philosophy. That the terrors of religion should thus enforce the natural sense of duty, was of too much importance to the happiness of mankind, for nature to leave it dependent upon the slowness and uncertainty of philosophical researches.

These researches, however, when they came to take place, confirmed those original anticipations of nature. Upon whatever we suppose that our moral faculties are founded, whether upon a certain modification of reason, upon an original instinct, called a moral sense, or upon some other principle of our nature, it cannot be doubted, that they were given us for the direction of our conduct in this life. They carry along with them the most evident badges of this authority, which denote that they were set up within us to be the supreme arbiters of all our actions, to superintend all our senses, passions, and appetites, and to judge how far each of them was either to be indulged or restrained. Our moral faculties are by no means, as some have pretended, upon a level in this respect with the other faculties and appetites of our nature, endowed with no more right to restrain these last, than these last are to restrain them. No other faculty or principle of action judges of any other. Love does not judge of resentment, nor resentment of love. Those two passions may be opposite to one another, but cannot, with any propriety, be said to approve or disapprove of one another. But it is the peculiar office of those faculties now under our consideration to judge, to bestow censure or applause upon all the other principles of our nature. They 213 may be considered as a sort of senses of which those principles are the objects. Every sense is supreme over its own objects. There is no appeal from the eye with regard to the beauty of colours, nor from the ear with regard to the harmony of sounds, nor from the taste with regard to the agreeableness of flavours. Each of those senses judges in the last resort of its own objects. Whatever gratifies the taste is sweet, whatever pleases the eye is beautiful, whatever sooths the ear is harmonious. The very essence of each of those qualities consists in being fitted to please the sense to which it is addressed. It belongs to our moral faculties, in the same manner to determine when the ear ought to be soothed, when the eye ought to be indulged, when the taste ought to be gratified, when and how far every other principle of our nature ought to be indulged or restrained. What is agreeable to our moral faculties, is fit, and right, and proper to be done; the contrary wrong, unfit, and improper. The sentiments which they approve of, are graceful and unbecoming. The very words, right, wrong, fit, improper, graceful, unbecoming, mean only what pleases or displeases those faculties.

Since these, therefore, were plainly intended to be the governing principles of human nature, the rules which they prescribe, are to be regarded as the commands and laws of the Deity, promulgated by those vicegerents which he has thus set up within us. All general rules are commonly denominated laws: thus the general rules which bodies observe in the communication of motion, are called the laws of motion. But those general rules which our moral faculties observe in approving or condemning whatever sentiment 214 or action is subjected to their examination, may much more justly be denominated such. They have a much greater resemblance to what are properly called laws, those general rules which the sovereign lays down to direct the conduct of his subjects. Like them they are rules to direct the free actions of men: they are prescribed most surely by a lawful superior, and are attended to in the sanction of rewards and punishments. Those vicegerents of God within us, never fail to punish the violation of them, by the torments of inward shame, and self-condemnation; and on the contrary, always reward obedience with tranquillity of mind, with contentment, and self-satisfaction.

There are innumerable other considerations which serve to confirm the same conclusion. The happiness of mankind, as well as of all other rational creatures, seems to have been the original purpose intended by the Author of nature, when he brought them into existence. No other end seems worthy of that supreme wisdom and divine benignity which we necessarily ascribe to him; and this opinion, which we are led to by the abstract consideration of his infinite perfections, is still more confirmed by the examination of the works of nature, which seem all intended to promote happiness, and to guard against misery. But by acting according to the dictates of our moral faculties, we necessarily pursue the most effectual means for promoting the happiness of mankind, and may therefore be said, in some sense, to co-operate with the Deity, and to advance as far as in our power the plan of Providence. By acting otherways, on the contrary, we seem to obstruct, in some measure, the scheme which the Author of nature has established for the 215 happiness and perfection of the world, and to declare ourselves, if I may say so, in some measure the enemies of God. Hence we are naturally encouraged to hope for his extraordinary favour and reward in the one case, and to dread his vengeance and punishment in the other.

There are besides many other reasons, and many other natural principles, which all tend to confirm and inculcate the same salutary doctrine. If we consider the general rules by which external prosperity and adversity are commonly distributed in this life, we shall find, that notwithstanding the disorder in which all things appear to be in this world, yet even here every virtue naturally meets with its proper reward, with the recompense which is most fit to encourage and promote it; and this too so surely, that it requires a very extraordinary concurrence of circumstances entirely to disappoint it. What is the reward most proper for encouraging industry, prudence, and circumspection? Success in every sort of business. And is it possible that in the whole of life these virtues should fail of attaining it? Wealth and external honours are their proper recompense, and the recompense which they can seldom fail of acquiring. What reward is most proper for promoting the practice of truth, justice, and humanity? The confidence, the esteem, and love of those we live with. Humanity does not desire to be great, but to be beloved. It is not in being rich that truth and justice would rejoice, but in being trusted and believed, recompenses which those virtues must almost always acquire. By some very extraordinary and unlucky circumstance, a good man may come to be suspected of a crime of which he was altogether 216 incapable, and upon that account be most unjustly exposed for the remaining part of his life to the horror and aversion of mankind. By an accident of this kind he may be said to lose his all, notwithstanding his integrity and justice; in the same manner as a cautious man, notwithstanding his utmost circumspection, may be ruined by an earthquake or an inundation. Accidents of the first kind, however, are perhaps still more rare, and still more contrary to the common course of things than those of the second; and still it remains true, that the practice of truth, justice, and humanity, is a certain and almost infallible method of acquiring what those virtues chiefly aim at, the confidence and love of those we live with. A person may be very easily misrepresented with regard to a particular action; but it is scarce possible that he should be so with regard to the general tenor of his conduct. An innocent man may be believed to have done wrong: this, however, will rarely happen. On the contrary, the established opinion of the innocence of his manners, will often lead us to absolve him where he has really been in the fault, notwithstanding very strong presumptions. A knave, in the same manner may escape censure, or even meet applause, for a particular knavery, in which his conduct is not understood. But no man was ever habitually such, without being almost universally known to be so, and without being even frequently suspected of guilt, when he was in reality perfectly innocent. And so far as vice and virtue can be either punished or rewarded by the sentiments and opinions of mankind, they both, according to the common course of things, meet even here with something more than exact and impartial justice.

217 But though the general rules by which prosperity and adversity are commonly distributed, when considered in this cool and philosophical light, appear to be perfectly suited to the situation of mankind in this life, yet they are by no means suited to some of our natural sentiments. Our natural love and admiration for some virtues is such, that we should wish to bestow on them all sorts of honours and rewards, even those which we must acknowledge to be the proper recompenses of other qualities with which those virtues are not always accompanied. Our detestation, on the contrary, for some vices is such, that we should desire to heap upon them every sort of disgrace and disaster, those not excepted which are the natural consequences of very different qualities. Magnanimity, generosity, and justice command so high a degree of admiration, that we desire to see them crowned with wealth, and power, and honours of every kind, the natural consequences of prudence, industry, and application; qualities with which those virtues are not inseparably connected. Fraud, falsehood, brutality, and violence, on the other hand, excite in every human breast such scorn and abhorrence, that our indignation rouses to see them possess those advantages which they may in some sense be said to have merited, by the diligence and industry with which they are sometimes attended. The industrious knave cultivates the soil; the indolent good man leaves it uncultivated. Who ought to reap the harvest? Who starve, and who live in plenty? The natural course of things decides it in favour of the knave: the natural sentiments of mankind in favour of the man of virtue. Man judges, that the good qualities of the one are greatly over-recompensed by those advantages which they tend to 218 procure him, and that the omissions of the other are by far too severely punished by the distress which they naturally bring upon him; and human laws, the consequences of human sentiments, forfeit the life and the estate of the industrious and cautious traitor, and reward, by extraordinary recompenses, the fidelity and public spirit of the improvident and careless good citizen. Thus man is by Nature directed to correct, in some measure, that distribution of things which she herself would otherwise have made. The rules which for this purpose she prompts him to follow, are different from those which she herself observes. She bestows upon every virtue, and upon every vice, that precise reward or punishment which is best fitted to encourage the one, or to restrain the other. She is directed by this sole consideration, and pays little regard to the different degrees of merit and demerit, which they may seem to possess in the sentiments and passions of man. Man, on the contrary pays regard to this only, and would endeavour to render the state of every virtue precisely

proportioned to that degree of love and esteem, and of every vice to that degree of contempt and abhorrence, which he himself conceives for it. The rules which she follows are fit for her, those which he follows for him: but both are calculated to promote the same great end, the order of the world, and the perfection and happiness of human nature.

But though man is thus employed to alter that distribution of things which natural events would make, if left to themselves; though, like the gods of the poets, he is perpetually interposing, by extraordinary means, in favour of virtue, and in opposition to vice, and like them, endeavours to turn away 219 the arrow that is aimed at the head of the righteous, but accelerates the sword of destruction that is lifted up against the wicked; yet he is by no means able to render the fortune of either quite suitable to his own sentiments and wishes. The natural course of things cannot be entirely controuled by the impotent endeavours of man: the current is too rapid and too strong for him to stop it; and though the rules which direct it appear to have been established for the wisest and best purposes, they sometimes produce effects which shock all his natural sentiments. That a great combination of men, should prevail over a small one; that those who engage in an enterprise with fore-thought and all necessary preparation, should prevail over such as oppose them without any; and that every end should be acquired by those means only which Nature has established for acquiring it, seems to be a rule not only necessary and unavoidable in itself, but even useful and proper for rousing the industry and attention of mankind. Yet, when, in consequence of this rule, violence and artifice prevail over sincerity and justice, what indignation does it not excite in the breast of every humane spectator? What sorrow and compassion for the sufferings of the innocent, and what furious resentment against the success of the oppressor? We are equally grieved and enraged, at the wrong that is done, but often find it altogether out of our power to redress it. When we thus despair of finding any force upon earth which can check the triumph of injustice, we naturally appeal to Heaven, and hope, that the great Author of our nature will himself execute hereafter, what all the principles which he has given us for the direction of our conduct, prompt us to attempt even here; that he will complete the 220 plan which he himself has thus taught us to begin; and will, in a life to come, render to every one according to the works which he has performed in this world. And thus we are led to the belief of a future state, not only by the weaknesses, by the hopes and fears of human nature, but by the noblest and best principles which belong to it, by the love of virtue, and by the abhorrence of vice and injustice.

"Does it suit the greatness of God," says the eloquent and philosophical bishop of Clermont, with that passionate and exaggerating force of imagination, which seems sometimes to exceed the bounds of decorum; "does it suit the greatness of God, to leave the world which he has created in so universal a disorder? To see the wicked prevail almost always over the just; the innocent dethroned by the usurper; the father become the victim of the ambition of an unnatural son; the husband expiring under the stroke of a barbarous and faithless wife? From the height of his greatness ought God to behold those melancholy events as a fantastical amusement, without taking any share in them? Because he is great, should he be weak, or unjust, or barbarous? Because men are little, ought they to be allowed either to be dissolute without punishment, or virtuous without reward? O God! if this is the character of your Supreme Being; if it is you whom we adore under such dreadful ideas; I can no longer acknowledge you for my father, for my protector, for the comforter of my sorrow, the support of my weakness, the rewarder of my fidelity. You would then be no more than an indolent and fantastical tyrant, who sacrifices mankind to his insolent vanity, and who [221] has brought them out of nothing, only to make them serve for the sport of his leisure, and of his caprice."

When the general rules which determine the merit and demerit of actions, come thus to be regarded, as the laws of an All-powerful Being, who watches over our conduct, and who, in a life to come, will reward the observance, and punish the breach of them; they necessarily acquire a new sacredness from this consideration. That our regard to the will of the Deity, ought to be the supreme rule of our conduct, can be doubted of by no body who believes his existence. The very thought of disobedience appears to involve in it the most shocking impropriety. How vain, how absurd would it be for man, either to oppose or to neglect the commands that were laid upon him by Infinite Wisdom, and Infinite Power! How unnatural, how impiously ungrateful not to reverence the precepts that were prescribed to him by the infinite goodness of his Creator, even though no punishment was to follow their violation. The sense of propriety too is here well supported by the strongest motives of self-interest. The idea that, however we may escape the observation of man, or be placed above the reach of human punishment, yet we are always acting under the eye, and exposed to the punishment of God, the great avenger of injustice, is a motive capable of restraining the most headstrong passions, with those at least who, by constant reflection, have rendered it familiar to them.

It is in this manner that religion enforces the natural sense of duty: and hence it is, that mankind [222] are generally disposed to place great confidence in the probity of those who seem deeply impressed with religious sentiments. Such persons, they imagine, act under an additional tye, besides those which regulate the conduct of other men. The regard to the propriety of action as well as to reputation, the regard to the applause of his own breast, as well as that of others, are motives which they suppose have the same influence over the religious man, as over the man of the world. But the former lies under another restraint, and never acts deliberately but as in the presence of that Great Superior who is finally to recompense him according to his deeds. A greater trust is reposed, upon this account, in the regularity and exactness of his conduct. And wherever the natural principles of religion are not corrupted by the factious and party zeal of some worthless cabal; wherever the first duty which it requires, is to fulfil all the obligations of morality; wherever men are not taught to regard frivolous observances, as more immediate duties of religion, than acts of justice and beneficence; and to imagine, that by sacrifices, and ceremonies, and vain supplications, they can bargain with the Deity for fraud, and perfidy, and violence, the world undoubtedly judges right in this respect, and justly places a double confidence in the rectitude of the religious man's behaviour.

[223]

CHAP. IV.
In what cases the sense of duty ought to be the sole principle of our conduct; and in what cases it ought to concur with other motives.

Religion affords such strong motives to the practice of virtue, and guards us by such powerful restraints from the temptations of vice, that many have been led to suppose, that religious principles were the sole laudable motives of action. We ought neither, they said, to reward from gratitude, nor punish from resentment; we ought neither to protect the helplessness of our children, nor afford support to the infirmities of our parents, from natural affection. All affections for particular objects, ought to be extinguished in our breast, and one great affection take the place of all others, the love of the Deity, the desire of rendering ourselves agreeable to him, and of directing our conduct in every respect according to his will. We ought not to be grateful from gratitude, we ought not to be charitable from humanity, we ought not to be public-spirited from the love of our country, nor generous and just from the love of mankind. The sole principle and motive of our conduct in the performance of all those different duties, ought to be a sense that God has commanded us to perform them. I shall not at present take time to examine this opinion particularly; I shall only observe, that we should not have expected to have found it entertained by any sect, who professed themselves of a religion in which, as it is the first precept to love the Lord our God with all our heart, with all our soul, and with all our strength, so it is the second to love our neighbour as we love ourselves; and we love ourselves surely for our own sakes, and not merely because we are commanded to do so. That the sense of duty should be the sole principle of our conduct, is no where the precept of Christianity; but that it should be the ruling and governing one, as philosophy, and as, indeed, common sense directs. It may be a question however, in what cases our actions ought to arise chiefly or entirely from a sense of duty, or from a regard to general rules; and in what cases some other sentiment or affection ought to concur, and have a principal influence.

The decision of this question, which cannot, perhaps, be given with any very great accuracy, will depend upon two different circumstances; first, upon the natural agreeableness or deformity of the sentiment or affection which would prompt us to any action independent of all regard to general rules; and secondly, upon the precision and exactness, or the looseness and inaccuracy of the general rules themselves.

I. First, I say, it will depend upon the natural agreeableness or deformity of the affection itself, how far our actions ought to arise from it, or entirely proceed from a regard to the general rule.

All those graceful and admired actions, to which the benevolent affections would prompt us, ought to proceed as much from the passions themselves, as from any regard to the general rules of conduct. A benefactor thinks himself but ill requited, if the person upon whom he has bestowed his good offices, repays them merely from a cold sense of duty, and without any affection to his person. A husband is dissatisfied with the most obedient wife, when he imagines her conduct is animated by no other principle besides her regard to what the relation she stands in requires. Though a son should fail in none of the offices of filial duty, yet if he wants that affectionate reverence which it so well becomes him to feel, the parent may justly complain of his indifference. Nor could a son be quite satisfied with a parent who, though he performed all the duties of his situation, had nothing of that fatherly fondness which might have been expected from him. With regard to all such benevolent and social affections, it is agreeable to see the sense of duty employed rather to restrain than to enliven them, rather to hinder us from doing too much, than to prompt us to do what we ought. It gives us pleasure to see a father obliged to check his own fondness, a friend obliged to set bounds to his natural generosity, a person who has received a benefit, obliged to restrain the too sanguine gratitude of his own temper.

The contrary maxim takes place with regard to the malevolent and unsocial passions. We ought to reward from the gratitude and generosity of our own hearts, without any reluctance, and without being obliged to reflect how great the propriety of rewarding: but we ought always to punish with reluctance, 226 and more from a sense of the propriety of punishing than from any savage disposition to revenge. Nothing is more graceful than the behaviour of the man who appears to resent the greatest injuries, more from a sense that they deserve, and are the proper objects of resentment, than from feeling himself the furies of that disagreeable passion; who, like a judge, considers only the general rule, which determines what vengeance is due for each particular offence; who, in executing that rule, feels less for what himself has suffered, than what the offender is about to suffer; who, though in wrath remembers mercy, and is disposed to interpret the rule in the most gentle and favourable manner, and to allow all the alleviations which the most candid humanity could, consistently with good sense, admit of.

As the selfish passions, according to what has formerly been observed, hold in other respects a sort of middle place, between the social and unsocial affections, so do they likewise in this. The pursuit of the objects of private interest, in all common, little, and ordinary cases, ought to flow rather from a regard to the general rules which prescribe such conduct, than from any passion for the objects themselves; but upon more important and extraordinary occasions, we should be awkward, insipid, and ungraceful, if the objects themselves did not appear to animate us with a considerable degree of passion. To be anxious, or to be laying a plot either to gain or to save a single shilling, would degrade the most vulgar tradesman in the opinion of all his neighbours. Let his circumstances be ever so mean, no attention to any such small matters, for the sake of the things themselves, must appear in his conduct. His situation 227 may require the most severe œconomy, and the most exact assiduity: but each particular exertion of that œconomy and assiduity must proceed not so much from a regard for that particular saving or gain, as for the general rule which to him prescribes, with the utmost rigour, such a tenour of conduct. His parsimony to-day must not arise from a desire of the particular three-pence which he will save by it, nor his attendance in his shop from a passion for the particular ten-pence which he will acquire by it: both the one and the other ought to proceed solely from a regard to the general rule, which prescribes, with the most unrelenting severity, this plan of conduct to all persons in his way of life. In this consists the difference between the character of a miser, and that of a person of exact œconomy and assiduity. The one is anxious about small matters for their own sake; the other attends to them only in consequence of the scheme of life which he has laid down to himself.

It is quite otherwise with regard to the more extraordinary and important objects of self-interest. A person appears mean-spirited, who does not pursue these with some degree of earnestness for their own sake. We should despise a prince who was not anxious about conquering or defending a province. We should have little respect for a private gentleman who did not exert himself to gain an estate, or even a considerable office, when he could acquire them without either meanness or injustice. A member of parliament who shews no keenness about his own election, is abandoned by his friends, as altogether unworthy of their attachment. Even a tradesman is 228 thought a poor-spirited fellow among his neighbours, who does not bestir himself to get what they call an extraordinary job, or some uncommon advantage. This spirit and keenness constitutes the difference between the man of enterprise and the man of dull regularity. Those great objects of self-interest, of which the loss or acquisition quite changes the rank of the person, are the objects of the passion properly called ambition; a passion, which when it keeps within the bounds of prudence and justice, is always admired in the world, and has even sometimes a certain irregular greatness, which dazzles the imagination, when it passes the limits of both these virtues, and is not only unjust but extravagant. Hence the general admiration for Heroes and Conquerors, and even for Statesmen, whose projects have been very daring and extensive, though altogether devoid of justice; such as those of the Cardinals of Richlieu and of Retz. The objects of avarice and ambition differ only in their greatness. A miser is as furious about a halfpenny, as a man of ambition about the conquest of a kingdom.

II. Secondly, I say, it will depend partly upon the precision and exactness, or the looseness and inaccuracy of the general rules themselves, how far our conduct ought to proceed entirely from a regard to them.

The general rules of almost all the virtues, the general rules which determine what are the offices of prudence, of charity, of generosity, of gratitude, of friendship, are in many respects loose and inaccurate, admit of many exceptions, and require so many modifications, that it is scarce possible to regulate our 229 conduct entirely by a regard to them. The common proverbial maxims of prudence, being founded in universal experience, are perhaps the best general rules which can be given about it. To affect, however, a very strict and literal adherence to them would evidently be the most absurd and ridiculous pedantry. Of all the virtues I have just now mentioned, gratitude is that, perhaps, of which the rules are the most precise, and admit of the fewest exceptions. That as soon as we can we should make a return of equal, and if possible of superior value to the services we have received, would seem to be a pretty plain rule, and one which admitted of scarce any exceptions. Upon the most superficial examination, however, this rule will appear to be in the highest degree loose and inaccurate, and to admit of ten thousand exceptions. If your benefactor attended you in your sickness, ought you to attend him in his? or can you fulfil the obligation of gratitude, by making a return of a different kind? If you ought to attend him, how long ought you to attend him? The same time which he attended you, or longer, and how much longer? If your friend lent you money in your distress, ought you to lend him money in his? How much ought you to lend him? When ought you to lend him? Now, or to-morrow, or next month? And for how long a time? It is evident, that no general rule can be laid down, by which a precise answer can, in all cases, be given to any of these questions. The difference between his character and yours, between his circumstances and yours, may be such, that you may be perfectly grateful, and justly refuse to lend him a halfpenny: and, on the contrary, you may be willing to lend, or even to give him ten times the sum which he lent 230 you, and yet justly be accused of the blackest ingratitude, and of not having fulfilled the hundredth part of the obligation you lie under. As the duties of gratitude, however, are perhaps the most sacred of all those which the beneficent virtues prescribe to us, so the general rules which determine them are, as I said before, the most accurate. Those which ascertain the actions required by friendship, humanity, hospitality, generosity, are still more vague and indeterminate.

There is, however, one virtue of which the general rules determine with the greatest exactness every external action which it requires. This virtue is justice. The rules of justice are accurate in the highest degree, and admit of no exceptions or modifications, but such as may be ascertained as accurately as the rules themselves, and which generally, indeed, flow from the very same principles with them. If I owe a man ten pounds, justice requires that I should precisely pay him ten pounds, either at the time agreed upon, or when he demands it. What I ought to perform, how much I ought to perform, when and where I ought to perform it, the whole nature and circumstances of the action prescribed, are all of them precisely fixt and determined. Though it may be awkward and pedantic, therefore, to affect too strict an adherence to the common rules of prudence or generosity, there is no pedantry in sticking fast by the rules of justice. On the contrary, the most sacred regard is due to them; and the actions which this virtue requires are never so properly performed, as when the chief motive for performing them is a reverential and religious regard to those general rules which require them. In the practice of 231 the other virtues, our conduct should rather be directed by a certain idea of propriety, by a certain taste for a particular tenour of conduct, than by any regard to a precise maxim or rule; and we should consider the end and foundation of the rule, more than the rule itself. But it is otherwise with regard to justice: the man who in that refines the least, and adheres with the most obstinate stedfastness, to the general rules themselves, is the most commendable, and the most to be depended upon. Though the end of the rules of justice be, to hinder us from hurting our neighbour, it may frequently be a crime to violate them, though we could pretend, with some pretext of reason, that this particular violation could do no hurt. A man often becomes a villain the moment he begins even in his own heart, to chicane in this manner. The moment he thinks of departing from the most staunch and positive adherence to what those inviolable precepts prescribe to him, he is no longer to be trusted, and no man can say what degree of guilt he may not arrive at. The thief imagines he does no evil, when he steals from the rich, what he supposes they may easily want, and what possibly they may never even know has been stolen from them. The adulterer imagines he does no evil, when he corrupts the wife of his friend, provided he covers his intrigue from the suspicion of the husband, and does not disturb the peace of the family. When once we begin to give way to such refinements, there is no enormity so gross of which we may not be capable.

The rules of justice may be compared to the rules of grammar; the rules of the other virtues to the 232 rules which critics lay down for the attainment of what is sublime and elegant in composition. The one, are precise, accurate, and indispensable. The other, are loose, vague, and indeterminate, and present us rather with a general idea of the perfection we ought to aim at, than afford us any certain and infallible directions for acquiring it. A man may learn to write grammatically by rule, with the most absolute infallibility; and so, perhaps, he may be taught to act justly. But there are no rules whose observance will infallibly lead us to the attainment of elegance or sublimity in writing, though there are some which may help us, in some measure, to correct and ascertain the vague ideas which we might otherwise have entertained of those perfections: and there are no rules by the knowledge of which we can infallibly be taught to act upon all occasions with prudence, with just magnanimity, or proper beneficence. Though there are some which may enable us to correct and ascertain in several respects, the imperfect ideas which we might otherwise have entertained of those virtues.

It may sometimes happen, that with the most serious and earnest desire of acting so as to deserve approbation, we may mistake the proper rules of conduct, and thus be misled by that very principle which ought to direct us. It is in vain to expect, that in this case mankind should entirely approve of our behaviour. They cannot enter into that absurd idea of duty which influenced us, nor go along with any of the actions which follow from it. There is still, however, something respectable in the character and behaviour of one who is thus betrayed into 233 vice, by a wrong sense of duty, or by what is called an erroneous conscience. How fatally soever he may be misled by it, he is still, with the generous and humane, more the object of commiseration than of hatred or resentment. They lament the weakness of human nature, which exposes us to such unhappy delusions, even while we are most sincerely labouring after perfection, and endeavouring to act according to the best principle which can possibly direct us. False notions of religion are almost the only causes which can occasion any very gross perversion of our natural sentiments in this way; and that principle which gives the greatest authority to the rules of duty, is alone capable of distorting our ideas of them in any considerable degree. In all other cases common sense is sufficient to direct us, if not to the most exquisite propriety of conduct, yet to something which is not very far from it; and provided we are in earnest desirous to do well, our behaviour will always, upon the whole, be praise-worthy. That to obey the will of the Deity, is the first rule of duty, all men are agreed. But concerning the particular commandments which that will may impose upon us, they differ widely from one another. In this, therefore, the greatest mutual forbearance and toleration is due; and though the defence of society requires that crimes should be punished, from whatever motives they proceed, yet a good man will always punish them with reluctance, when they evidently proceed from false notions of religious duty. He will never feel against those who commit them that indignation which he feels against other criminals, but will rather regret, and sometimes even admire their unfortunate firmness and magnanimity, at the very time that he punishes 234 their crime. In the tragedy of Mahomet, one of the finest of Mr. Voltaire's, it is well represented, what ought to be our sentiments for crimes which proceed from such motives. In that tragedy, two young people of different sexes, of the most innocent and virtuous dispositions, and without any other weakness except what endears them the more to us, a mutual fondness for one another, are instigated by the strongest motives of a false religion, to commit a horrid murder, that shocks all the principles of human nature: a venerable old man, who had expressed the most tender affection for them both, for whom, notwithstanding he was the avowed enemy of their religion, they had both conceived the highest reverence and esteem, and who was in reality their father, though they did not know him to be such, is pointed out to them as a sacrifice which God had expressly required at their hands, and they are commanded to kill him. While they are about executing this crime, they are tortured with all the agonies which can arise from the struggle between the idea of the indispensableness of religious duty on the one side, and compassion, gratitude, reverence for the age, and love for the humanity and virtue of the person whom they are going to destroy, on the other. The representation of this exhibits one of the most interesting, and perhaps the most instructive spectacle that was ever introduced upon any theatre. The sense of duty, however, at last prevails over all the amiable weaknesses of human nature. They execute the crime imposed upon them; but immediately discover their error, and the fraud which had deceived them, and are distracted with horror, remorse, and resentment. Such as are our sentiments for the unhappy Seid and Palmira, such ought we 235 to feel for every person who is in this manner misled by religion, when we are sure that it is really religion which misleads him, and not the pretence of it, which is made a cover to some of the worst of human passions.

As a person may act wrong by following a wrong sense of duty, so nature may sometimes prevail, and lead him to act right in opposition to it. We cannot in this case be displeased to see that motive prevail, which we think ought to prevail, though the person himself is so weak as to think otherwise. As his conduct, however, is the effect of weakness, not principle, we are far from bestowing upon it any thing that approaches to complete approbation. A bigotted Roman Catholic, who, during the massacre of St. Bartholomew, had been so overcome by compassion, as to save some unhappy protestants, whom he thought it his duty to destroy, would not seem to be entitled to that high applause which we should have bestowed upon him, had he exerted the same generosity with complete self-approbation. We might be pleased with the humanity of his temper, but we should still regard him with a sort of pity which is altogether inconsistent with the admiration that is due to perfect virtue. It is the same case with all the other passions. We do not dislike to see them exert themselves properly, even when a false notion of duty would direct the person to restrain them. A very devout Quaker, who upon being struck upon one cheek, instead of turning up the other, should so far forget his literal interpretation of our Saviour's precept, as to bestow some good discipline upon the brute that insulted him, 236 would not be disagreeable to us. We should laugh and be diverted with his spirit, and rather like him the better for it. But we should by no means regard him with that respect and esteem which would seem due to one who, upon a like occasion, had acted properly from a just sense of what was proper to be done. No action can properly be called virtuous, which is not accompanied with the sentiment of self-approbation.

PART IV.
Of the EFFECT of UTILITY upon the sentiment of approbation.

CONSISTING OF ONE SECTION.

CHAP. I.
Of the beauty which the appearance of UTILITY *bestows upon all the productions of art, and of the extensive influence of this species of beauty.*

That utility is one of the principal sources of beauty has been observed by every body, who has considered with any attention what constitutes the nature of beauty. The conveniency of a house gives pleasure to the spectator as well as its regularity, and he is as much hurt when he observes the contrary defect, as when he sees the correspondent windows of different forms, or the door not placed exactly in the middle of the building. That the fitness of any system or machine to produce the end for which it was intended, bestows a certain propriety and beauty upon the whole, and renders the very thought and contemplation of it agreeable, is so very obvious that nobody has overlooked it.

238 The cause too, why utility pleases, has of late been assigned by an ingenious and agreeable philosopher, who joins the greatest depth of thought to the greatest elegance of expression, and possesses the singular and happy talent of treating the abstrusest subjects not only with the most perfect perspicuity, but with the most lively eloquence. The utility of any object, according to him, pleases the master by perpetually suggesting to him the pleasure or conveniency which it is fitted to promote. Every time he looks at it, he is put in mind of this pleasure; and the object in this manner becomes a source of perpetual satisfaction and enjoyment. The spectator enters by sympathy into the sentiments of the master, and necessarily views the object under the same agreeable aspect. When we visit the palaces of the great, we cannot help conceiving the satisfaction we should enjoy if we ourselves were the masters, and were possessed of so much artful and ingeniously contrived accommodation. A similar account is given why the appearance of inconveniency should render any object disagreeable both to the owner and to the spectator.

But that this fitness, this happy contrivance of any production of art, should often be more valued, than the very end for which it was intended; and that the exact adjustment of the means for attaining any conveniency or pleasure, should frequently be more regarded, than that very conveniency or pleasure, in the attainment of which their whole merit would seem to consist, has not, so far as I know, been yet taken notice of by any body. That this however is very frequently the case, may be observed 239 in a thousand instances, both in the most frivolous and in the most important concerns of human life.

When a person comes into his chamber, and finds the chairs all standing in the middle of the room, he is angry with his servant, and rather than see them continue in that disorder, perhaps takes the trouble himself to set them all in their places with their backs to the wall. The whole propriety of this new situation arises from its superior conveniency in leaving the floor free and disengaged. To attain this conveniency he voluntarily puts himself to more trouble than all he could have suffered from the want of it; since nothing was more easy, than to have set himself down upon one of them, which is probably what he does when his labour is over. What he wanted therefore, it seems, was not so much this conveniency, as that arrangement of things which promotes it. Yet it is this conveniency which ultimately recommends that arrangement, and bestows upon it the whole of its propriety and beauty.

A watch, in the same manner, that falls behind above two minutes in a day, is despised by one curious in watches. He sells it perhaps for a couple of guineas, and purchases another at fifty, which will not lose above a minute in a fortnight. The sole use of watches however, is to tell us what o'clock it is, and to hinder us from breaking any engagement, or suffering any other inconveniency by our ignorance in that particular point. But the person so nice with regard to this machine, will not always be found either more scrupulously punctual than other men, or more anxiously concerned upon any other account, to know precisely what time of day 240 it is. What interests him is not so much the attainment of this piece of knowledge, as the perfection of the machine which serves to attain it.

How many people ruin themselves by laying out money on trinkets of frivolous utility? What pleases these lovers of toys is not so much the utility, as the aptness of the machines which are fitted to promote it. All their pockets are fluffed with little conveniencies. They contrive new pockets, unknown in the clothes of other people, in order to carry a greater number. They walk about loaded with a multitude of baubles, in weight and sometimes in value not inferior to an ordinary Jew's-box, some of which may sometimes be of some little use, but all of which might at all times be very well spared, and of which the whole utility is certainly not worth the fatigue of bearing the burden.

Nor is it only with regard to such frivolous objects that our conduct is influenced by this principle; it is often the secret motive of the most serious and important pursuits of both private and public life.

The poor man's son, whom Heaven in its anger has visited with ambition, when he begins to look around him admires the condition of the rich. He finds the cottage of his father too small for his accommodation, and fancies he should be lodged more at his ease in a palace. He is displeased with being obliged to walk a-foot, or to endure the fatigue of riding on horseback. He sees his superiors carried about in machines, and imagines that in one of these he could travel with less inconveniency. He 241 feels himself naturally indolent, and willing to serve himself with his own hands as little as possible; and judges, that a numerous retinue of servants would save him from a great deal of trouble. He thinks if he had attained all these, he would sit still contentedly, and be quiet, enjoying himself in the thought of the happiness and tranquillity of his situation. He is enchanted with the distant idea of this felicity. It appears in his fancy like the life of some superior rank of beings, and in order to arrive at it, he devotes himself for ever to the pursuit of wealth and greatness. To obtain the conveniencies which these afford, he submits in the first year nay in the first month of his application, to more fatigue of body and more uneasiness of mind than he could have suffered through the whole of his life from the want of them. H studies to distinguish himself in some laborious profession. With the most unrelenting industry he labours night and day to acquire talents superior to all his competitors. He endeavours next to bring those talents into public view, and with equal assiduity solicits every opportunity of employment. For this purpose he makes his court to all mankind, he serves those whom he hates, and is obsequious to those whom he despises. Through the whole of his life he pursues the idea of a certain artificial and elegant repose which he may never arrive at, for which he sacrifices a real tranquillity that is at all times in his power, and which, if in the extremity of old age he should at last attain to it, he will find to be in no respect preferable to that humble security and contentment which he had abandoned for it. It is then, in the last dregs of life, his body wailed with toil and diseases, his mind galled and ruffled by the memory of a thousand 242 injuries and disappointments which he imagines he has met with from the injustice of his enemies, or from the perfidy and ingratitude of his friends, that he begins at last to find that wealth and greatness are mere trinkets of frivolous utility, no more adapted for procuring ease of body or tranquillity of mind than the tweezer-cases of the lover of toys; and like them too, more troublesome to the person who carries them about with him than all the advantages they can afford him are commodious. There is no other real difference between them, except that the conveniencies of the one are somewhat more observable than those of the other. The palaces, the gardens, the equipage, the retinue of the great are objects of which the obvious conveniency strikes every body. They do not require that their masters should point out to us wherein consists their utility. Of our own accord we readily enter into it, and by sympathy enjoy and thereby applaud the satisfaction which they are fitted to afford him. But the curiosity of a tooth-pick, of an ear-picker, of a machine for cutting the nails, or of any other trinket of the same kind, is not so obvious. Their convenience may perhaps be equally great, but it is not so striking, and we do not so readily enter into the satisfaction of the man who possesses them. They are therefore less reasonable subjects of vanity than the magnificence of wealth and greatness; and in this consists the sole advantage of these last. They more effectually gratify that love of distinction so natural to man. To one who was to live alone in a desolate island it might be a matter of doubt, perhaps, whether a palace, or a collection of such small conveniencies as are commonly contained in a tweezer-case, would contribute most to his happiness and enjoyment. 243 If he is to live in society, indeed, there can be no comparison, because in this, as in all other cases, we constantly pay more regard to the sentiments of the spectator, than to those of the person principally concerned, and consider rather how his situation will appear to other people, than how it will appear to himself. If we examine, however, why the spectator distinguishes with such admiration the condition of the rich and the great, we shall find that it is not so much upon account of the superior ease or pleasure which they are supposed to enjoy, as of the numberless artificial and elegant contrivances for promoting this ease or pleasure. He does not even imagine that they are really happier than other people: but he imagines that they possess more means of happiness. And it is the ingenious and artful adjustment of those means to the end for which they were intended, that is the principal source of his admiration. But in the languor of disease, and the weariness of old age, the pleasures of the vain and empty distinctions of greatness disappear. To one, in this situation, they are no longer capable of recommending those toilsome pursuits in which they had formerly engaged him. In his heart he curses ambition, and vainly regrets the ease and the indolence of youth, pleasures which are fled for ever, and which he has foolishly sacrificed for what, when he has got it, can afford him no real satisfaction. In this miserable aspect does greatness appear to every man when reduced either by spleen or disease to observe with attention his own situation, and to consider what it is that is really wanting to his happiness. Power and riches appear then to be what they are, enormous and operose machines contrived to produce a few trifling conveniencies to 244 the body, consisting of springs the most nice and delicate, which must be kept in order with the most anxious attention, and which in spite of all our care are ready every moment to burst into pieces, and to crush in their ruins their unfortunate possessor. They are immense fabrics, which it requires the labour of a life to raise, which threaten every moment to overwhelm the person that dwells in them, and which while they stand, though they may save him from some smaller inconveniencies, can protect him from none of the severer inclemencies of the season. They keep off the summer shower, not the winter storm, but leave him always as much, and sometimes more exposed than before, to anxiety, to fear, and to sorrow; to diseases, to danger, and to death.

But though this splenetic philosophy, which in time of sickness or low spirits is familiar to every man, thus entirely depreciates those great objects of human desire, when in better health and in better humour, we never fail to regard them under a more agreeable aspect. Our imagination, which in pain and sorrow seems to be confined and cooped up within our own persons, in times of ease and prosperity expands itself to every thing around us. We are then charmed with the beauty of that accommodation which reigns in the palaces and œconomy of the great; and admire how every thing is adapted to promote their ease, to prevent their wants, to gratify their wishes, and to amuse and entertain their most frivolous desires. If we consider the real satisfaction which all these things are capable of affording, by itself and separated from the beauty of that arrangement which is fitted to promote it, it will always appear in the highest 245 degree contemptible and trifling. But we rarely view it in this abstract and philosophical light. We naturally confound it in our imagination with the order, the regular and harmonious movement of the system, the machine or œconomy by means of which it is produced. The pleasures of wealth and greatness, when considered in this complex view, strike the imagination as something grand and beautiful and noble, of which the attainment is well worth all the toil and anxiety which we are so apt to bestow upon it.

And it is well that nature imposes upon us in this manner. It is this deception which rouses and keeps in continual motion the industry of mankind. It is this which first prompted them to cultivate the ground, to build houses, to found cities and commonwealths, and to invent and improve all the sciences and arts, which ennoble and embellish human life; which have entirely changed the whole face of the globe, have turned the rude forests of nature into agreeable and fertile plains, and made the trackless and barren ocean a new fund of subsistence, and the great high road of communication to the different nations of the earth. The earth by these labours of mankind has been obliged to redouble her natural fertility, and to maintain a greater multitude of inhabitants. It is to no purpose, that the proud and unfeeling landlord views his extensive fields, and without a thought for the wants of his brethren, in imagination consumes himself the whole harvest that grows upon them. The homely and vulgar proverb, that the eye is larger than the belly, never was more fully verified than with regard to him. The capacity of his stomach bears no proportion to 246 the immensity of his desires, and will receive no more than that of the meanest peasant. The rest he is obliged to distribute among those, who prepare, in the nicest manner, that little which he himself makes use of, among those who sit up the palace in which this little is to be consumed, among those who provide and keep in order all the different baubles and trinkets, which are employed in the œconomy of greatness; all of whom thus derive from his luxury and caprice, that share of the necessaries of life, which they would in vain have expected from his humanity or his justice. The produce of the soil maintains at all times nearly that number of inhabitants, which it is capable of maintaining. The rich only select from the heap what is most precious and agreeable. They consume little more than the poor, and in spite of their natural selfishness and rapacity, though they mean only their own conveniency, though the sole end which they propose from the labours of all the thousands whom they employ, be the gratification of their own vain and insatiable desires, they divide with the poor the produce of all their improvements. They are led by an invisible hand to make nearly the same distribution of the necessaries of life, which would have been made, had the earth been divided into equal portions among all its inhabitants, and thus without intending it, without knowing it, advance the interest of the society, and afford means to the multiplication of the species. When Providence divided the earth among a few lordly masters, it neither forgot nor abandoned those who seemed to have been left out in the partition. These last too enjoy their share of all that it produces. In what constitutes [247] the real happiness of human life, they are in no respect inferior to those who would seem so much above them. In ease of body and peace of mind, all the different ranks of life are nearly upon a level, and the beggar, who suns himself by the side of the highway, possesses that security which kings are fighting for.

The same principle, the same love of system, the same regard to the beauty of order, of art and contrivance, frequently serves to recommend those institutions, which tend to promote the public welfare. When a patriot exerts himself for the improvement of any part of the public police, his conduct does not always arise from pure sympathy with the happiness of those who are to reap the benefit of it. It is not commonly from a fellow-feeling with carriers and waggoners that a public-spirited man encourages the mending of high roads. When the legislature establishes premiums and other encouragements to advance the linen or woollen manufactures, its conduct seldom proceeds from pure sympathy with the wearer of cheap or fine cloth, and much less from that with the manufacturer, or merchant. The perfection of police, the extension of trade and manufactures, are noble and magnificent objects. The contemplation of them pleases us, and we are interested in whatever can tend to advance them. They make part of the great system of government, and the wheels of the political machine seem to move with more harmony and ease by means of them. We take pleasure in beholding the perfection of so beautiful and grand a system, and we are uneasy till we remove any obstruction that can in the least disturb or encumber the regularity of its motions. All [248] constitutions of government, however, are valued only in proportion, as they tend to promote the happiness of those who live under them. This is their sole use and end. From a certain spirit of system, however, from a certain love of art and contrivance, we sometimes seem to value the means more than the end, and to be eager to promote the happiness of our fellow-creatures, rather from a view to perfect and improve a certain beautiful and orderly system, than from any immediate sense or feeling of what they either suffer or enjoy. There have been men of the greatest public spirit, who have shewn themselves in other respects not very sensible to the feelings of humanity. And on the contrary, there have been men of the greatest humanity, who seem to have been entirely devoid of public spirit.

Every man may find in the circle of his acquaintance instances both of the one kind and the other. Who had ever less humanity, or more public spirit, than the celebrated legislator of Muscovy? The social and well natured James the First of Great Britain seems, on the contrary, to have had scarce any passion, either for the glory, or the interest of his country. Would you awaken the industry of the man, who seems almost dead to ambition, it will often be to no purpose to describe to him the happiness of the rich and the great; to tell him that they are generally sheltered from the sun and the rain, that they are seldom hungry, that they are seldom cold, and that they are rarely exposed to weariness, or to want of any kind. The most eloquent exhortation of this kind will have little effect upon him. If you would hope to succeed, you must describe to him the conveniency and arrangement of the different apartments in their palaces, you must explain to him the propriety of 249 their equipages, and point out to him the number, the order, and the different offices of all their attendants. If any thing is capable of making impression upon him, this will. Yet all these things tend only to keep off the sun and the rain, to save them from hunger and cold, from want and weariness. In the same manner, if you would implant public virtue in the breast of him, who seems heedless of the interest of his country, it will often be to no purpose to tell him, what superior advantages the subjects of a well-governed state enjoy; that they are better lodged, that they are better clothed, that they are better fed. These considerations will commonly make no great impression. You will be more likely to persuade, if you describe the great system of public police which procures these advantages, if you explain the connexions and dependencies of its several parts, their mutual subordination to one another, and their general subserviency to the happiness of the society; if you show how this system might be introduced into his own country, what it is that hinders it from taking place there at present, how those obstructions might be removed, and all the several wheels of the machine of government be made to move with more harmony and smoothness, without grating upon one another, or mutually retarding one another's motions. It is scarce possible that a man should listen to a discourse of this kind, and not feel himself animated to some degree of public spirit. He will, at least for the moment, feel some desire to remove those obstructions, and to put into motion so beautiful and so orderly a machine. Nothing tends so much to promote public spirit as the study of politics, of the several systems of civil government, their advantages and disadvantages, of the constitution of our own 250 country, its situation, and interest with regard to foreign nations, its commerce, its defence, the disadvantages it labours under, the dangers to which it may be exposed, how to remove the one, and how to guard against the other. Upon this account political disquisitions, if just and reasonable, and practicable, are of all the works of speculation the most useful. Even the weakest and the worst of them are not altogether without their utility. They serve at least to animate the public passions of men, and rouse them to seek out the means of promoting the happiness of the society.

CHAP. II.
Of the beauty which the appearance of utility bestows upon the characters and actions of men; and how far

the perception of this beauty may be regarded as one of the original principles of approbation.

The characters of men, as well as the contrivances of art, or the institutions of civil government, may be fitted either to promote or to disturb the happiness both of the individual and of the society. The prudent, the equitable, the active, resolute, and sober character promises prosperity and satisfaction, both to the person himself and to every one connected with him. The rash, the insolent, the slothful, effeminate, and voluptuous, on the contrary, forebodes ruin to the individual, and misfortune to all who have any thing to do with him. The first turn of mind has at least all the beauty 251 which can belong to the most perfect machine that was ever invented for promoting the most agreeable purpose: and the second all the deformity of the most awkward and clumsy contrivance. What institution of government could tend so much to promote the happiness of mankind as the general prevalence of wisdom and virtue? All government is but an imperfect remedy for the deficiency of these. Whatever beauty, therefore, can belong to civil government upon account of its utility, must in a far superior degree belong to these. On the contrary, what civil policy can be so ruinous and destructive as the vices of men? The fatal effects of bad government arise from nothing, but that it does not sufficiently guard against the mischiefs which human wickedness gives occasion to.

This beauty and deformity which characters appear to derive from their usefulness or inconveniency, are apt to strike, in a peculiar manner, those who consider, in an abstract and philosophical light, the actions and conduct of mankind. When a philosopher goes to examine why humanity is approved of, or cruelty condemned, he does not always form to himself, in a very clear and distinct manner, the conception of any one particular action either of cruelty or of humanity, but is commonly contented with the vague and indeterminate idea which the general names of those qualities suggest to him. But it is in particular instances only that the propriety or impropriety, the merit or demerit of actions is very obvious and discernible. It is only when particular examples are given that we perceive distinctly either the concord or disagreement between our own affections and those of the agent, or feel a social gratitude arise 252 towards him in the one case, or a sympathetic resentment in the other. When we consider virtue and vice in an abstract and general manner, the qualities by which they excite these several sentiments seem in a great measure to disappear, and the sentiments themselves become less obvious and discernible. On the contrary, the happy effects of the one and the fatal consequences of the other seem then to rise up to the view, and as it were to stand out and distinguish themselves from all the other qualities of either.

The same ingenious and agreeable author who first explained why utility pleases, has been so struck with this view of things, as to resolve our whole approbation of virtue into a perception of this species of beauty which results from the appearance of utility. No qualities of the mind, he observes, are approved of as virtuous, but such as are useful or agreeable either to the person himself or to others; and no qualities are disapproved of as vicious but such as have a contrary tendency. And Nature, indeed, seems to have so happily adjusted our sentiments of approbation and disapprobation, to the conveniency both of the individual and of the society, that after the strictest examination it will be found, I believe, that this is universally the case. But still I affirm, that it is not the view of this utility or hurtfulness which is either the first or principal source of our approbation and disapprobation. These sentiments are no doubt enhanced and enlivened by the perception of the beauty or deformity which results from this utility or hurtfulness. But still, I say, they are originally and essentially different from this perception.

253 For first of all, it seems impossible that the approbation of virtue should be a sentiment of the same kind with that by which we approve of a convenient and well contrived building, or that we should have no other reason for praising a man than that for which we commend a chest of drawers.

And secondly, it will be found, upon examination, that the usefulness of any disposition of mind is seldom the first ground of our approbation; and that the sentiment of approbation always involves in it a sense of propriety quite distinct from the perception of utility. We may observe this with regard to all the qualities which are approved of as virtuous, both those which, according to this system, are originally valued as useful to ourselves, as well as those which are esteemed on account of their usefulness to others.

The qualities most useful to ourselves are, first of all, superior reason and understanding, by which we are capable of discerning the remote consequences of all our actions, and of foreseeing the advantage or detriment which is likely to result from them: and secondly, self-command, by which we are enabled to abstain from present pleasure or to endure present pain, in order to obtain a greater pleasure or to avoid a greater pain in some future time. In the union of those two qualities consists the virtue of prudence, of all the virtues that which is most useful to the individual.

With regard to the first of those qualities, it has been observed on a former occasion, that superior reason and understanding are originally approved of 254 as just and right and accurate, and not merely as useful or advantageous. It is in the abstruser sciences, particularly in the higher parts of mathematics, that the greatest and most admired exertions of human reason have been displayed. But the utility of those sciences, either to the individual or to the public, is not very obvious, and to prove it requires a discussion which is not always very easily comprehended. It was not, therefore, their utility which first recommended them to the public admiration. This quality was but little insisted upon, till it became necessary to make some reply to the reproaches of those, who, having themselves no taste for such sublime discoveries, endeavoured to depreciate them as useless.

That self-command, in the same manner, by which we restrain our present appetites, in order to gratify them more fully upon another occasion, is approved of, as much under the aspect of propriety, as under that of utility. When we act in this manner, the sentiments which influence our conduct seem exactly to coincide with those of the spectator. The spectator does not feel the felicitations of our present appetites. To him the pleasure which we are to enjoy a week hence, or a year hence, is just as interesting as that which we are to enjoy this moment. When for the sake of the present, therefore, we sacrifice the future, our conduct appears to him absurd and extravagant in the highest degree, and he cannot enter into the principles which influence it. On the contrary, when we abstain from present pleasure, in order to secure greater pleasure to come, when we act as if the remote object interests us as much as that which immediately presses upon the senses, as 255 our affections exactly correspond with his own, he cannot fail to approve of our behaviour: and as he knows from experience, how few are capable of this self command, he looks upon our conduct with a considerable degree of wonder and admiration. Hence arises that eminent esteem with which all men naturally regard a steady perseverance in the practice of frugality, industry, and application, though directed to no other purpose than the acquisition of fortune. The resolute firmness of the person who acts in this manner, and in order to obtain a great though remote advantage, not only gives up all present pleasures, but endures the greatest labour both of mind and body, necessarily commands our approbation. That view of his interest and happiness which appears to regulate his conduct, exactly tallies with the idea which we naturally form of it. There is the most perfect correspondence between his sentiments and our own, and at the same time, from our experience of the common weakness of human nature, it is a correspondence which we could not reasonably have expected. We not only approve, therefore, but in some measure admire his conduct, and think it worthy of a considerable degree of applause. It is the consciousness of this merited approbation and esteem which is alone capable of supporting the agent in this tenour of conduct. The pleasure which we are to enjoy ten years hence interests us so little in comparison with that which we may enjoy to-day, the passion which the first excites, is naturally so weak in comparison with that violent emotion which the second is apt to give occasion to, that one could never be any balance to the other, unless it was supported by the sense of propriety, by the consciousness that we merited the esteem and 256 approbation of every body, by acting in the one way, and that we became the proper objects of their contempt and derision by behaving in the other.

Humanity, justice, generosity, and public spirit, are the qualities most useful to others. Wherein consists the propriety of humanity and justice has been explained upon a former occasion, where it was shewn how much our esteem and approbation of those qualities depended upon the concord between the affections of the agent and those of the spectators.

The propriety of generosity and public spirit is founded upon the same principle with that of justice. Generosity is different from humanity. Those two qualities, which at first sight seem so nearly allied, do not always belong to the same person. Humanity is the virtue of a woman, generosity of a man. The fair sex, who have commonly much more tenderness than ours, have seldom so much generosity. That women rarely make considerable donations is an observation of the civil law. Humanity consists merely in the exquisite fellow-feeling which the spectator entertains with the sentiments of the persons principally concerned, so as to grieve for their sufferings, to resent their injuries, and to rejoice at their good fortune. The most humane actions require no self-denial, no self-command, no great exertion of the sense of propriety. They consist only in doing what this exquisite sympathy would of its own accord prompt us to do. But it is otherwise 257 with generosity. We never are generous except when in some respect we prefer some other person to ourselves, and sacrifice some great and important interest of our own to an equal interest of a friend or of a superior. The man who gives up his pretensions to an office that was the great object of his ambition, because he imagines that the services of another are better entitled to it, the man who exposes his life to defend that of his friend, which he judges to be of more importance, neither of them act from humanity, or because they feel more exquisitely what concerns that other person than what concerns themselves. They both consider those opposite interests not in the light in which they naturally appear to themselves, but in that in which they appear to others. To every by-stander, the success or preservation of this other person may justly be more interesting than their own; but it cannot be so to themselves. When to the interest of this other person, therefore, they sacrifice their own, they accommodate themselves to the sentiments of the spectator, and by an effort of magnanimity act according to those views of things which they feel, must naturally occur to any third person. The soldier who throws away his life in order to defend that of his officer, would perhaps be but little affected by the death of that officer, if it should happen without any fault of his own; and a very small disaster which had befallen himself might excite a much more lively sorrow. But when he endeavours to act so as to deserve applause, and to make the impartial spectator enter into the principles of his conduct, he feels, that to every body but himself, his own life is a trifle compared with that of his officer, and that when he sacrifices the one to the other, he acts quite properly and agreeably to what 258 would be the natural apprehensions of every impartial by-stander.

7. Raro mulieres donare solent.

It is the same case with the greater exertions of public spirit. When a young officer exposes his life to acquire some inconsiderable addition to the dominions of his sovereign, it is not, because the acquisition of the new territory is, to himself, an object more desireable than the preservation of his own life. To him his own life is of infinitely more value than the conquest of a whole kingdom for the state which he serves. But when he compares those two objects with one another, he does not view them in the light in which they naturally appear to himself, but in that in which they appear to the nation he fights for. To them the success of the war is of the highest importance; the life of a private person of scarce any consequence. When he puts himself in their situation, he immediately feels that he cannot be too prodigal of his blood, if by shedding it, he can promote so valuable a purpose. In thus thwarting, from a sense of duty and propriety, the strongest of all natural propensities, consists the heroism of his conduct. There is many an honest Englishman, who, in his private station, would be more seriously disturbed by the loss of a guinea, than by the national loss of Minorca, who yet, had it been in his power to defend that fortress, would have sacrificed his life a thousand times rather than, through his fault, have let it fall into the hands of the enemy. When the first Brutus led forth his own sons to a capital punishment, because they had conspired against the rising liberty of Rome, he sacrificed what, if he had consulted his own breast only, would appear to be the stronger to the weaker 259 affection. Brutus ought naturally to have felt much more for the death of his own sons, than for all that probably Rome could have suffered from the want of so great an example. But he viewed them, not with the eyes of a father, but with those of a Roman citizen. He entered so thoroughly into the sentiments of this last character, that he paid no regard to that tye, by which he himself was connected with them; and to a Roman citizen, the sons even of Brutus seemed contemptible, when put into the balance with the smallest interest of Rome. In these and in all other cases of this kind, our admiration is not so much founded upon the utility, as upon the unexpected and on that account the great, the noble, and exalted propriety of such actions. This utility when we come to view it, bestows upon them, undoubtedly, a new beauty, and upon that account still further recommends them, to our approbation. This beauty, however, is chiefly perceived by men of reflection and speculation, and is by no means the quality which first recommends such actions to the natural sentiments of the bulk of mankind.

It is to be observed, that so far as the sentiment of approbation arises from the perception of this beauty of utility, it has no reference of any kind to the sentiments of others. If it was possible, therefore, that a person should grow up to manhood without any communication with society, his own actions might, notwithstanding, be agreeable or disagreeable to him on account of their tendency to his happiness or disadvantage. He might perceive a beauty of this kind in prudence, temperance, and good conduct, and a deformity in the opposite behaviour: He might view his own temper and character with that sort of satisfaction with which we consider a well contrived machine, in the one case; or with that sort of distaste and dissatisfaction with which we regard a very awkward and clumsy contrivance, in the other. As these perceptions, however, are merely a matter of taste, and have all the feebleness and delicacy of that species of perceptions, upon the justness of which what is properly called taste is founded, they probably would not be much attended to by one in his solitary and miserable condition. Even though they should occur to him, they would by no means have the same effect upon him, antecedent to his connexion with society, which they would have in consequence of that connexion. He would not be cast down with inward shame at the thought of this deformity; nor would he be elevated with secret triumph of mind from the consciousness of the contrary beauty. He would not exult from the notion of deserving reward in the one case, nor tremble from the suspicion of meriting punishment in the other. All such sentiments suppose the idea of some other being, who is the natural judge of the person that feels them; and it is only by sympathy with the decisions of this arbiter of his conduct, that he can conceive, either the triumph of self-applause, or the shame of self-condemnation.

PART V.
Of the INFLUENCE of CUSTOM and FASHION upon the sentiments of moral approbation and disapprobation.

CONSISTING OF ONE SECTION.

CHAP. I.
Of the influence of custom and fashion upon our notions of beauty and deformity.

There are other principles besides those already enumerated, which have a considerable influence upon the moral sentiments of mankind, and are the chief causes of the many irregular and discordant opinions which prevail in different ages and nations concerning what is blameable or praise-worthy. These principles are custom and faction, principles which extend their dominion over our judgments concerning beauty of every kind.

When two objects have frequently been seen together, the imagination acquires a habit of passing easily from the one to the other. If the first appear, we lay our account that the second is to follow. Of 262 their own accord they put us in mind of one another, and the attention glides easily along them. Though, independent of custom, there should be no real beauty in their union, yet when custom has thus connected them together, we feel an impropriety in their reparation. The one we think is awkward when it appears without its usual companion. We miss something which we expected to find, and the habitual arrangement of our ideas is disturbed by the disappointment. A suit of clothes, for example, seems to want something if they are without the most insignificant ornament which usually accompanies them, and we find a meanness or awkwardness in the absence even of a haunch button. When there is any natural propriety in the union, custom increases our sense of it, and makes a different arrangement appear still more disagreeable than it would otherwise seem to be. Those who have been accustomed to see things in a good taste, are more disgusted by whatever is clumsy or awkward. Where the conjunction is improper, custom either diminishes, or takes away altogether, our sense of the impropriety. Those who have been accustomed to slovenly disorder lose all sense of neatness or elegance. The modes of furniture or dress which seem ridiculous to strangers, give no offence to the people who are used to them.

Fashion is different from custom, or rather is a particular species of it. That is not the fashion which every body wears, but which those wear who are of a high rank, or character. The graceful, the easy, and commanding manners of the great, joined to the usual richness and magnificence of their dress, give a grace to the very form which they happen to bestow 263 upon it. As long as they continue to use this form, it is connected in our imaginations with the idea of something that is genteel and magnificent, and though in itself it should be indifferent, it seems, on account of this relation, to have something about it that is genteel and magnificent too. As soon as they drop it, it loses all the grace, which it had appeared to possess before, and being now used only by the inferior ranks of people, seems to have something of their meanness and awkwardness.

Dress and furniture are allowed by all the world to be entirely under the dominion of custom and fashion. The influence of those principles, however, is by no means confined to so narrow a sphere, but extends itself to whatever is in any respect the object of taste, to music, to poetry, to architecture. The modes of dress and furniture are continually changing, and that fashion appearing ridiculous to-day which was admired five years ago, we are experimentally convinced that it owed its vogue chiefly or entirely to custom and fashion. Clothes and furniture are not made of very durable materials. A well fancied coat is done in a twelve-month, and cannot continue longer to propagate, as the fashion, that form according to which it was made. The modes of furniture change less rapidly than those of dress; because furniture is commonly more durable. In five or six years, however, it generally undergoes an entire revolution, and every man in his own time sees the fashion in this respect change many different ways. The productions of the other arts are much more lasting, and, when happily imagined, may continue to propagate the fashion of their make for a much longer time. A well contrived building may endure many 264 centuries: a beautiful air may be delivered down by a sort of tradition, through many successive generations: a well written poem may last as long as the world; and al of them continue for ages together, to give the vogue to that particular style, to that particular taste or manner, according to which each of them was composed. Few men have an opportunity of seeing in their own times the fashion in any of these arts change very considerably. Few men have so much experience and acquaintance with the different modes which have obtained in remote ages and nations, as to be thoroughly reconciled to them, or to judge with impartiality between them, and what takes place in their own age and country. Few men therefore are willing to allow that custom or fashion have much influence upon their judgments concerning what is beautiful, or otherwise, in the productions of any of those arts; but imagine, that all the rules, which they think ought to be observed in each of them, are founded upon reason and nature, not upon habit or prejudice. A very little attention, however, may convince them of the contrary, and satisfy them, that the influence of custom and fashion over dress and furniture, is not more absolute than over architecture, poetry, and music.

Can any reason, for example, be assigned why the Doric capital should be appropriated to a pillar, whose height is equal to eight diameters; the Ionic volute to one of nine; and the Corinthian foliage to one of ten? The propriety of each of those appropriations can be founded upon nothing but habit and custom. The eye having been used to see a particular proportion connected with a particular ornament, would be offended if they were not joined together. 205 Each of the five orders has its peculiar ornaments, which cannot be changed for any other, without giving offence to all those who know any thing of the rules of architecture. According to some architects, indeed, such is the exquisite judgment with which the ancients have assigned to each order its proper ornaments, that no others can be found which are equally suitable. It seems, however, a little difficult to be conceived that these forms, though, no doubt, extremely agreeable, should be the only forms which can suit those proportions, or that there should not be five hundred others which, antecedent to established custom, would have fitted them equally well. When custom, however, has established particular rules of building, provided they are not absolutely unreasonable, it is absurd to think of altering them for others which are only equally good, or even for others which, in point of elegance and beauty, have naturally some little advantage over them. A man would be ridiculous who should appear in public with a suit of clothes quite different from those which are commonly worn, though the new dress should in itself be ever so graceful or convenient. And there seems to be an absurdity of the same kind in ornamenting a house after a quite different manner from that which custom and fashion have prescribed; though the new ornaments should in themselves be somewhat superior to the common ones.

According to the ancient rhetoricians, a certain measure or verse was by nature appropriated to each particular species of writing, as being naturally expressive of that character, sentiment, or passion, 206 which ought to predominate in it. One verse, they said, was fit for grave and another for gay works, which could not, they thought, be interchanged without the greatest impropriety. The experience of modern times, however, seems to contradict this principle, though in itself it would appear to be extremely probable. What is the burlesque verse in English is the heroic verse in French. The tragedies of Racine and the Henriad of Voltaire, are in the same verse with,

Thus said to my lady the knight full of care.

The burlesque verse in French, on the contrary, is pretty much the same with the heroic verse of ten syllables in English. Custom has made the one nation associate the ideas of gravity, sublimity, and seriousness, to that measure which the other has connected with whatever is gay, flippant, and ludicrous. Nothing would appear more absurd in English than a tragedy written in the Alexandrine verses of the French, or in French, than a work of the same kind in verses of ten syllables.

An eminent artist will bring about a considerable change in the established modes of each of those arts, and introduce a new fashion of writing, music, or architecture. As the dress of an agreeable man of high rank recommends itself, and how peculiar and fantastical soever, comes soon to be admired and imitated; so the excellencies of an eminent matter recommend his peculiarities, and his manner becomes the fashionable style in the art which he practises. The taste of the Italians in music and architecture, has, within these fifty years, undergone a considerable 267 change, from imitating the peculiarities of some eminent masters in each of those arts. Seneca is accused by Quintilian of having corrupted the taste of the Romans, and of having introduced a frivolous prettiness in the room of majestic reason and masculine eloquence. Sallust and Tacitus have by others been charged with the same accusation, tho' in a different manner. They gave reputation, it is pretended, to a style, which though in the highest degree concise, elegant, expressive, and even poetical, wanted, however, ease, simplicity, and nature, and was evidently the production of the most laboured and studied affectation. How many great qualities must that writer possess who can thus render his very faults agreeable? After the praise of refining the taste of a nation, the highest eulogy, perhaps, which can be bestowed upon any author is to say, that he corrupted it. In our own language, Mr. Pope and Dr. Swift have each of them introduced a manner different from what was practised before, into all works that are written in rhyme, the one in long verses, the other in short. The quaintness of Butler has given place to the plainness of Swift. The rambling freedom of Dryden, and the correct but often tedious and prosaic languor of Addison, are no longer the objects of imitation, but all long verses are now written after the manner of the nervous precision of Mr. Pope.

Neither is it only over the productions of the arts, that custom and fashion exert their dominion. They influence our judgments, in the same manner, with regard to the beauty of natural objects. What various and opposite forms are deemed beautiful in different species of things? The proportions which are 268 admired in one animal, are altogether different from those which are esteemed in another. Every class of things has its own peculiar conformation, which is approved of, and has a beauty of its own, distinct from that of every other species. It is upon this account that a learned Jesuit, father Buffier, has determined that the beauty of every object consists in that form and colour, which is most usual among things of that particular sort to which it belongs. Thus, in the human form, the beauty of each feature lies in a certain middle equally removed from a variety of other forms that are ugly. A beautiful nose, for example, is one that is neither very long, nor very short, neither very straight, nor very crooked, but a sort of middle among all these extremes, and less different from any one of them, than all of them are from one another. It is the form which Nature seems to have aimed at in them all, which, however, she deviates from in a great variety of ways, and very seldom hits exactly; but to which all those deviations still bear a very strong resemblance. When a number of drawings are made after one pattern, though they may all miss it in some respects, yet they will all resemble it more than they resemble one another; the general character of the pattern will run through them all; the most singular and odd will be those which are most wide of it and though very few will copy it exactly, yet the most accurate delineations will bear a greater resemblance to the most careless, than the careless ones will bear to one another. In the same manner, in each species of creatures, what is most beautiful bears the strongest characters of the general fabric of the species, and has the strongest resemblance to the greater part of the individuals with which it is 269 classed. Monsters, on the contrary, or what is perfectly deformed, are always most singular and odd, and have the least resemblance to the generality of that species to which they belong. And thus the beauty of each species, though in one sense the rarest of all things, because few individuals hit this middle form exactly, yet in another, is the most common, because all the deviations from it resemble it more than they resemble one another. The most customary form, therefore, is in each species of things, according to him, the most beautiful. And hence it is that a certain practice and experience in contemplating each species of objects is requisite, before we can judge of its beauty, or know wherein the middle and most usual form consists. The nicest judgment concerning the beauty of the human species, will not help us to judge of that of flowers, or horses, or any other species of things. It is for the same reason that in different climates and where different customs and ways of living take place, as the generality of any species receives a different conformation from those circumstances, so different ideas of its beauty prevail. The beauty of a Moorish is not exactly the same with that of an English horse. What different ideas are formed in different nations concerning the beauty of the human shape and countenance? A fair complexion is a shocking deformity upon the coast of Guinea. Thick lips and a flat nose are a beauty. In some nations long ears that hang down upon the shoulders are the objects of universal admiration. In China if a lady's foot is so large as to be fit to walk upon, she is regarded as a monster of ugliness. Some of the savage nations in North America tie four boards round the heads of their children, and thus squeeze them, while the 270 bones are tender and gristly, into a form that is almost perfectly square. Europeans are astonished at the absurd barbarity of this practice, to which some missionaries have imputed the singular stupidity of those nations among whom it prevails. But, when they condemn those savages, they do not reflect that the ladies in Europe had, till within these very few years, been endeavouring, for near a century past, to squeeze the beautiful roundness of their natural shape into a square form of the same kind. And that notwithstanding the many distortions and diseases which this practice was known to occasion, custom had rendered it agreeable among some of the most civilized nations, which, perhaps, the world ever beheld.

Such is the system of this learned and ingenious father, concerning the nature of beauty; of which the whole charm, according to him, would thus seem to arise from its falling in with the habits which custom had impressed upon the imagination, with regard to things of each particular kind. I cannot, however, be induced to believe that our sense even of external beauty is founded altogether on custom. The utility of any form, its fitness for the useful purposes for which it was intended, evidently recommends it, and renders it agreeable to us independent of custom. Certain colours are more agreeable than others, and give more delight to the eye the first time it ever beholds them. A smooth surface is more agreeable than a rough one. Variety is more pleasing than a tedious undiversified uniformity. Connected variety, in which each new appearance seems to be introduced by what went before it, and in which all the adjoining parts seem to have some natural 271 relation to one another, is more agreeable than a disjointed and disorderly assemblage of unconnected objects. But though I cannot admit that custom is the sole principle of beauty, yet I can so far allow the truth of this ingenious system as to grant, that there is scarce any one external form so beautiful as to please, if quite contrary to custom and unlike whatever we have been used to in that particular species of things: or so deformed as not to be agreeable, if custom uniformly supports it, and habituates us to see it in every single individual of the kind.

CHAP. II.
Of the influence of custom and fashion upon moral sentiments.

Since our sentiments concerning beauty of every kind are so much influenced by custom and fashion, it cannot be expected, that those, concerning the beauty, of conduct, should be entirely exempted from the dominion of those principles. Their influence here, however, seems to be much less than it is every where else. There is, perhaps, no form of external objects, how absurd and fantastical soever, to which custom will not reconcile us, or which fashion will not render even agreeable. But the characters and conduct of a Nero, or a Claudius, are what no custom will ever reconcile us to, what no fashion will ever render agreeable; but the one will always be the object of dread and hatred; the other of scorn and derision. The principles of the imagination, upon which our sense of beauty depends, 272 are of a very nice and delicate nature, and may easily be altered by habit and education: but the sentiments of moral approbation and disapprobation, are founded on the strongest and most vigorous passions of human nature; and though they may be somewhat warpt, cannot be entirely perverted.

But though the influence of custom and fashion, upon moral sentiments, is not altogether so great, it is however perfectly similar to what it is every where else. When custom and fashion coincide with the natural principles of right and wrong, they heighten the delicacy of our sentiments, and increase our abhorrence for every thing which approaches to evil. Those who have been educated in what is really good company, not in what is commonly called such, who have been accustomed to see nothing in the persons whom they esteemed and lived with, but justice, modesty, humanity, and good order, are more shocked with whatever seems to be inconsistent with the rules which those virtues prescribe. Those, on the contrary, who have had the misfortune to be brought up amidst violence, licentiousness, falsehood, and injustice, lose, though not all sense of the impropriety of such conduct, yet all sense of its dreadful enormity, or of the vengeance and punishment due to it. They have been familiarized with it from their infancy, custom has rendered it habitual to them, and they are very apt to regard it as, what is called the way of the world, something which either may, or must be practised, to hinder us from being the dupes of our own integrity.

273 Fashion too will sometimes give reputation to a certain degree of disorder, and on the contrary discountenance qualities which deserve esteem. In the reign of Charles II. a degree of licentiousness was deemed the characteristic of a liberal education. It was connected, according to the notions of those times, with generosity, sincerity

magnanimity, loyalty, and proved that the person who acted in this manner, was a gentleman, and not a puritan; severity of manners, and regularity of conduct, on the other hand, were altogether unfashionable, and were connected, in the imagination of that age, with cant, cunning, hypocrisy, and low manners. To superficial minds, the vices of the great seem at all times agreeable. They connect them, not only with the splendour of fortune, but with many superiour virtues, which they ascribe to their superiors; with the spirit of freedom and independency, with frankness, generosity, humanity, and politeness. The virtues of the inferior ranks of people, on the contrary, their parsimonious frugality, their painful industry, and rigid adherence to rules, seem to them mean and disagreeable. They connect them, both with the meanness of the station to which those qualities commonly belong, and with many great vices, which, they suppose, usually accompany them; such as an abject, cowardly, ill-natured, lying, pilfering disposition.

The objects with which men in the different professions and states of life are conversant, being very different, and habituating them to very different passions, naturally form in them very different characters and manners. We expect in each rank and procession, 274 a degree of those manners, which, experience has taught us, belong to it. But as in each species of things, we are particularly pleased with the middle conformation, which in every part and feature agrees most exactly with the general standard which nature seems to have established for things of that kind; so in each rank, or, if I may say so, in each species of men, we are particularly pleased, if they have neither too much, nor too little of the character which usually accompanies their particular condition and situation. A man, we say, should look like his trade and profession; yet the pedantry of every profession is disagreeable. The different periods of life have, for the same reason, different manners assigned to them. We expect in old age, that gravity and sedateness which its infirmities, its long experience, and its worn-out sensibility seem to render both natural and respectable; and we lay our account to find in youth that sensibility, that gaiety and sprightly vivacity which experience teaches us to expect from the lively impressions that all interesting objects are apt to make upon the tender and unpractised senses of that early period of life. Each of those two ages, however, may easily have too much of these peculiarities which belong to it. The flirting levity of youth, and the immoveable insensibility of old age, are equally disagreeable. The young, according to the common saying, are most agreeable when in their behaviour there is something of the manners of the old, and the old, when they retain something of the gaiety of the young. Either of them, however, may easily have too much of the manners of the other. The extreme coldness, and dull formality, which are pardoned in old age, make youth ridiculous. The levity, the carelessness, and the vanity, 275 which are indulged in youth, render old age contemptible.

The peculiar character and manners which we are led by custom to appropriate to each rank and profession, have sometimes perhaps a propriety independent of custom; and are what we should approve of for their own sakes, if we took into consideration all the different circumstances which naturally affect those in each different state of life. The propriety of a person's behaviour, depends not upon its suitableness to any one circumstance of his situation, but to all the circumstances, which, when we bring his case home to ourselves we feel, should naturally call upon his attention. If he appears to be so much occupied by any one of them, as entirely to neglect the rest, we disapprove of his conduct, as something which we cannot entirely go along with, because not properly adjusted to all the circumstances of his situation: yet, perhaps, the emotion he expresses for the object which principally interests him, does not exceed what we should entirely sympathize with, and approve of, in one whose attention was not required by any other thing. A parent in private life might, upon the loss of an only son, express without blame, a degree of grief and tenderness, which would be unpardonable in a general at the head of an army, when glory, and the public safety demanded so great a part of his attention. As different objects ought, upon common occasions, to occupy the attention of men of different professions, so different passions ought, naturally to become habitual to them; and when we bring home to ourselves their situation in this particular respect, we must be sensible, that every occurrence should naturally affect them more or less, according 276 as the emotion which it excites, coincides or disagrees with the fixt habit and temper of their minds. We cannot expect the same sensibility to the gay pleasures and amusements of life in a clergyman which we lay our account with in an officer. The man whose peculiar occupation it is to keep the world in mind of that awful futurity which awaits them, who is to announce what may be the fatal consequences of every deviation from the rules of duty, and who is himself to set the example of the most exact conformity, seems to be the messenger of tidings, which cannot, in propriety, be delivered either with levity or indifference. His mind is supposed to be continually occupied with what is too grand and solemn, to leave any room for the impressions of those frivolous objects, which fill up the attention of the dissipated and the gay. We readily feel therefore, that, independent of custom, there is a propriety in the manners which custom has allotted to this profession; and that nothing can be more suitable to the character of a clergyman, than that grave, that austere and abstracted severity, which we are habituated to expect in his behaviour. These reflections are so very obvious, that there is scarce any man so inconsiderate, as not, at some time, to have made them, and to have accounted to himself in this manner for his approbation of the usual character of this order.

The foundation of the customary character of some other professions is not so obvious, and our approbation of it is founded entirely in habit, without being either confirmed, or enlivened by any reflections of this kind. We are led by custom, for example, to annex the character of gaiety, levity, and sprightly 277 freedom, as well as of some degree of dissipation, to the military profession: yet, if we were to consider what mood or tone of temper would be most suitable to this situation, we should be apt to determine, perhaps, that the most serious and thoughtful turn of mind, would best become those whose lives are continually exposed to uncommon danger; and who should therefore be more constantly occupied with the thoughts of death and its consequences than other men. It is this very circumstance, however, which is not improbably the occasion why the contrary turn of mind prevails so much among men of this profession. It requires so great an effort to conquer the fear of death, when we survey it with steadiness and attention, that those who are constantly exposed to it, find it easier to turn away their thoughts from it altogether, to wrap themselves up in careless security and indifference, and to plunge themselves, for this purpose, into every sort of amusement and dissipation. A camp is not the element of a thoughtful or a melancholy man: persons of that cast, indeed, are often abundantly determined, and are capable, by a great effort, of going on with inflexible resolution to the most unavoidable death. But to be exposed to continual, though less imminent danger, to be obliged to exert, for a long time, a degree of this effort, exhaust. and depresses the mind, and renders it incapable of all happiness and enjoyment. The ga' and careless, who have occasion to make no effort at all, who fairly resolve never to loo] before them, but to lose in continual pleasures and amusements, all anxiety about their situation, more easily support such circumstances. Whenever, by any peculiar circumstances, an officer has no reason to lay his account with being exposed to any uncommon 278 danger, he is very apt to lose the gaiety and dissipated thoughtlessness of his character. The captain of a city guard is commonly as sober, careful, and penurious an animal as the rest of his fellow-citizens. A long peace is, for the same reason, very apt to diminish the difference between the civil and the military character. The ordinary situation, however, of men of this profession, renders gaiety, and a degree of dissipation, so much their usual character; and custom has, in our imagination, so strongly connected this character with this state of life, that we are very apt to despise any man, whose peculiar humour or situation, renders him incapable of acquiring it. We laugh at the grave and careful faces of a city guard, which, so little resemble those of their profession. They themselves seem often to be ashamed of the regularity of their own manners, and, not to be out of the fashion of their trade, are fond of affecting that levity, which is by no means natural to them. Whatever is the deportment which we have been accustomed to see in a respectable order of men, it comes to be so associated in our imagination with that order, that whenever we see the one, we lay our account that we are to meet with the other, and when disappointed, miss something which we expected to find. We are embarrassed, and put to a stand, and know not how to address ourselves to a character, which plainly affects to be of a different species from those with which we should have been disposed to class it.

The different situations of different ages and countries, are apt, in the same manner, to give different characters to the generality of those who live in them, and their sentiments concerning the particular 279 degree of each quality, that is either blameable, or praise-worthy, vary according to that degree, which is usual in their own country, and in their own times. That degree of politeness, which would be highly esteemed, perhaps, would be thought effeminate adulation, in Russia, would be regarded as rudeness and barbarism at the court of France. That degree of order and frugality, which, in a Polish nobleman, would be considered as excessive parsimony, would be regarded as extravagance in a citizen of Amsterdam. Every age and country look upon that degree of each quality, which is commonly to be met with in those who are esteemed among themselves, as the golden mean of that particular talent or virtue. And as this varies, according as their different circumstances render different qualities more or less habitual to them, their sentiments concerning the exact propriety of character and behaviour vary accordingly.

Among civilized nations, the virtues which are founded upon humanity, are more cultivated than those which are founded upon self-denial and the command of the passions. Among rude and barbarous nations, it is quite otherwise, the virtues of self-denial are more cultivated than those of humanity. The general security and happiness which prevail in ages of civility and politeness afford little exercise to the contempt of danger, to patience in enduring labour, hunger, and pain. Poverty may easily be avoided, and the contempt of it therefore, almost ceases to be a virtue. The abstinence from pleasure, becomes less necessary, and the mind is more at liberty to unbend itself, and to indulge 280 its natural inclinations in all those particular respects.

Among savages and barbarians it is quite otherwise. Every savage undergoes a sort of Spartan discipline, and by the necessity of his situation is inured to every sort of hardship. He is in continual danger: He is often exposed to the greatest extremities of hunger, and frequently dies of pure want. His circumstances not only habituate him to every sort of distress, but teach him to give way to none of the passions which that distress is apt to excite. He can expect from his countrymen no sympathy or indulgence for such weakness. Before we can feel much for others, we must in some measure be at ease ourselves. If our own misery pinches us very severely, we have no leisure to attend to that of our neighbour: And all savages are too much occupied with their own wants and necessities, to give much attention to those of another person. A savage, therefore, whatever be the nature of his distress, expects no sympathy from those about him, and disdains, upon that account, to expose himself, by allowing the least weakness to escape him. His passions, how furious and violent soever, are never permitted to disturb the serenity of his countenance or the composure of his conduct and behaviour. The savages in North America, we are told, assume upon all occasions the greatest indifference, and would think themselves degraded if they should ever appear in any respect to be overcome, either by love, or grief, or resentment. Their magnanimity and self-command, in this respect, are almost beyond the conception of Europeans. In a country in which all men are upon a level, with regard to rank and 281 fortune, it might be expected that the mutual inclinations of the two parties should be the only thing considered in marriages, and should be indulged without any sort of controul. This, however, is the country in which all marriages, without exception, are made up by the parents, and in which a young man would think himself disgraced for ever, if he shewed the least preference of one woman above another, or did not express the most complete indifference, both about the time when, and the person to whom he was to be married. The weakness of love, which is so much indulged in ages of humanity and politeness, is regarded among savages as the most unpardonable effeminacy. Even after the marriage the two parties seem to be ashamed of a connexion which is founded upon so sordid a necessity. They do not live together. They see one another by stealth only. They both continue to dwell in the houses of their respective fathers, and the open cohabitation of the two sexes, which is permitted without blame in all other countries, is here considered as the most indecent and unmanly sensuality. Nor is it only over this agreeable passion that they exert this absolute self-command. They often bear in the sight of all their countrymen with injuries, reproach, and the grossest insults with the appearance of the greatest insensibility, and without expressing the smallest resentment. When a savage is made prisoner of war, and receives, as is usual, the sentence of death from his conquerors, he hears it without expressing any emotion, and afterwards submits to the most dreadful torments, without ever bemoaning himself, or discovering any other passion but contempt of his enemies. While he is hung by the shoulders over a slow fire, he derides his tormentors, and tells them 282 with how much more ingenuity he himself had tormented such of their countrymen as had fallen into his hands. After he has been scorched and burnt, and lacerated in all the most tender and sensible parts of his body for several hours together, he is often allowed, in order to prolong his misery, a short respite, and is taken down from the stake: he employs this interval in talking upon all indifferent subjects, inquires after the news of the country, and seems indifferent about nothing but his own situation. The spectators express the same insensibility; the sight of so horrible an object seems to make no impression upon them, they scarce look at the prisoner, except when they lend a hand to torment him. At other times they smoke tobacco, and amuse themselves with any common object, as if no such matter was going on. Every savage is said to prepare himself from his earliest youth for this dreadful end. He composes, for this purpose, what they call the song of death, a song which he is to sing when he has fallen into the hands of his enemies, and is expiring under the tortures which they inflict upon him. It consists of insults upon his tormentors, and expresses the highest contempt of death and pain. He sings this song upon all extraordinary occasions, when he goes out to war, when he meets his enemies in the field, or whenever he has a mind to show that he has familiarised his imagination to the most dreadful misfortunes, and that no human event can daunt his resolution, or alter his purpose. The same contempt of death and torture prevails among all other savage nations. There is not a negro from the coast of Africa who does not, in this respect, possess a degree of magnanimity which the soul of his sordid master is 283 too often scarce capable of conceiving. Fortune never exerted more cruelly her empire over mankind, than when she subjected those nations of heroes to the refuse of the jails of Europe, to wretches who possess the virtues neither of the countries which they come from, nor of those which they go to, and whose levity, brutality, and baseness, so justly expose them to the contempt of the vanquished.

This heroic and unconquerable firmness, which the custom and education of his country demand of every savage, is not required of those who are brought up to live in civilized societies. If these last complain when they are in pain, if they grieve when they are in distress, if they allow themselves either to be overcome by love, or to be discomposed by anger, they are easily pardoned. Such weaknesses are not apprehended to affect the essential parts of their character. As long as they do not allow themselves to be transported to do any thing contrary to justice or humanity, they lose but little reputation, though the serenity of their countenance or the composure of their discourse and behaviour should be somewhat ruffled and disturbed. A humane and polished people, who have more sensibility to the passions of others, can more readily enter into an animated and passionate behaviour, and can more easily pardon some little excess. The person principally concerned is sensible of this; and being assured of the equity of his judges, indulges himself in stronger expressions of passion, and is less afraid of exposing himself to their contempt by the violence of his emotions. We can venture to express more emotion in the presence of a friend than in that of a stranger, because we expect more indulgence from the one than from the 284 other. And in the same manner the rules of decorum among civilized nations, admit of a more animated behaviour, than is approved of among barbarians. The first converse together with the openness of friends; the second with the reserve of strangers. The emotion and vivacity with which the French and the Italians, the two most polished nations upon the continent, express themselves on occasions that are at all interesting, surprise at first those strangers who happen to be travelling among them, and who, having been educated among a people of duller sensibility, cannot enter into this passionate behaviour, of which they have never seen any example in their own country. A young French nobleman will weep in the presence of the whole court upon being refused a regiment. An Italian, says the abbot Dû Bos, expresses more emotion on being condemned in a fine of twenty shillings, than an Englishman on receiving the sentence of death. Cicero, in the times of the highest Roman politeness, could, without degrading himself, weep with all the bitterness of sorrow in the sight of the whole senate and the whole people; as it is evident he must have done in the end of almost every oration. The orators of the earlier and ruder ages of Rome could not probably, consistent with the manners of the times, have expressed themselves with so much motion. It would have been regarded, I suppose, as a violation of nature and propriety in the Scipios, in the Leliuses, and in the elder Cato, to have exposed so much tenderness to the view of the public. Those ancient warriors could express themselves, with order, gravity, and good judgment; but are said to have been strangers to that sublime and passionate eloquence which was first introduced into Rome, not many years before the 285 birth of Cicero, by the two Gracchi, by Crassus, and by Sulpitius. This animated eloquence, which has been long practiced, with or without success, both in France and Italy, is but just beginning to be introduced into England. So wide is the difference between the degrees of self-command which are required in civilized and in barbarous nations, and by such different standards do they judge of the propriety of behaviour.

This difference gives occasion to many others that are not less essential. A polished people being accustomed to give way, in some measure, to the movements of nature, become frank, open, and sincere. Barbarians, on the contrary, being obliged to smother and conceal the appearance of every passion, necessarily acquire the habits of falsehood and dissimulation. It is observed by all those who have been conversant with savage nations, whether in Asia, Africa, or America, that they are all equally impenetrable, and that, when they have a mind to conceal the truth, no examination is capable of drawing it from them. They cannot be trepanned by the most artful questions. The torture itself is incapable of making them confess any thing which they have no mind to tell. The passions of a savage too, though they never express themselves by any outward emotion, but lie concealed in the breast of the sufferer, are, notwithstanding, all mounted to the highest pitch of fury. Though he seldom shows any symptoms of anger, yet his vengeance, when he comes to give way to it, is always sanguinary and dreadful. The least affront drives him to despair. His countenance and discourse indeed are still sober and composed, and express nothing but the most perfect 286 tranquillity of mind: But his actions are often the most furious and violent. Among the North-Americans it is not uncommon for persons of the tenderest age and more fearful sex to drown themselves upon receiving only a slight reprimand from their mothers, and this too without expressing any passions or saying any thing, except, *you shall no longer have a daughter*. In civilized nations the passions of men are not commonly so furious or so desperate. They are often clamorous and noisy, but are seldom very hurtful; and seem frequently to aim at no other satisfaction, but that of convincing the spectator, that they are in the right to be so much moved, and of procuring his sympathy and approbation.

All these effects of custom and fashion, however, upon the moral sentiments of mankind, are inconsiderable in comparison of those which they give occasion to in some other cases; and it is not concerning the general style of character and behaviour, that those principles produce the greatest perversion of judgment, but concerning the propriety or impropriety of particular usages.

The different manners which custom teaches us to approve of in the different professions and states of life, do not concern things of the greatest importance. We expect truth and justice from an old man as well as from a young, from a clergyman as well as from an officer; and it is in matters of small moment only that we look for the distinguishing marks of their respective characters. With regard to these too, there is often some unobserved circumstance which, if it was attended to, would show us, that, independent 287 of custom there was a propriety in the character which custom had taught us to allot to each profession. We cannot complain, therefore, in this case, that the perversion of natural sentiment is very great. Though the manners of different nations require different degrees of the same quality, in the character which they think worthy of esteem, yet the worst that can be said to happen even here, is that the duties of one virtue are sometimes extended so as to encroach a little upon the precincts of some other. The rustic hospitality that is in fashion among the Poles encroaches, perhaps, a little upon œconomy and good order; and the frugality that is esteemed in Holland, upon generosity and good-fellowship. The hardiness demanded of savages diminishes their humanity; and, perhaps, the delicate sensibility required in civilized nations sometimes destroys the masculine firmness of the character. In general, the style of manners which takes place in any nation, may commonly upon the whole be said to be that which is most suitable to its situation. Hardiness is the character most suitable to the circumstances of a savage; sensibility to those of one who lives in a very civilized society. Even here, therefore, we cannot complain that the moral sentiments of men are very grossly perverted.

It is not therefore in the general style of conduct or behaviour that custom authorizes the widest departure from what is the natural propriety of action. With regard to particular usages its influence is often much more destructive of good morals, and it is capable of establishing, as lawful and blameless, particular actions, which shock the plainest principles of right and wrong.

288 Can there be greater barbarity, for example, than to hurt an infant? Its helplessness, its innocence, its amiableness, call forth the compassion even of an enemy, and not to spare that tender age is regarded as the most furious effort of an enraged and cruel conqueror. What then should we imagine must be the heart of a parent who could injure that weakness which even a furious enemy is afraid to violate? Yet the exposition, that is, the murder of newborn infants, was a practice allowed of in almost all the states of Greece, even among the polite and civilized Athenians; and whenever the circumstances of the parent rendered it inconvenient to bring up the child, to abandon it to hunger, or to wild beasts, was regarded without blame or censure. This practice had probably begun in times of the most savage barbarity. The imaginations of men had been first made familiar with it in that earliest period of society, and the uniform continuance of the custom had hindered them afterwards from perceiving its enormity. We find, at this day, that this practice prevails among all savage nations; and in that rudest and lowest state of society it is undoubtedly more pardonable than in any other. The extreme indigence of a savage is often such that he himself is frequently exposed to the greatest extremity of hunger, he often dies of pure want, and it is frequently impossible for him to support both himself and his child. We cannot wonder, therefore, that in this case he should abandon it. One who in flying from an enemy, whom it was impossible to resist, should throw down his infant, because it retarded his flight, would surely be excusable; since, by attempting to save it, he could only hope for the consolation of 289 dying with it. That in this state of society, therefore, a parent should be allowed to judge whether he can bring up his child, ought not to surprise us so greatly. In the latter ages of Greece, however, the same thing was permitted from views of remote interest or conveniency, which could by no means excuse it. Uninterrupted custom had by this time so thoroughly authorized the practice, that not only the loose maxims of the world tolerated this barbarous prerogative, but even the doctrine of philosophers, which ought to have been more just and accurate, was led away by the established custom, and upon this, as upon many other occasions, instead of censuring, supported the horrible abuse, by far-fetched considerations of public utility. Aristotle talks of it as of what the magistrate ought upon many occasions to encourage. The humane Plato is of the same opinion, and, with all that love of mankind which seems

to animate all his writings, no where marks this practice with disapprobation. When custom can give sanction to so dreadful a violation of humanity, we may well imagine that there is scarce any particular practice so gross which it cannot authorize. Such a thing, we hear men every day saying, is commonly done, and they seem to think this a sufficient apology for what, in itself, is the most unjust and unreasonable conduct.

There is an obvious reason why custom should never pervert our sentiments with regard to the general style and character of conduct and behaviour, in the same degree as with regard to the propriety or unlawfulness of particular usages. There 290 never can be any such custom. No society could subsist a moment, in which the usual strain of mens conduct and behaviour was of a piece with the horrible practice I just now mentioned.

PART VI.
Of Systems of MORAL PHILOSOPHY.

CONSISTING OF FOUR SECTIONS.

SECTION I.
Of the questions which ought to be examined in a theory of moral sentiments.

If we examine the most celebrated and remarkable of the different theories which have been given concerning the nature and origin of our moral sentiments, we shall find that almost all of them coincide with some part or other of that which I have been endeavouring to give an account of; and that if every thing which has already been said be fully considered, we shall be at no loss to explain what was the view or aspect of nature which led each particular author to form his particular system. From some one or other of those principles which I have been endeavouring to unfold, every system of morality that ever had any reputation in the world has, perhaps, ultimately been derived. As they are all of them, in this respect, founded upon natural principles, they are all of them in some measure in the right. But as many of them are derived from a partial 292 and imperfect view of nature, there are many of them too in some respects in the wrong.

In treating of the principles of morals there are two questions to be considered. First, wherein does virtue consist? Or what is the tone of temper, and tenour of conduct, which constitutes the excellent and praise-worthy character, the character which is the natural object of esteem, honour, and approbation? and secondly, by what power or faculty in the mind is it, that this character, whatever it be, is recommended to us? Or in other words, how and by what means does it come to pass, that the mind prefers one tenour of conduct to another, denominates the one right and the other wrong; considers the one as the object of approbation, honour, and reward, and the other of blame, censure, and punishment?

We examine the first question when we consider whether virtue consists in benevolence, as Dr. Hutcheson imagines; or in acting suitably to the different relations we stand in, as Dr. Clarke supposes; or in the wise and prudent pursuit of our own real and solid happiness, as has been the opinion of others.

We examine the second question, when we consider, whether the virtuous character, whatever it consists in, be recommended to us by self-love, which makes us perceive that this character, both in ourselves and others, tends most to promote our own private interest or by reason, which points out to us the difference between one character and another, in the same manner as it does that between truth and falsehood; or by a peculiar power of perception, 293 called a moral sense, which this virtuous character gratifies and pleases, as the contrary disgusts and displeases it; or last of all, by some other principle in human nature, such as a modification of sympathy, or the like.

I shall begin with considering the systems which have been formed concerning the first of these questions, and shall proceed afterwards to examine those concerning the second.

SECTION II.
Of the different accounts which have been given of the nature of virtue.

INTRODUCTION.

The different accounts which have been given of the nature of virtue, or of the temper of mind which constitutes the excellent and praise-worthy character, may be reduced to three different classes. According to some, the virtuous temper of mind does not consist in any one species of affections, but in the proper government and direction of all our affections, which may be either virtuous or vicious according to the objects which they pursue, and the degree of vehemence with which they pursue them. According to these authors, therefore, virtue consists in propriety.

According to others, virtue consists in the judicious pursuit of our own private interest and happiness, or in the proper government and direction of those selfish affections which aim solely at this end. In the opinion of these authors, therefore, virtue consists in prudence.

Another set of authors make virtue consist in those affections only which aim at the happiness of others, not in those which aim at our own. According to them, therefore disinterested benevolence 295 is the only motive which can stamp upon any action the character of virtue.

The character of virtue, it is evident, must either be ascribed indifferently to all our affections, when under proper government and direction; or it must be confined to some one class or division of them. The great division of our affections is into the selfish and the benevolent. If the character of virtue, therefore, cannot be ascribed indifferently to all our affections, when under proper government and direction, it must be confined either to those which aim directly at our own private happiness, or to those which aim directly at that of others. If virtue, therefore, does not consist in propriety, it must consist either in prudence or in benevolence. Besides these three, it is scarce possible to imagine that any other account can be given of the nature of virtue. I shall endeavour to shew hereafter how all the other accounts, which are seemingly different from any of these, coincide at bottom with some one or other of them.

CHAP. I.
Of those systems which make virtue consist in propriety.

According to Plato, to Aristotle, and to Zeno, virtue consists in the propriety of conduct, or in the suitableness of the affection from which we act to the object which excites it.

I. In the system of Plato[8] the soul is considered as something like a little state or republic, composed of three different faculties or orders.

8. See Plato de Rep. lib. iv.

296 The first is the judging faculty, the faculty which determines not only what are the proper means for attaining any end, but also what ends are fit to be pursued, and what degree of relative value we ought to put upon each. This faculty Plato called, as it is very properly called reason, and considered it as what had a right to be the governing principle of the whole. Under this appellation, it is evident, he comprehended not only that faculty by which we judge of truth and falsehood, but that by which we judge of the propriety or impropriety of desires and affections.

The different passions and appetites, the natural subject of this ruling principle, but which are so apt to rebel against their master, he reduced to two different classes or orders. The first consisted of those passions, which are founded in pride and resentment, or in what the schoolmen called the irascible part of the soul; ambition, animosity, the love of honour, and the dread of shame, the desire of victory, superiority, and revenge; all those passions, in short, which are supposed either to rise from, or to denote what, by a metaphor in our language, we commonly call spirit or natural fire. The second consisted of those passions which are founded in the love of pleasure, or in what the schoolmen called the concupiscible part of the soul. It comprehended all the appetites of the body, the love of ease and security, and of all sensual gratifications.

It rarely happens that we break in upon that plan of conduct, which the governing principle prescribes, and which in all our cool hours we had laid down to ourselves as what was most proper for us to pursue, [297] but when prompted by one or other of those two different sets of passions; either by ungovernable ambition and resentment, or by the importunate solicitations of present ease and pleasure. But though these two orders of passions are so apt to mislead us, they are still considered as necessary parts of human nature: the first having been given to defend us against injuries, to assert our rank and dignity in the world, to make us aim at what is noble and honourable, and to make us distinguish those who act in the same manner; the second to provide for the support and necessities of the body.

In the strength, acuteness, and perfection of the governing principle was placed the essential virtue of prudence, which, according to Plato, consisted in a just and clear discernment, founded upon general and scientific ideas, of the ends which were proper to be pursued, and of the means which were proper for attaining them.

When the first set of passions, those of the irascible part of the soul, had that degree of strength and firmness, which enabled them, under the direction of reason, to despise all dangers in the pursuit of what was honourable and noble; it constituted the virtue of fortitude and magnanimity. This order of passions, according to this system, was of a more generous and noble nature than the other. They were considered upon many occasions as the auxiliaries of reason, to check and restrain the inferior and brutal appetites. We are often angry at ourselves, it was observed, we often become the objects of our own resentment and indignation, when the love of pleasure prompts to do what we disapprove of; and the irascible [298] part of our nature is in this manner called in to assist the rational against the concupiscible.

When all those three different parts of our nature were in perfect concord with one another, when neither the irascible nor concupiscible passions ever aimed at any gratification which reason did not approve of, and when reason never commanded any thing, but what these of their own accord were willing to perform; this happy composure, this perfect and complete harmony of soul, constituted that virtue which in their language is expressed by a word which we commonly translate temperance, but which might more properly be translated good temper, or sobriety and moderation of mind.

Justice, the last and greatest of the four cardinal virtues, took place, according to this system, when each of those three faculties of the mind confined itself to its proper office, without attempting to encroach upon that of any other; when reason directed and passion obeyed, and when each passion performed its proper duty, and exerted itself towards its proper object easily and without reluctance, and with that degree of force and energy, which was suitable to the value of what it pursued. In this consisted that complete virtue, that perfect propriety of conduct, which Plato, after some of the ancient Pythagoreans, denominated Justice.

The word, it is to be observed, which expresses justice in the Greek language, has several different meanings; and as the correspondent word in all other languages, so far as I know, has the same, there must be some natural affinity among those various significations. [299] In one sense we are said to do justice to our neighbour when we abstain from doing him any positive harm, and do not directly hurt him, either in his person, or in his estate, or in his reputation. This is that justice which I have treated of above, the observance of which may be extorted by force, and the violation of which exposes to punishment. In another sense we are said not to do justice to our neighbour unless we conceive for him all that love, respect and esteem, which his character, his situation, and his connexion with ourselves, render suitable and proper for us to feel, and unless we act accordingly. It is in this sense that we are said to do injustice to a man of merit who is connected with us, tho' we abstain from hurting him in every respect, if we do not exert ourselves to serve him and to place him in that situation in which the impartial spectator would be pleased to see him. The first sense of the word coincides with what Aristotle and the Schoolmen call commutative justice, and with what Grotius calls the *justitia expletrix*, which consists in abstaining from what is another's, and in doing voluntarily whatever we can with propriety be forced to do. The second sense of the word coincides with what some have called distributive justice[a], and with the *justitia attributrix* of Grotius, which consists in proper beneficence, in the becoming use of what is our own, and in the applying it to those purposes either of charity or generosity, to which it is most suitable, in our situation, that it should be applied. In this sense justice comprehends all the social virtues. [300] There is yet another sense in which the word justice is sometimes taken, still more extensive than either of the former, though very much akin to the last; and which runs too, so far as I know, through all languages. It is in this last sense that we are said to be unjust, when we do not seem to value any particular object with that degree of esteem, or to pursue it with that degree of ardour which to the impartial spectator it may appear to deserve or to be naturally fitted for exciting. Thus we are said to do injustice to a poem or a picture, when we do not admire them enough, and we are said to do them more than justice when we admire them too much. In the same manner we are said to do injustice to ourselves when we appear not to give sufficient attention to any particular object of self-interest. In this last sense, what is called justice means the same thing with exact and perfect propriety of conduct and behaviour, and comprehends in it, not only the offices of both commutative and distributive justice, but of every other virtue, of prudence, of fortitude, of temperance. It is in this last sense that Plato evidently understands what he calls justice, and which, therefore, according to him, comprehends in it the perfection of every sort of virtue.

9. The distributive justice of Aristotle is somewhat different. It consists in the proper distribution of rewards from the public stock of a community. See Aristotle Ethic. Nic. l. 5. c. 2.

Such is the account given by Plato of the nature of virtue, or of that temper of mind which is the proper object of praise and approbation. It consists, according to him, in that state of mind in which every faculty confines itself within its proper sphere without encroaching upon that of any other, and performs its proper office with that precise degree of strength and vigour which belongs to it. His account, it is evident, coincides in every respect with [301] what we have said above concerning the propriety of conduct.

II. Virtue, according to Aristotle[10], consists in the habit of mediocrity according to right reason. Every particular virtue, according to him, lies in a kind of middle between two opposite vices, of which the one offends from being too much, the other from being too little affected by a particular species of objects. Thus the virtue of fortitude or courage lies in the middle between the opposite vices of cowardice and of presumptuous rashness, of which the one offends from being too much, and the other from being too little affected by the objects of fear. Thus too the virtue of frugality lies in a middle between avarice and profusion, of which the one consists in an excess, the other in a defect of the proper attention to the objects of self interest. Magnanimity, in the same manner, lies in a middle between the excess of arrogance and the defect of pusillanimity, of which the one consists in too extravagant, the other in too weak a sentiment of our own worth and dignity. It is unnecessary to observe that this account of virtue corresponds too pretty exactly with what has been said above concerning the propriety and impropriety of conduct.

10. See Aristotle Ethic. Nic. l. 2. c. 5. et seq. et l. 3. c. 5. et seq.

According to Aristotle[10], indeed, virtue did not so much consist in those moderate and right affections, as in the habit of this moderation. In order to understand this, it is to be observed, that virtue may be considered either as the quality of an action, or [302] as the quality of a person. Considered as the quality of an action, it consists, even according to Aristotle, in the reasonable moderation of the affection from which the action proceeds, whether this disposition be habitual to the person or not. Considered as the quality of a person, it consists in the habit of this reasonable moderation, in its having become the customary and usual disposition of the mind. Thus the action which proceeds from an occasional fit of generosity is undoubtedly a generous action, but the man who performs it, is not necessarily a generous person, because it may be the single action of the kind which he ever performed. The motive and disposition of heart, from which this action was performed, may have been quite just and proper: but as this happy mood seems to have been the effect rather of accidental humour than of any thing steady or permanent in the character, it can reflect no great honour on the performer. When we denominate a character generous or charitable, or virtuous in any respect, we mean to signify that the disposition expressed by each of those appellations is the usual and customary disposition of the person. But single actions of any kind, how proper and suitable soever, are of little consequence to show that this is the case. If a single action was sufficient to stamp the character of any virtue upon the person who performed it, the most worthless of mankind might lay claim to all the virtues; since there is no man who has not, upon some occasions, acted with prudence, justice, temperance, and fortitude. But though single actions, how laudable soever, reflect very little praise upon the person who performs them, a single vicious action performed by one whose conduct is usually very regular, greatly diminishes and sometimes destroys altogether [303] our opinion of his virtue. A single action of this kind sufficiently shows that his habits are not perfect, and that he is less to be depended upon, than, from the usual train of his behaviour, we might have been apt to imagine.

11. See Aristotle Ethic. Nic. lib. ii. ch. 1., 2., 3. and 4.

Aristotle too[11], when he made virtue to consist in practical habits, had it probably in his view to oppose the doctrine of Plato, who seems to have been of opinion that just sentiments and reasonable judgments concerning what was fit to be done or to be avoided, were alone sufficient to constitute the most perfect virtue. Virtue, according to Plato, might be considered as a species of science, and no man, he thought, could see clearly and demonstratively what was right and what was wrong, and not act accordingly. Passion might make us act contrary to doubtful and uncertain opinions, not to plain and evident judgments. Aristotle, on the contrary, was of opinion, that no conviction of the understanding was capable of getting the better of inveterate habits, and that good morals arose not from knowledge but from action.

12. See Aristotle Mag. Mor. lib. i. ch. 1.

III. According to Zeno[12], the founder of the stoical doctrine, every animal was by nature recommended to its own care, and was endowed with the principle of self-love, that might endeavour to preserve, not only its existence, but all the different parts of its nature, in the best and most perfect state of which they were capable.

13. See Cicero de finibus, lib. iii. also Diogenes Laertius in Zenone, lib. vii. segment 84.

304 The self-love of man embraced, if I may say so, his body and all its different members, his mind and all its different faculties and powers, and desired the preservation and maintenance of them all in their best and most perfect condition. Whatever tended to support this state of existence was, therefore, by nature pointed out to him as fit to be chosen; and whatever tended to destroy it, as fit to be rejected. Thus health, strength, agility, and ease of body, as well as the external conveniencies which could promote these, wealth, power, honours, the respect and esteem of those we live with, were naturally pointed out to us as things eligible, and of which the possession was preferable to the contrary. On the other hand, sickness, infirmity, unwieldiness, pain of body, as well as all the external inconveniencies which tended to occasion or bring on any of them, poverty, the want of authority, the contempt or hatred of those we live with; were, in the same manner, pointed out to us as things to be shunned and avoided. In each of those two different classes of objects there were some which appeared to be more the objects either of choice or rejection than others in the same class. Thus, in the first class, health appeared evidently preferable to strength, and strength to agility; reputation to power, and power to riches. And thus too, in the second class, sickness was more to be avoided than unwieldiness of body, ignominy than poverty, and poverty than the want of authority. Virtue and the propriety of conduct consisted in choosing and rejecting all different objects and circumstances according as they were by nature rendered more or less the objects of choice or rejection; in selecting always from among the several objects of choice presented to us, that which was most to be 305 chosen, when we could not obtain them all: and in selecting too out of the several objects of rejection offered to us, that which was least to be avoided, when it was not in our power to avoid them all. By choosing and rejecting with this just and accurate discernment, by thus bestowing upon every object the precise degree of attention it deserved, according to the place which it held in this natural scale of things, we maintained, according to the Stoics, that perfect rectitude of conduct which constituted the essence of virtue. This was what they called to live consistently, to live according to nature, and to obey those laws and directions which nature, or the Author of nature, had prescribed for our conduct.

So far the Stoical idea of propriety and virtue is not very different from that of Aristotle and the ancient peripatetics. What chiefly distinguished those two systems from one another was the different degrees of self-command which they required. The peripatetics allowed of some degree of perturbation as suitable to the weakness of human nature, and as useful to so imperfect a creature as man. If his own misfortunes excited no passionate grief, if his own injuries called forth no lively resentment, reason, or a regard to the general rules which determined what was right and fit to be done, would commonly, they thought, be too weak to prompt him to avoid the one or to beat off the other. The Stoics, on the contrary, demanded the most perfect apathy, and regarded every emotion which could in the smallest degree disturb the tranquillity of the mind, as the effect of levity and folly. The Peripatetics seem to have thought that no passion exceeded the bounds of propriety as long as the spectator, by the utmost effort 306 of humanity, could sympathize with it. The Stoics, on the contrary, appear to have regarded every passion as improper, which made any demand upon the sympathy of the spectator, or required him to alter in any respect the natural and ordinary state of his mind, in order to keep time with the vehemence of its emotions. A man of virtue, they seem to have thought, ought not to depend upon the generosity of those he lives with for pardon or approbation.

According to the Stoics, every event should, to a wise man, appear indifferent, and what for its own sake could be the object neither of desire, nor aversion, neither of joy, nor sorrow. If he preferred some events to others, if some situations were the objects of his choice, and others of his rejection, it was not, because he regarded the one as, in themselves, in any respect better than the other, or thought that his own happiness would be more complete in, what is called, the fortunate, than in what is commonly regarded as the distressful situation; but because the propriety of action, the rule which the gods had given him for the direction of his conduct, required him to choose and reject in this manner. Among the primary objects of natural inclination, or among those things which nature had originally recommended to us as eligible, was the prosperity, of our family, of our relations, of our friends, of our country, of mankind, and of the universe in general. Nature too had taught us that as the prosperity of [307] two was preferable to that of one, that of many or of all must be infinitely more so. That we ourselves were but one, and that consequently wherever our prosperity was inconsistent with that, either of the whole, or of any considerable part of the whole, it ought, even in our own choice, to yield to what was so vastly preferable. As all the events in this world were conducted by the providence of a wise, powerful and good God, we might be assured that whatever happened, tended to the prosperity and perfection of the whole, if we ourselves, therefore, were in poverty, in sickness, or in any other calamity, we ought, first of all, to use our utmost endeavours, so far as justice and our duty to others would allow, to rescue ourselves from this disagreeable circumstance. But if after all we could do, we found this impossible, we ought to rest satisfied that the order and perfection of the universe required that we should in the mean time continue in this situation. And as the prosperity of the whole should, even to us, appear preferable to so insignificant a part as ourselves, our situation, whatever it was, ought from that moment to become the object of our choice, and even of our desire, if we would maintain that complete propriety and rectitude of sentiment and conduct in which the perfection of our nature consists. If, indeed, any opportunity of extricating ourselves should offer, it became our duty to embrace it. The order of the universe, it was evident, no longer required our continuance in this situation, and the great director of the world plainly called upon us to leave it, by so clearly pointing out the road which we were to follow. It was the same case with the adversity of our relations, our friends, our country. If without violating [308] any more sacred obligation, it was in our power to prevent or to put an end to their calamity, it undoubtedly was our duty to do so. The propriety of action, the rule which Jupiter had given us for the direction of our conduct, evidently required this of us. But if it was altogether out of our power to do either, we ought then to consider this event as the most fortunate which could possibly have happened: Because we might be assured that it tended most to the prosperity and order of the whole: which was what we ourselves, if we were wise and equitable, ought most of all to desire. "In what sense, says Epictetus, are some things said to be according to our nature, and others contrary to it? It is in that sense in which we consider ourselves as separated and detached from all other things. For thus it may be said to be according to the nature of the foot to be always clean. But if you consider it as a foot, and not as something detached from the rest of the body, it must behove it sometimes to trample in the dirt, and sometimes to tread upon thorns, and sometimes too to be cut off for the sake of the whole body; and if it refuses this, it is no longer a foot. Thus too ought we to conceive with regard to ourselves. What are you? A man. If you consider yourself as something separated and detached, it is agreeable to your nature to live to old age, to be rich, to be in health. But if you consider yourself as a man, and as a part of a whole, upon account of that whole it will behoove you sometimes to be in sickness, sometimes to be exposed to the inconveniency of a sea voyage, sometimes to be in want; and at last, perhaps, to die before your time. Why then do you complain? [309]Don't you know that by doing so, as the foot ceases to be a foot, so you cease to be a man?"[15]

14. Some of these expressions sound a little awkward in the English language: they are literal translations of the technical terms of the Stoics.

15. Arrian. lib. II. c. 5.

This submission to the order of the universe, this entire indifference with regard to whatever concerns ourselves, when put into the balance with the interest of the whole, could derive its propriety, it is evident, from no other principle besides that, upon which I have endeavoured to show, the propriety of justice was founded. As long as we view our own interests with our own eyes, it is scarce possible that we should willingly acquiesce in their being thus sacrificed to the interests of the whole. It is only when we view those opposite interests with the eyes of others, that what concerns ourselves can appear to be so contemptible in the comparison, as to be resigned without any reluctance. To every body but the person principally concerned, nothing can appear more agreeable to reason and propriety than that the part should give place to the whole. But what is agreeable to the reason of all other men, ought not to appear contrary to his. He himself therefore ought to approve of this sacrifice, and acknowledge its conformity to reason. But all the affections of a wise man, according to the stoics, are perfectly agreeable to reason and propriety, and of their own accord coincide with whatever these ruling principles prescribe. A wise man, therefore, could never feel any reluctance to comply with this disposition of things.

IV. Besides these ancient, there are some modern systems, according to which virtue consists in propriety; or in the suitableness of the affection from which [310]we act, to the cause or object which excites it. The system of Dr. Clarke, which places virtue in acting according to the relations of things, in regulating our conduct according to the fitness or incongruity which there may be in the application of certain actions to certain things, or to certain relations: That of Mr. Woolaston, which places it in acting according to the truth of things, according to their proper nature and essence, or in treating them as what they really are, and not as what they are not: that of my lord Shaftesbury, which places it in maintaining a proper balance of the affections, and in allowing no passion to go beyond its proper sphere; are all of them more or less inaccurate descriptions of the same fundamental idea.

The description of virtue which is either given, or at least meant and intended to be given in each of those systems, for some of the modern authors are not very fortunate in their manner of expressing themselves, is no doubt quite just, so far as it goes. There is no virtue without propriety, and wherever there is propriety, some degree of approbation is due. But still this description is imperfect. For though propriety is an essential ingredient in every virtuous action, it is not always the sole ingredient. Beneficent actions have in them another quality by which they appear not only to deserve approbation but recompense. None of those systems account either easily or sufficiently for that superior degree of esteem which seems due to such actions, or for that diversity of sentiment which they naturally excite. Neither is the description of vice more complete. For in the same manner, though impropriety is a necessary ingredient in every vicious action, it is [311] not always the sole ingredient, and there is often the highest degree of absurdity and impropriety in very harmless and insignificant actions. Deliberate actions, of a pernicious tendency to those we live with, have, besides their impropriety, a peculiar quality of their own by which they appear to deserve, not only disapprobation, but punishment; and to be the objects, not of dislike merely, but of resentment and revenge: and none of those systems easily and sufficiently account for that superior degree of detestation which we feel for such actions.

CHAP. II.
Of those systems which make virtue consist in prudence.

The most ancient of those systems which make virtue consist in prudence, and of which any considerable remains have come down to us, is that of Epicurus, who is said, however, to have borrowed all the leading principles of his philosophy, from some of those who had gone before him, particularly From Aristippus; though it is very probable, notwithstanding this allegation of his enemies, that at least his manner of applying those principles was altogether his own.

According to Epicurus,[16] bodily pleasure and pain were the sole ultimate objects of natural desire and aversion. That they were always the natural objects of those passions, he thought required no [312] proof. Pleasure might, indeed, appear sometimes to be avoided; not, however, because it was pleasure, but because, by the enjoyment of it, we should either forfeit some greater pleasure, or expose ourselves to some pain that was more to be avoided than this pleasure was to be desired. Pain, in the same manner, might appear sometimes to be eligible; not, however, because it was pain, but because by enduring it we might either avoid a still greater pain, or acquire some pleasure of much more importance. That bodily pain and pleasure, therefore, were always the natural objects of desire and aversion, was, he thought, abundantly evident. Nor was it less so, he imagined that they were the sole ultimate objects of those passions. Whatever else was either desired or avoided was so, according to him, upon account of its tendency to produce one or other of those sensations. The tendency to procure pleasure rendered power and riches desirable, as the contrary tendency to produce pain made poverty and insignificancy the objects of aversion. Honour and reputation were valued, because the esteem and love of those we live with were of the greatest consequence both to procure pleasure and to defend us from pain. Ignominy and bad fame, on the contrary, were to be avoided because the hatred, contempt, and resentment of those we lived with destroyed all security, and necessarily exposed us to the greatest bodily evils.

16. See Cicero de finibus, lib. i. Diogenes Laert. 1. x.

All the pleasures and pains of the mind were, according to Epicurus, ultimately derived from those of the body. The mind was happy when it thought of the past pleasures of the body, and hoped for others to come: and it was miserable when it thought ₃₁₃ of the pains which the body had formerly endured, and dreaded the same or greater thereafter.

But the pleasures and pains of the mind, though ultimately derived from those of the body, were vastly greater than their originals. The body felt only the sensation of the present instant, whereas the mind felt also the past and the future, the one by remembrance, the other by anticipation, and consequently both suffered and enjoyed much more. When we are under the greatest bodily pain, he observed, we shall always find, if we attend to it, that it is not the suffering of the present instant which chiefly torments us, but either the agonizing remembrance of the past, or the yet more horrible dread of the future. The pain of each instant, considered by itself, and cut off from all that goes before and all that comes after it, is a trifle not worth the regarding. Yet this is all which the body can ever be said to suffer. In the same manner, when we enjoy the greatest pleasure, we shall always find that the bodily sensation, the sensation of the present instant makes but a small part of our happiness, that our enjoyment chiefly arises either from the chearful recollection of the past, or the still more joyous anticipation of the future, and that the mind always contributes by much the largest share of the entertainment.

Since our happiness and misery, therefore, depended chiefly on the mind, if this part of our nature was well disposed, if our thoughts and opinions were as they should be, it was of little importance in what manner our body was affected. Though under great bodily pain, we might still enjoy a considerable share of happiness, if our reason and judgment [314] maintained their superiority. We might entertain ourselves with the remembrance of past, and with the hopes of future pleasure; we might soften the rigour of our pains, by recollecting what it was which, even in this situation, we were under any necessity of suffering. That this was merely the bodily sensation, the pain of the present instant, which by itself could never be very great. That whatever agony we suffered from the dread of its continuance was the effect of an opinion of the mind, which might be corrected by juster sentiments; by considering that, if our pains were violent, they would probably be of short duration; and that if they were of long continuance, they would probably be moderate, and admit of many intervals of ease; and that, at any rate, death was always at hand and within call to deliver us, which as, according to him, it put an end to all sensation, either of pain or pleasure, could not be regarded as an evil. When we are, said he, death is not; and when death is, we are not; death therefore can be nothing to us.

If the actual sensation of positive pain was in itself so little to be feared, that of pleasure was still less to be desired. Naturally the sensation of pleasure was much less pungent than that of pain. If, therefore, this last could take so very little from the happiness of a well-disposed mind, the other could add scarce any thing to it. When the body was free from pain and the mind from fear and anxiety, the superadded sensation of bodily pleasure could be of very little importance; and though it might diversify, could not be properly be said to increase the happiness of this situation.

[315] In ease of body, therefore, and in security or tranquillity of mind, consisted, according to Epicurus, the most perfect state of human nature, the most complete happiness which man was capable of enjoying. To obtain this great end of natural desire was the sole object

of all the virtues, which, according to him, were not desirable upon their own account, but upon account of their tendency to bring about this situation.

Prudence, for example, though according to this philosophy, the source and principle of all the virtues, was not desirable upon its own account. That careful and laborious and circumspect state of mind, ever watchful and ever attentive to the most distant consequences of every action, could not be a thing pleasant or agreeable for its own sake, but upon account of its tendency to procure the greatest goods and to keep off the greatest evils.

To abstain from pleasure too, to curb and restrain our natural passions for enjoyment, which was the office of temperance, could never be desirable for its own sake. The whole value of this virtue arose from its utility, from its enabling us to postpone the present enjoyment for the sake of a greater to come, or to avoid a greater pain that might ensue from it. Temperance, in short, was nothing but prudence with regard to pleasure.

To support labour, to endure pain, to be exposed to danger or to death, the situations which fortitude would often lead us into, were surely still less the objects of natural desire. They were chosen only to avoid greater evils. We submitted to labour, in order 316 to avoid the greater shame and pain of poverty, and we exposed ourselves to danger and to death in defence of our liberty and property, the means and instruments of pleasure and happiness; or in defence of our country, in the safety of which our own was necessarily comprehended. Fortitude enabled us to do all this chearfully, as the best which, in our present situation, could possibly be done, and was in reality no more than prudence, good judgment, and presence of mind in properly appreciating pain, labour, and danger, always choosing the less in order to avoid the greater.

It is the same case with justice. To abstain from what is anothers was not desirable on its own account, and it could not surely be better for you, that I should possess what is my own, than that you should possess it. You ought however, to abstain from whatever belongs to me, because by doing otherwise you will provoke the resentment and indignation of mankind. The security and tranquillity of your mind will be entirely destroyed. You will be filled with fear and consternation at the thought of that punishment which you will imagine that men are at all times ready to inflict upon you, and from which no power, no art, no concealment, will ever, in your own fancy, be sufficient to protect you. That other species of justice which consists in doing proper good offices to different persons, according to the various relations of neighbours, kinsmen, friends, benefactors, superiors, or equals, which they may stand in to us, is recommended by the same reasons. To act properly in all these different relations procures us the esteem and love of those we live with; as to do otherwise excites their contempt and hatred. By the 317 one we naturally secure, by the other we necessarily endanger our own ease and tranquillity, the great and ultimate objects of all our desires. The whole virtue of justice, therefore, the most important of all the virtues, is no more than discreet and prudent conduct with regard to our neighbours.

Such is the doctrine of Epicurus concerning the nature of virtue. It may seem extraordinary that this philosopher, who is described as a person of the most amiable manners, should never have observed, that, whatever may be the tendency of those virtues, or of the contrary vices, with regard to our bodily ease and security, the sentiments which they naturally excite in others are the objects of a much more passionate desire or aversion than all their other consequences; That to be amiable, to be respectable to be the proper object of esteem, is by every well-disposed mind more valued than all the ease and security which love, respect, and esteem can procure us; That, on the contrary, to be odious, to be contemptible, to be the proper object of indignation, is more dreadful than all that we can suffer in our body from hatred, contempt, or indignation; and that consequently our desire of the one character, and our aversion to the other, cannot arise from any regard to the effects which either of them is likely to produce upon the body.

This system is, no doubt, altogether inconsistent with that which I have been endeavouring to establish. It is not difficult, however, to discover from what phasis, if I may say so, from what particular view or aspect of nature, this account of things derives its probability. By the wise contrivance of the [318]Author of nature, virtue is upon all ordinary occasions, even with regard to this life, real wisdom, and the surest and readiest means of obtaining both safety and advantage. Our success or disappointment in our undertakings must very much depend upon the good or bad opinion which is commonly entertained of us, and upon the general disposition of those we live with, either to assist or to oppose us. But the best, the surest, the easiest, and the readiest way of obtaining the advantageous and of avoiding the unfavourable judgments of others, is undoubtedly to render ourselves the proper objects of the former and not of the latter. "Do you desire, said Socrates, the reputation of a good musician? The only sure way of obtaining it, is to become a good musician. Would you desire in the same manner to be thought capable of serving your country either as a general or as a statesman? The best way in this case too is really to acquire the art and experience of war and government, and to become really fit to be a general or a statesman. And in the same manner if you would be reckoned sober, temperate, just, and equitable, the best way of acquiring this reputation is to become sober, temperate, just, and equitable. If you can really render yourself amiable, respectable, and the proper object of esteem, there is no fear of your not soon acquiring the love, the respect, and esteem of those you live with." Since the practice of virtue, therefore, is in general so advantageous, and that of vice so contrary to our interest, the consideration of those opposite tendencies undoubtedly stamps an additional beauty and propriety upon the one, and a new deformity and impropriety upon the other. Temperance, magnanimity, justice, and beneficence, come thus to [319]be approved of, not only under their proper characters, but under the additional character of the highest wisdom and most real prudence. And in the same manner the contrary vices of intemperance, pusillanimity, injustice, and either malevolence or sordid selfishness, come to be disapproved of, not only under their proper characters, but under the additional character of the most short-sighted folly and weakness. Epicurus appears in every virtue to have attended to this species of propriety only. It is that which is most apt to occur to those who are endeavouring to persuade others to regularity of conduct. When men by their practice, and perhaps too by their maxims, manifestly show that the natural beauty of virtue is not like to have much effect upon them, how is it possible to move them but by representing the folly of their conduct, and how much they themselves are in the end likely to suffer by it?

By running up all the different virtues too to this one species of propriety, Epicurus indulged a propensity, which is natural to all men, but which philosophers in particular are apt to cultivate with a peculiar fondness, as the great means of displaying their ingenuity, the propensity to account for all appearances from as few principles as possible. And he, no doubt, indulged this propensity still further, when he referred all the primary objects of natural desire and aversion to the pleasures and pains of the body. The great patron of the atomical philosophy, who took so much pleasure in deducing all the powers and qualities of bodies from the most obvious and familiar, the figure, motion, and arrangement of the small parts of matter, felt no doubt a similar satisfaction, when he accounted, in the same manner, for 320 all the sentiments and passions of the mind from those which are most obvious and familiar.

The system of Epicurus agreed with those of Plato, Aristotle, and Zeno, in making virtue consist in acting in the most suitable manner to obtain the ᴸᵀᴸprimary objects of natural desire. It differed from all of them in two other respects; first, in the account which it gave of those primary objects of natural desire; and secondly, in the account which it gave of the excellence of virtue, or of the reason why that quality ought to be esteemed.

17. Prima naturæ.

The primary objects of natural desire consisted, according to Epicurus, in bodily pleasure and pain, and in nothing else whereas, according to the other three philosophers, there were many other objects, such as knowledge, such as the happiness of our relations, of our friends, of our country, which were ultimately desirable for their own sakes.

Virtue too, according to Epicurus, did not deserve to be pursued for its own sake, nor was itself one of the ultimate objects of natural appetite, but was eligible only upon account of its tendency to prevent pain and to procure ease and pleasure. In the opinion of the other three, on the contrary, it was desirable, not merely as the means of procuring the other primary objects of natural desire, but as something which was in itself more valuable than them all. Man, they thought, being born for action, his happiness must consist, not merely in the agreeableness of his passive sensations, but also in the propriety of his active exertions.

321

CHAP. III.
Of those systems which make virtue consist in benevolence.

The system which makes virtue consist in benevolence, though I think not so ancient as all of those which I have already given an account of, is, however, of very great antiquity. It seems to have been the doctrine of the greater part of those philosophers who, about and after the age of Augustus, called themselves Eclectics, who pretended to follow chiefly the opinions of Plato and Pythagoras, and who upon that account are commonly known by the name of the later Platonists.

In the divine nature, according to these authors, benevolence or love was the sole principle of action, and directed the exertion of all the other attributes. The wisdom of the Deity was employed in finding out the means for bringing about those ends which his goodness suggested, as his infinite power was exerted to execute them. Benevolence however, was still the supreme and governing attribute, to which the others were subservient, and from which the whole excellency, or the whole morality, if I may be allowed such an expression, of the divine operations, was ultimately derived. The whole perfection and virtue of the human mind consisted in some resemblance or participation of the divine perfections, and, consequently, in being filled with the same principle [322] of benevolence and love which influenced all the actions of the deity. The actions of men which flowed from this motive were alone truly praise-worthy, or could claim any merit in the sight of the deity. It was by actions of charity and love only that we could imitate, as became us, the conduct of God, that we could express our humble and devout admiration of his infinite perfections, that by fostering in our own minds the same divine principle, we could bring our own affections to a greater resemblance with his holy attributes, and thereby become more proper objects of his love and esteem; till at last we arrived at that immediate converse and communication with the deity to which it was the great object of this philosophy to raise us.

This system, as it was much esteemed by many ancient fathers of the christian church, so after the reformation it was adopted by several divines of the most eminent piety and learning, and of the most amiable manners; particularly, by Dr. Ralph Cudworth, by Dr. Henry More, and by Mr. John Smith of Cambridge. But of all the patrons of this system, ancient or modern, the late Dr. Hutcheson, was undoubtedly beyond all comparison, the most acute, the most distinct, the most philosophical, and what is of the greatest consequence of all, the soberest and most judicious.

That virtue consists in benevolence is a notion supported by many appearances in human nature. It has been observed already that proper benevolence is the most graceful and agreeable of all the affections, that it is recommended to us by a double sympathy, that as its tendency is necessarily beneficent, [323] it is the proper object of gratitude and reward, and that upon all these accounts it appears to our natural sentiments to possess a merit superior to any other. It has been observed too that even the weakness of benevolence are not very disagreeable to us, whereas those of every other passion are always extremely disgusting. Who does not abhor excessive malice, excessive selfishness, or excessive resentment? But the most excessive indulgence even of partial friendship is not so offensive. It is the benevolent passions only which can exert themselves without any regard or attention to propriety, and yet retain something about them which is engaging. There is something pleasing even in mere instinctive good-will which goes on to do good offices without once reflecting whether by this conduct it is the proper object either of blame or approbation. It is not so with the other passions. The moment they are deserted, the moment they are unaccompanied by the sense of propriety, they cease to be agreeable.

As benevolence bestows upon those actions which proceed from it, a beauty superior to all others, so the want of it, and much more the contrary inclination, communicates a peculiar deformity to whatever evidences such a disposition. Pernicious actions are often punishable for no other reason than because they show a want of sufficient attention to the happiness of our neighbour.

Besides all this, Dr. Hutcheson[18] observed, that whenever in any action, supposed to proceed from benevolent affections, some other motive had been [324] discovered, our sense of the merit of this action was just so far diminished as this motive was believed to have influenced it. If an action, supposed to proceed, from gratitude, should be discovered to have arisen from an expectation of some new favour, or if what was apprehended to proceed from public spirit, should be found out to have taken its origin from the hope of pecuniary reward, such a discovery would entirely destroy all notion of merit or praise-worthiness in either of these actions. Since, therefore, the mixture of any selfish motive, like that of a base alloy, diminished or took away altogether the merit which would otherwise have belonged to any action, it was evident, he imagined, that virtue must consist in pure and disinterested benevolence alone.

<u>18</u>. See Inquiry concerning virtue, sect. 1. and 2.

When those actions, on the contrary, which are commonly supposed to proceed from a selfish motive, are discovered to have arisen from a benevolent one, it greatly enhances our sense of their merit. If we believed of any person that he endeavoured to advance his fortune from no other view but that of doing friendly offices, and of making proper returns to his benefactors, we should only love and esteem him the more. And this observation seemed still more to confirm the conclusion, that it was benevolence only which could stamp upon any action the character of virtue.

Last of all, what, he imagined, was an evident proof of the justness of this account of virtue, in all the disputes of casuists concerning the rectitude of conduct, the public good, he observed, was the standard to which they constantly referred; thereby universally acknowledging that whatever tended to 325 promote the happiness of mankind was right and laudable and virtuous, and the contrary, wrong, blameable, and vicious. In the late debates about passive obedience and the right of resistance, the sole point in controversy among men of sense was, whether universal submission would probably be attended with greater evils than temporary insurrections when privileges were invaded. Whether what, upon the whole, tended most to the happiness of mankind, was not also morally good, was never once, he said, made a question.

Since benevolence, therefore, was the only motive which could bestow upon any action the character of virtue, the greater the benevolence which was evidenced by any action, the greater the praise which must belong to it.

Those actions which aimed at the happiness of a great community, as they demonstrated a more enlarged benevolence than those which aimed only at that of a smaller system, so were they, likewise, proportionally the more virtuous. The most virtuous of all affections, therefore, was that which embraced as its object the happiness of all intelligent beings. The lead virtuous, on the contrary, of those to which the character of virtue could in any respect belong, was that which aimed no further than at the happiness of an individual, such as a son, a brother, a friend.

In directing all our actions to promote the greatest possible good, in submitting all inferior affections to the desire of the general happiness of mankind, in regarding ones self but as one of the many, whose 326 prosperity was to be pursued no further than it was consistent with, or conducive to that of the whole, consisted the perfection of virtue.

Self-love was a principle which could never be virtuous in any degree or in any direction It was vicious whenever it obstructed the general good. When it had no other effect than to make the individual take care of his own happiness, it was merely innocent, and tho' i deserved no praise, neither ought it to incur any blame. Those benevolent actions which were performed, notwithstanding some strong motive from self-interest, were the more virtuous upon that account. They demonstrated the strength and vigour of the benevolen principle.

Dr. Hutcheson[19] was so far from allowing self-love to be in any case a motive of virtuou actions, that even a regard to the pleasure of self-approbation, to the comfortabl applause of our own consciences, according to him, diminished the merit of a benevolent action. This was a selfish motive, he thought, which, so far as it contributed to any action, demonstrated the weakness of that pure and disinterested benevolence which could alone stamp upon the conduct of man the character of virtue. In the common judgments of mankind, however, this regard to the approbation of our own minds is so far from being considered as what can in any respect diminish the virtue of any action, that it is rather looked upon as the sole motive which deserves the appellation of virtuous.

19. Inquiry concerning virtue, sect 2. art. 4. also illustrations on the moral sense, sect. 5. last paragraph.

Such is the account given of the nature of virtue in this amiable system, a system which has a peculiar tendency to nourish and support in the human heart the noblest and the most agreeable of all affections, and not only to check the injustice of self-love, but in some measure to discourage that principle altogether, by representing it as what could never reflect any honour upon those who were influenced by it.

As some of the other systems which I have already given an account of, do not sufficiently explain from whence arises the peculiar excellency of the supreme virtue of beneficence, so this system seems to have the contrary defect, of not sufficiently explaining from whence arises our approbation of the inferior virtues of prudence, vigilance, circumspection, temperance, constancy, firmness. The view and aim of our affections, the beneficent and hurtful effects which they tend to produce, are the only qualities at all attended to in this system. Their propriety and impropriety, their suitableness and unsuitableness, to the cause which excites them, are disregarded altogether.

Regard to our own private happiness and interest too, appear upon many occasions very laudable principles of action. The habits of œconomy, industry, discretion, attention, and application of thought, are generally supposed to be cultivated from self-interested motives, and at the same time are apprehended to be very praise-worthy qualities, which deserve the esteem and approbation of every body. The mixture of a selfish motive, it is true, seems often to sully the beauty of those actions which ought to arise from a benevolent affection. The cause of this, however, is not that self-love can never be the motive of a virtuous action, but that the benevolent principle appears in this particular case to want its due degree of strength, and to be altogether unsuitable to its object. The character, therefore, seems evidently imperfect, and upon the whole to deserve blame rather than praise. The mixture of a benevolent motive in an action to which self-love alone ought to be sufficient to prompt us, is not so apt indeed to diminish our sense of its propriety, or of the virtue of the person who performs it. We are not ready to suspect any person of being defective in selfishness. This is by no means the weak side of human nature, or the failing of which we are apt to be suspicious. If we could really believe, however, of any man, that, was it not from a regard to his family and friends, he would not take that proper care of his health, his life, or his fortune, to which self-preservation alone ought to be sufficient to prompt him, it would undoubtedly be a failing, tho' one of those amiable failings, which render a person rather the object of pity than of contempt or hatred. It would still, however, somewhat diminish the dignity and respectableness of his character. Carelessness and want of œconomy are universally disapproved of, not, however as proceeding from a want of benevolence, but from a want of the proper attention to the objects of self-interest.

Though the standard by which casuists frequently determine what is right or wrong in human conduct, be its tendency to the welfare or disorder of society, it does not follow that a regard to the 329 welfare of society should be the sole virtuous motive of action, but only that, in any competition, it ought to cast the balance against all other motives.

Benevolence may, perhaps, be the sole principle of action in the Deity, and there are several, not improbable, arguments which tend to persuade us that it is so. It is not easy to conceive what other motive an independent and all perfect being, who stands in need of nothing external, and whose happiness is complete in himself, can act from. But whatever may be the case with the Deity, so imperfect a creature as man, the support of whose existence requires so many things external to him, must often act from many other motives. The condition of human nature were peculiarly hard, if those affections, which, by the very nature of our being, ought frequently to influence our conduct, could upon no occasion appear virtuous, or deserve esteem and commendation from any body.

Those three systems, that which places virtue in propriety, that which places it in prudence, and that which makes it consist in benevolence, are the principal accounts which have been given of the nature of virtue. To one or other of them, all the other descriptions of virtue, how different soever they may appear, are easily reducible.

That system which places virtue in obedience to the will of the Deity, may be counted either among those which make it consist in prudence, or among those which make it consist in propriety. When it is asked, why we ought to obey the will of the Deity, this question, which would be impious and absurd in the highest degree, if asked from any doubt that 330 we ought to obey him, can admit but of two different answers. It must either be said that we ought to obey the will of the Deity because he is a being of infinite power, who will reward us eternally if we do so, and punish us eternally if we do otherwise: Or it must be said, that independent of any regard to our own happiness, or to rewards and punishments of any kind, there is a congruity and fitness that a creature should obey its creator, that a limited and imperfect being should submit to one of infinite and incomprehensible perfections. Besides one or other of these two it is impossible to conceive that any other answer can be given to this question. If the first answer be the proper one, virtue consists in prudence, or in the proper pursuit of our own final interest and happiness; since it is upon this account that we are obliged to obey the will of the Deity. If the second answer be the proper one, virtue must consist in propriety, since the ground of our obligation to obedience is the suitableness or congruity of the sentiments of humility and submission to the superiority of the object which excites them.

That system which places virtue in utility coincides too with that which makes it consist in propriety. According to this system all those qualities of the mind which are agreeable or advantageous, either to the person himself or to others, are approved of as virtuous and the contrary disapproved of as vicious. But the agreeableness or utility of any affection depends upon the degree which it is allowed to subsist in. Every affection is useful when it is confined to a certain degree of moderation, and every affection is disadvantageous when it exceeds the proper bounds. According to this system therefore, virtue consists, 331 not in any one affection, but in the proper degree of all the affections, The only difference between it and that which I have been endeavouring to establish, is, that it makes utility, and not sympathy, or the correspondent affection of the spectator, the natural and original measure of this proper degree.

CHAP. IV.
Of licentious systems.

All those systems, which I have hitherto given an account of, suppose that there is a real and essential distinction between vice and virtue, whatever these qualities may consist in. There is a real and essential difference between the propriety and impropriety of any affection, between benevolence and any other principle of action, between real prudence and short-sighted folly or precipitate rashness. In the main too all of them contribute to encourage the praise-worthy, and to discourage the blameable disposition.

It may be true perhaps, of some of them, that they tend, in some measure, to break the balance of the affections, and to give the mind a particular bias to some principles of action, beyond the proportion that is due to them. The ancient systems which place virtue in propriety, seem chiefly to recommend the great, the awful, and the respectable virtues, the virtues of self-government and self-command; fortitude, magnanimity, independency upon fortune, the contempt of all outward accidents, of pain, poverty, exile, and death. It is in these great exertions that the noblest propriety of conduct is displayed. The soft, the amiable, the gentle virtues, all the virtues of indulgent humanity are, in comparison, but little insisted upon, and seem, on the contrary, by the Stoics in particular, to have been often regarded as mere weaknesses which it behoved a wise man not to harbour in his breast.

The benevolent system, on the other hand, while it fosters and encourages all those milder virtues in the highest degree, seems entirely to neglect the more awful and respectable qualities of the mind. It even denies them the appellation of virtues. It calls them moral abilities, and treats them as qualities which do not deserve the same sort of esteem and approbation, that is due to what is properly denominated virtue. All those principles of action which aim only at our own interest, it treats, if that be possible, still worse. So far from having any merit of their own, they diminish, it pretends, the merit of benevolence, when they co-operate with it: and prudence, it is asserted, when employed only in promoting private interest, can never even be imagined a virtue.

That system, again, which makes virtue consist in prudence only, while it gives the highest encouragement to the habits of caution, vigilance, sobriety, and judicious moderation, seems to degrade equally both the amiable and respectable virtues, and to strip the former of all their beauty, and the latter of all their grandeur.

But notwithstanding these defects, the general tendency of each of those three systems is to encourage the best and most laudable habits of the human mind: and it were well for society, if, either mankind in general, or even those few who pretend to live according to any philosophical rule, were to regulate their conduct by the precepts of any one of them. We may learn from each of them something that is both valuable and peculiar. If it was possible, by precept and exhortation, to inspire the mind with fortitude and magnanimity, the ancient systems of propriety would seem sufficient to do this. Or if it was possible, by the same means, to soften it into humanity, and to awaken the affections of kindness and general love towards those we live with, some of the pictures with which the benevolent system presents us, might seem capable of producing this effect. We may learn from the system of Epicurus, though undoubtedly the worst of all the three, how much the practice of both the amiable and respectable virtues is conducive to our own interest, to our own ease and safety and quiet even in this life. As Epicurus placed happiness in the attainment of ease and security, he exerted himself in a particular manner to show that virtue was, not merely the best and the surest, but the only means of acquiring those invaluable possessions. The good effects of virtue, upon our inward tranquility and peace of mind, are what other philosophers have chiefly celebrated. Epicurus, without neglecting this topic, has chiefly insisted upon the influence of that amiable quality on our outward prosperity and safety. It was upon this account that his writings were so much studied in the ancient world by men of all different philosophical parties. It is from him that Cicero, the great enemy of the Epicurean system, borrows his most agreeable proofs that virtue alone is sufficient to secure happiness. Seneca, though a Stoic, the sect most opposite 334 to that of Epicurus, yet quotes this philosopher more frequently than any other.

There are, however, some other systems which seem to take away altogether the distinction between vice and virtue, and of which the tendency is, upon that account, wholly pernicious: I mean the systems of the duke of Rochefoucault and Dr. Mandeville. Though the notions of both these authors are in almost every respect erroneous, there are, however, some appearances in human nature which, when viewed in a certain manner, seem at first sight to favour them. These, first slightly sketched out with the elegance and delicate precision of the duke of Rochefoucault, and afterwards more fully represented with the lively and humorous, though coarse and rustic eloquence of Dr. Mandeville, have thrown upon their doctrines an air of truth and probability which is very apt to impose upon the unskilful.

Dr. Mandeville, the most methodical of those two authors, considers whatever is done from a sense of propriety, from a regard to what is commendable and praise-worthy, as being done from a love of praise and commendation, or as he calls it from vanity. Man, he observes, is naturally much more interested in his own happiness than in that of others, and it is impossible that in his heart he can ever really prefer their prosperity to his own. Whenever he appears to do so, we may be assured that he imposes upon us, and that he is then acting from the same selfish motives as at all other times. Among his other selfish passions, vanity is one of the strongest, and he is always easily flattered and greatly delighted with the applauses of those about him. When he 335 appears to sacrifice his own interest to that of his companions, he knows that this conduct will be highly agreeable to their self-love, and that they will not fail to express their satisfaction by bellowing upon him the most extravagant praises. The pleasure which he expects from this, over-balances, in his opinion, the interest which he abandons in order to procure it. His conduct, therefore, upon this occasion, is in reality just as selfish, and arises from just as mean a motive as upon any other. He is flattered, however, and he flatters himself with the belief that it is entirely disinterested; since, unless this was supposed, it would not seem to merit any commendation either in his own eyes or in those of others. All public spirit, therefore, all preference of public to private interest, is, according to him a mere cheat and imposition upon mankind; and that human virtue which is so much boasted of and which is the occasion of so much emulation among men, is the mere offspring of flattery begot upon pride.

Whether the most generous and public-spirited actions may not, in some sense, be regarded as proceeding from self-love, I shall not at present examine. The decision of this question is not, I apprehend, of any importance towards establishing the reality of virtue since self-love may frequently be a virtuous motive of action. I shall only endeavour to show that the desire of doing what is honourable and noble, of rendering ourselves the proper objects of esteem and approbation, cannot with any propriety be called vanity. Even the love of well-grounded fame and reputation, the desire of acquiring esteem by what is really estimable, does not deserve that name. The first is the love of virtue, the noblest 336 and the best passion of human nature. The second is the love of true glory, a passion inferior no doubt to the former, but which in dignity appears to come immediately after it. He is guilty of vanity who desires praise for qualities which are either not praise-worthy in any degree, or not in that degree which he expects to be praised for them; who sets his character upon the frivolous ornaments of dress and equipage, or the equally frivolous accomplishments of ordinary behaviour. He is guilty of vanity who desires praise for what indeed very well deserves it, but what he perfectly knows does not belong to him. The empty coxcomb who gives himself airs of importance which he has no title to, the silly liar who assumes the merit of adventures which never happened, the foolish plagiary who gives himself out for the author of what he has no pretensions to, are properly accused of this passion. He too is said to be guilty of vanity who is not contented with the silent sentiments of esteem and approbation, who seems to be fonder of their noisy expressions and acclamations than of the sentiments themselves, who is never satisfied but when his own praises are ringing in his ears, and who solicits with the most anxious importunity all external marks of respect, is fond of titles, of compliments, of being visited, of being attended, of being taken notice of in public places with the appearance of deference and attention. This frivolous passion is altogether different from either of the two former, and is the passion of the lowest, and the least of mankind, as they are of the noblest and the greatest.

But though these three passions, the desire of rendering ourselves the proper objects of honour and esteem; or of becoming what is honourable and 337 estimable; the desire of acquiring honour and esteem by really deserving those sentiments; and the frivolous desire of praise at any rate, are widely different; though the two former are always approved of, while the latter never fails to be despised; there is, however, a certain remote affinity among them, which, exaggerated by the humorous and diverting eloquence of this lively author, has enabled him to impose upon his readers. There is an affinity between vanity and the love of true glory, as both these passions aim at acquiring esteem and approbation. But they are different in this, that the one is a just, reasonable, and equitable passion, while the other is unjust, absurd, and ridiculous. The man who desires esteem for what is really estimable, desires nothing but what he is justly entitled to, and what cannot be refused him without some sort of injury. He, on the contrary, who desires it upon any other terms, demands what he has no just claim to. The first is easily satisfied, is not apt to be jealous or suspicious that we do not esteem him enough, and is seldom solicitous about receiving many external marks of our regard. The other, on the contrary, is never to be satisfied, is full of jealousy and suspicion that we do not esteem him so much as he desires, because he has some secret consciousness that he desires more than he deserves. The least neglect of ceremony, he considers as a mortal affront, and as an expression of the most determined contempt. He is restless and impatient, and perpetually afraid that we have lost all respect for him, and is upon this account always anxious to obtain new expressions of esteem, and cannot be kept in temper but by continual attendance and adulation.

338 There is an affinity too between the desire of becoming what is honourable and estimable, and the desire of honour and esteem, between the love of virtue and the love of true glory. They resemble one another not only in this respect, that both aim at really being what is honourable and noble, but even in that respect in which the love of true glory resembles what is properly called vanity, some reference to the sentiments of others. The man of the greatest magnanimity, who desires virtue for its own sake, and is most indifferent about what actually are the opinions of mankind with regard to him, is still, however, delighted with the thoughts of what they should be, with the consciousness that though he may neither be honoured nor applauded, he is still the proper object of honour and applause, and that if mankind were cool and candid and consistent with themselves, and properly informed of the motives and circumstances of his conduct, they would not fail to honour and applaud him. Though he despises the opinions which are actually entertained of him, he has the highest value for those which ought to be entertained of him. That he might think himself worthy of those honourable sentiments, and, whatever was the idea which other men might conceive of his character, that when he should put himself in their situation, and consider, not what was, but what ought to be their opinion, he should always have the highest idea of it himself, was the great and exalted motive of his conduct. As even in the love of virtue, therefore, there is still some reference, though not to what is, yet to what in reason and propriety ought to be, the opinion of others, there is even in this respect some affinity between it, and the love of true glory. There is, however, at the same time, a very great difference 339 between them. The man who acts solely from a regard to what is right and fit to be done, from a regard to what is the proper object of esteem and approbation, though these sentiments should never be bestowed upon him, acts from the most sublime and godlike motive which human nature is even capable of conceiving. The man, on the other hand, who while he desires to merit approbation is at the same time anxious to obtain it, though he too is laudably in the main, yet his motives have a greater mixture of human infirmity. He is in danger of being mortified by the ignorance and injustice of mankind, and his happiness is exposed to the envy of his rivals, and the folly of the public. The happiness of the other, on the contrary, is altogether secure and independent of fortune, and of the caprice of those he lives with. The contempt and hatred which may be thrown upon him by the ignorance of mankind, he considers as not belonging to him, and is not at all mortified by it. Mankind despise and hate him from a false notion of his character and conduct. If they knew him better, they would esteem and love him. It is not him whom, properly speaking, they hate and despise, but another person whom they mistake him to be. Our friend, whom we should meet at a masquerade in the garb of our enemy, would be more diverted than mortified if under that disguise we should vent our indignation against him. Such are the sentiments of a man of real magnanimity, when exposed to unjust censure. It seldom happens however, that human nature arrives at this degree of firmness. Though none but the weakest and most worthless of mankind are much delighted with false glory, yet, by a strange inconsistency, false ignominy is often capable of mortifying those who appear the most resolute and determined.

340 Dr. Mandeville is not satisfied with representing the frivolous motive of vanity, as the source of all those actions which are commonly accounted virtuous. He endeavours to point out the imperfection of human virtue in many other respects. In every case, he pretends, it falls short of that complete self-denial which it pretends to, and, instead of conquest, is commonly no more than a concealed indulgence of our passions. Whereve

our reserve with regard to pleasure falls short of the most ascetic abstinence, he treats it as gross luxury and sensuality. Every thing, according to him, is luxury which exceeds what is absolutely necessary for the support of human nature, so that there is a vice even in the use of a clean shirt, or of a convenient habitation. The indulgence of the inclination to sex, in the most lawful union, he considers as the same sensuality with the most hurtful gratification of that passion, and derides that temperance and that chastity which can be practiced at so cheap a rate. The ingenious sophistry of his reasoning, is here, as upon many other occasions, covered by the ambiguity of language. There are some of our passions which have no other names except those which mark the disagreeable and offensive degree. The spectator is more apt to take notice of them in this degree than in any other. When they shock his own sentiments, when they give him some sort of antipathy and uneasiness, he is necessarily obliged to attend to them, and is from thence naturally led to give them a name. When they fall in with the natural state of his own mind, he is very apt to overlook them altogether, and either gives them no name at all, or, if he gives them any, it is one which marks rather the subjection and restraint of the passion than the degree which it still is allowed [341] to subsist in, after it is so subjected and restrained. Thus the common names of the [20] love of pleasure, and of the love of sex, denote a vicious and offensive degree of those passions. The words temperance and chastity, on the other hand, seem to mark rather the restraint and subjection which they are kept under, than the degree which they are still allowed to subsist in. When he can show, therefore, that they still subsist in some degree, he imagines, he has entirely demolished the reality of the virtues of temperance and chastity, and shown them to be mere impositions upon the inattention and simplicity of mankind. Those virtues, however, do not require an entire insensibility to the objects of the passions which they mean to govern. They only aim at restraining the violence of those passions so far as not to hurt the individual, and neither disturb nor offend the society.

20. Luxury and lust.

It is the great fallacy of Dr. Mandeville's book[a] to represent every passion as wholly vicious, which is so in any degree and in any direction. It is thus that he treats every thing as vanity which has any reference, either to what are, or to what ought to be the sentiments of others: and it is by means of this sophistry, that he establishes his favourite conclusion, that private vices are public benefits. If the love of magnificence, a taste for the elegant arts and improvements of human life, for whatever is agreeable in dress, furniture, or equipage, for architecture, statuary, painting, and music, is to be regarded as luxury, sensuality and ostentation, even in those whose situation allows, without any inconveniency, the indulgence [342] of those passions, it is certain that luxury, sensuality, and ostentation are public benefits: since, without the qualities upon which he thinks proper to bestow such opprobrious names, the arts of refinement could never find encouragement, and must languish for want of employment. Some popular ascetic doctrines which had been current before his time, and which placed virtue in the entire extirpation and annihilation of all our passions, were the real foundation of this licentious system. It was easy for Dr. Mandeville to prove, first, that this entire conquest never actually took place among men; and secondly, that, if it was to take place universally, it would be pernicious to society, by putting an end to all industry and commerce, and in a manner to the whole business of human life. By the first of these propositions he seemed to prove that there was no real virtue, and that what pretended to be such, was a mere cheat and imposition upon mankind; and by the second, that private vices were public benefits, since without them no society could prosper or flourish.

21. Fable of the Bees.

Such is the system of Dr. Mandeville, which once made so much noise in the world, and which, though perhaps, it never gave occasion to more vice than what would have been without it, at least taught that vice, which arose from other causes, to appear with more effrontery, and to avow the corruption of its motives with a profligate audaciousness which had never been heard of before.

But how destructive soever this system may appear, it could never have imposed upon so great a number of persons, nor have occasioned so general an alarm 343 among those who are the friends of better principles, had it not in some respects bordered upon the truth. A system of natural philosophy may appear very plausible, and be for a long time very generally received in the world, and yet have no foundation in nature, nor any sort of resemblance to the truth. The vortices of Des Cartes were regarded by a very ingenious nation, for near a century together, as a most satisfactory account of the revolutions of the heavenly bodies. Yet it has been demonstrated, to the conviction of all mankind, that these pretended causes of those wonderful effects, not only do not actually exist, but are utterly impossible, and if they did exist, could produce no such effects as are ascribed to them. But it is otherwise with systems of moral philosophy, and an author who pretends to account for the origin of our moral sentiments, cannot deceive us so grossly, nor depart so very far from all resemblance to the truth. When a traveller gives an account of some distant country, he may impose upon our credulity the most groundless and absurd fictions as the most certain matters of fact. But when a person pretends to inform us of what passes in our neighbourhood, and of the affairs of the very parish which we live in, though here too, if we are so careless as not to examine things with our own eyes, he may deceive us in many respects, yet the greatest falsehoods which he imposes upon us must bear some resemblance to the truth, and must even have a considerable mixture of truth in them. An author who treats of natural philosophy, and pretends to assign the causes of the great phenomena of the universe, pretends to give an account of the affairs of a very distant country, concerning which he may tell us what he pleases, and as long as his narration keeps within the bounds of seeming possibility, he need not 344 despair of gaining our belief. But when he proposes to explain the origin of our desires and affections, of our sentiments of approbation and disapprobation, he pretends to give an account, not only of the affairs of the very parish that we live in, but of our own domestic concerns. Though here too, like indolent masters who put their trust in a steward who deceives them, we are very liable to be imposed upon, yet we are incapable of passing any account which does not preserve some little regard to the truth. Some of the articles, at least, must be just, and even those which are most overcharged must have had some foundation, otherwise the fraud would be detected even by that careless inspection which we are disposed to give. The author who should assign, as the cause of any natural sentiment, some principle which neither had any connexion with it, nor resembled any other principle which had some such connexion, would appear absurd and ridiculous to the most injudicious and unexperienced reader.

SECTION III.
Of the different systems which have been formed concerning the principle of approbation.

INTRODUCTION.

After the inquiry concerning the nature of virtue, the next question of importance in Moral Philosophy, is concerning the principle of approbation, concerning the power or faculty of the mind which renders certain characters agreeable or disagreeable to us, makes us prefer one tenour of conduct to another, denominate the one right and the other wrong, and consider the one as the object of approbation, honour, and reward; the other as that of blame, censure, and punishment.

Three different accounts have been given of this principle of approbation. According to some, we approve and disapprove both of our own actions and of those of others, from self-love only, or from some view of their tendency to our own happiness or disadvantage; according to others, reason, the same faculty by which we distinguish between truth and falsehood, enables us to distinguish between what is fit and unfit both in actions and affections: according to others this distinction is altogether the effect of immediate sentiment and feeling, and arises from the satisfaction or disgust with which the view of certain actions or affections inspires us. Self-love, reason, and sentiment, therefore, are the three different sources which have been assigned for the principle of approbation.

Before I proceed to give an account of those different systems, I must observe, that the determination of this second question, though of the greatest importance in speculation, is of none in practice. The question concerning the nature of virtue necessarily has some influence upon our notions of right and wrong in many particular cases. That concerning the principle of approbation can possibly have no such effect. To examine from what contrivance or mechanism within, those different notions or sentiments arise, is a mere matter of philosophical curiosity.

CHAP. I.
Of those systems which deduce the principle of approbation from self-love.

Those who account for the principle of approbation from self-love, do not all account for it in the same manner, and there is a good deal of confusion and inaccuracy in all their different systems. According to Mr. Hobbes, and many of his followers,[aa] man is driven to take refuge in society, not by any natural love which he bears to his own kind, but because without the assistance of others he is incapable of subsisting with ease or safety. Society, upon this account, becomes necessary to him, and whatever tends to its support and welfare, he considers as having a remote tendency to his own interest, and, on the contrary, whatever is likely to disturb or destroy it, he regards as in some measure hurtful or pernicious to himself. Virtue is the great support, and vice the great disturber of human society. The former, therefore, is agreeable, and the latter offensive to every man; as from the one he foresees the prosperity, and from the other the ruin and disorder of what is so necessary for the comfort and security of his existence.

22. Puffendorff. Mandeville.

That the tendency of virtue to promote, and of vice to disturb the order of society, when we consider it coolly and philosophically, reflects a very great beauty upon the one, and a very great deformity upon the other, cannot, as I have observed upon a former occasion, be called in question. Human society, when we contemplate it in a certain abstract and philosophical light, appears like a great, an immense machine, whose regular and harmonious movements produce a thousand agreeable effects. As in any other beautiful and noble machine that was the production of human art, whatever tended to render its movements more smooth and easy, would derive a beauty from this effect, and, on the contrary, whatever tended to obstruct them would displease upon that account: so virtue, which is, as it were, the fine polish to the wheels of society, necessarily pleases; while vice, like the vile rust, which makes them jar and grate upon one another, is as necessarily offensive. This account, therefore, of the origin of approbation and disapprobation, so far as it derives them from a regard to the order of society, runs into 348 that principle which gives beauty to utility, and which I have explained upon a former occasion; and it is from thence that this system derives all that appearance of probability which it possesses. When those authors describe the innumerable advantages of a cultivated and social, above a savage and solitary life; when they expatiate upon the necessity of virtue and good order for the maintenance of the one, and demonstrate how infallibly the prevalence of vice and disobedience to the laws tend to bring back the other, the reader is charmed with the novelty and grandeur of those views which they open to him: he sees plainly a new beauty in virtue, and a new deformity in vice, which he had never taken notice of before, and is commonly so delighted with the discovery, that he seldom takes time to reflect, that this political view, having never occurred to him in his life before, cannot possibly be the ground of that approbation and disapprobation with which he has always been accustomed to consider those different qualities.

When those authors, on the other hand, deduce from self-love the interest which we take in the welfare of society, and the esteem which upon that account we bestow upon virtue, they do not mean, that when we in this age applaud the virtue of Cato, and detest the villainy of Catiline, our sentiments are influenced by the notion of any benefit we receive from the one, or of any detriment we suffer from the other. It was not because the prosperity or subversion of society, in those remote ages and nations, was apprehended to have any influence upon our happiness or misery in the present times; that according to those philosophers, we esteemed the virtuous, 349 and blamed the disorderly character. They never imagined that our sentiments were influenced by any benefit or damage which we supposed actually to redound to us, from either; but by that which might have redounded to us, had we lived in those distant ages and countries; or by that which might still redound to us, if in our own times we should meet with characters of the same kind. The idea, in short, which those authors were groping about, but which they were never able to unfold distinctly, was that indirect sympathy which we feel with the gratitude or resentment of those who received the benefit or suffered the damage resulting from such opposite characters: and it was this which they were indistinctly pointing at, when the said, that it was not the thought of what we had gained or suffered which prompted our applause or indignation, but the conception or imagination of what we might gain or suffer if we were to act in society with such associates.

Sympathy, however, cannot, in any sense, be regarded as a selfish principle. When I sympathize with your sorrow or your indignation, it may be pretended, indeed, that my emotion is founded in self-love, because it arises from bringing your case home to myself, from putting myself in your situation, and thence conceiving what I should feel in the like circumstances. But though sympathy is very properly said to arise from an imaginary change of situations with the person principally concerned, yet this imaginary change is not supposed to happen to me in my own person and character, but in that of the person with whom I sympathize. When I condole with you for the loss of your only son, in order to enter into your grief, I do not consider what I, a 350 person of such a character and profession, should suffer, if I had a son, and if that son was unfortunately to die: but I consider what I should suffer if I was really you, and I not only change circumstances with you, but I change persons and characters. My grief, therefore, is entirely upon your account, and not in the least upon my own. It is not, therefore, in the least selfish. How can that be regarded as a selfish passion, which does not arise even from the imagination of any thing that has befallen, or that relates to myself, in my own proper person and character, but which is entirely occupied about what relates to you? A man may sympathize with a woman in child-bed; though it is impossible that he should conceive himself as suffering her pains in his own proper person and character. That whole account of human nature, however, which deduces all sentiments and affections from self-love, which has made so much noise in the world, but which, so far as I know, has never yet been fully and distinctly explained, seems to me to have arisen from some confused misapprehension of the system of sympathy.

CHAP. II.
Of those systems which make reason the principle of approbation.

It is well known to have been the doctrine of Mr. Hobbes, that a state of nature, is a state of war; and that antecedent to the institution of civil government, there could be no safe or peaceable society among men. To preserve society, therefore, according 351 to him, was to support civil government, and to destroy civil government was the same thing as to put an end to society. But the existence of civil government depends upon the obedience that is paid to the supreme magistrate. The moment he loses his authority, all government is at an end. As self-preservation, therefore, teaches men to applaud whatever tends to promote the welfare of society, and to blame whatever is likely to hurt it; so the same principle, if they would think and speak consistently, ought to teach them to applaud upon all occasions obedience to the civil magistrate, and to blame all disobedience and rebellion. The very ideas of laudable and blameable, ought to be the same with those of obedience and disobedience. The laws of the civil magistrate, therefore, ought to be regarded as the sole ultimate standards of what was just and unjust, of what was right and wrong.

It was the avowed intention of Mr. Hobbes, by propagating these notions, to subject the consciences of men immediately to the civil, and not to the ecclesiastical powers, whose turbulence and ambition, he had been taught, by the example of his own times, to regard as the principal source of the disorders of society. His doctrine, upon this account, was peculiarly offensive to Theologians, who accordingly did not fail to vent their indignation against him with great asperity and bitterness. It was likewise offensive to all sound moralists, as it supposed that there was no natural distinction between right and wrong, that these were mutable and changeable, and depended upon the mere arbitrary will of the civil magistrate. This account of things, therefore, 352 was attacked from all quarters, and by all sorts of weapons, by sober reason as well as by furious declamation.

In order to confute so odious a doctrine, it was necessary to prove, that antecedent to all law or positive institution, the mind was naturally endowed with a faculty, by which it distinguished in certain actions and affections, the qualities of right, laudable, and virtuous, and in others those of wrong, blameable, and vicious.

Law, it was justly observed by Dr. Cudworth,[23] could not be the original source of those distinctions; since upon the supposition of such a law, it must either be right to obey it, and wrong to disobey it, or indifferent whether we obeyed it, or disobeyed it. That law which it was indifferent whether we obeyed or disobeyed, could not, it was evident, be the source of those distinctions; neither could that which it was right to obey and wrong to disobey, since even this still supposed the antecedent notions or ideas of right and wrong, and that obedience to the law was conformable to the idea of right, and disobedience to that of wrong.

23. Immutable Morality, l. 1.

Since the mind, therefore, had a notion of those distinctions antecedent to all law, it seemed necessarily to follow, that it derived this notion from reason, which pointed out the difference between right and wrong, in the same manner in which it did that between truth and falsehood: and this conclusion, which though true in some respects, is rather hasty 353 in others, was more easily received at a time when the abstract science of human nature was but in its infancy, and before the distinct offices and powers of the different faculties of the human mind had been carefully examined and distinguished from one another. When this controversy with Mr. Hobbes was carried on with the greatest warmth and keenness, no other faculty had been thought of from which any such ideas could possibly be supposed to arise. It became at this time, therefore, the popular doctrine, that the essence of virtue and vice did not consist in the conformity or disagreement of human actions with the law of a superior, but in their conformity or disagreement with reason which was thus considered as the original source and principle of approbation and disapprobation.

That virtue consists in conformity to reason, is true in some respects, and this faculty may very justly be considered, as in some sense, the source and principle of approbation and disapprobation, and of all solid judgments concerning right and wrong. It is by reason that we discover those general rules of justice by which we ought to regulate our actions and it is by the same faculty that we form those more vague and indeterminate ideas of what is prudent, of what is decent, of what is generous or noble, which we carry constantly about with us, and according to which we endeavour, as well as we can, to model the tenour of our conduct. The general maxims of morality are formed, like all other general maxims, from experience and induction. We observe in a great variety of particular cases what pleases or displeases our moral faculties, what these approve or disapprove of, and, by induction from this experience, 354 we establish those general rules. But induction is always regarded as one of the operations of reason. From reason, therefore, we are very properly said to derive all those general maxims and ideas. It is by these, however, that we regulate the greater part of our moral judgments, which would be extremely uncertain and precarious if they depended altogether upon what is liable to so many variations as immediate sentiment and feeling, which the different states of health and humour are capable of altering so essentially. As our most solid judgments, therefore, with regard to right and wrong, are regulated by maxims and ideas derived from an induction of reason, virtue may very properly be said to consist in a conformity to reason, and so far this faculty may be considered as the source and principle of approbation and disapprobation.

But though reason is undoubtedly the source of the general rules of morality, and of all the moral judgments which we form by means of them; it is altogether absurd and unintelligible to suppose that the first perceptions of right and wrong can be derived from reason, even in those particular cases upon the experience of which the general rules are formed. These first perceptions, as well all other experiments upon which any general rules are founded, cannot be the object of reason, but of immediate sense and feeling. It is by finding in a vast variety of instances that one tenour of conduct constantly pleases in a certain manner, and that another as constantly displeases the mind, that we form the general rules of morality. But reason cannot render any particular object either agreeable or disagreeable to the mind for its own sake. Reason may show that this object 355 is the means of obtaining some other which is naturally either pleasing or displeasing, and in this manner may render it either agreeable or disagreeable for the sake of something else. But nothing can be agreeable or disagreeable for its own sake, which is not rendered such by immediate sense and feeling. If virtue, therefore, in every particular instance, necessarily pleases for its own sake, and if vice as certainly displeases the mind, it cannot be reason, but immediate sense and feeling, which, in this manner, reconciles us to the one, and alienates us from the other.

Pleasure and pain are the great objects of desire and aversion: but these are distinguished not by reason, but by immediate sense and feeling. If virtue, therefore, is desirable for its own sake, and if vice is, in the same manner, the object of aversion, it cannot be reason which originally distinguishes those different qualities, but immediate sense and feeling.

As reason, however, in a certain sense, may justly be considered as the principle of approbation and disapprobation, these sentiments were, through inattention, long regarded as originally flowing from the operations of this faculty. Dr. Hutcheson had the merit of being the first who distinguished with any degree of precision in what respect all moral distinctions may be said to arise from reason, and in what respect they are founded upon immediate sense and feeling. In his illustrations upon the moral sense he has explained this so fully, and, in my opinion, so unanswerably, that, if any controversy is still kept up about this subject, I can impute it to nothing, 356 but either to inattention to what that gentleman has written, or to a superstitious attachment to certain forms of expression, a weakness not very uncommon among the learned, especially in subjects so deeply interesting as the present, in which a man of virtue is often loth to abandon, even the propriety of a single phrase which he has been accustomed to.

CHAP. III.
Of those systems which make sentiment the principle of approbation.

Those systems which make sentiment the principle of approbation may be divided into two different classes.

I. According to some the principle of approbation is founded upon a sentiment of a peculiar nature, upon a particular power of perception exerted by the mind at the view of certain actions or affections; some of which affecting this faculty in an agreeable and others in a disagreeable manner, the former are stampt with the characters of right, laudable, and virtuous; the latter with those of wrong, blameable and vicious. This sentiment being of a peculiar nature distinct from every other, and the effect of a particular power of perception, they give it a particular name, and call it a moral sense.

II. According to others, in order to account for the principle of approbation, there is no occasion for supposing any new power of perception which 357 had never been heard of before: Nature, they imagine, acts here, as in all other cases, with the strictest œconomy, and produces a multitude of effects from one and the same cause; and sympathy, a power which has always been taken notice of, and with which the mind is manifestly endowed, is, they think, sufficient to account for all the effects ascribed to this peculiar faculty.

I. Dr. Hutcheson[24] had been at great pains to prove that the principle of approbation was not founded on self-love. He had demonstrated too that it could not arise from any operation of reason. Nothing remained, he thought, but to suppose it a faculty of a peculiar kind, with which Nature had endowed the human mind, in order to produce this one particular and important effect. When self-love and reason were both excluded, it did not occur to him that there was any other known faculty of the mind which could in any respect answer this purpose.

24. Inquiry concerning Virtue.

This new power of perception he called a moral sense, and supposed it to be somewhat analogous to the external senses. As the bodies around us, by affecting these in a certain manner, appear to possess the different qualities of sound, taste, odour, colour; so the various affections of the human mind, by touching this particular faculty in a certain manner, appear to possess the different qualities of amiable and odious, of virtuous and vicious, of right and wrong.

The various senses or powers of perception,[25] from which the human mind derives all its simple ideas, 358 were, according to this system, of two different kinds, of which the one were called the direct or antecedent, the other, the reflex or consequent senses. The direct senses were those faculties from which the mind derived the perception of such species of things as did not presuppose the antecedent perception of any other. Thus sounds and colours were objects of the direct senses. To hear a sound or to see a colour does not presuppose the antecedent perception of any other quality or object. The reflex or consequent senses, on the other hand, were those faculties from which the mind derived the perception of such species of things as presupposed the antecedent perception of some other. Thus harmony and beauty were objects of the reflex senses. In order to perceive the harmony of a sound, or the beauty of a colour, we must first perceive the sound or the colour. The moral sense was considered as a faculty of this kind. That faculty, which M[r]

Locke calls reflection, and from which he derived the simple ideas of the different passions and emotions of the human mind, was, according to Dr. Hutcheson, a direct internal sense. That faculty again by which we perceived the beauty or deformity, the virtue or vice of those different passions and emotions, was a reflex, internal sense.

25. Treatise of the passions.

Dr. Hutcheson endeavoured still further to support this doctrine, by shewing that it was agreeable to the analogy of nature, and that the mind was endowed with a variety of other reflex senses exactly similar to the moral sense; such as a sense of beauty and deformity in external objects; a public sense, by which we sympathize with the happiness or misery of our [359] fellow-creatures; a sense of shame and honour, and a sense of ridicule.

But notwithstanding all the pains which this ingenious philosopher has taken to prove that the principle of approbation is founded in a peculiar power of perception, somewhat analogous to the external senses, there are some consequences, which he acknowledges to follow from this doctrine, that will, perhaps, be regarded by many as a sufficient confutation of it. The qualities, he allows,[26] which belong to the objects of any sense, cannot, without the greatest absurdity, be ascribed to the sense itself. Who ever thought of calling the sense of seeing black or white, the sense of hearing loud or low, or the sense of tasting sweet or bitter? And, according to him, it is equally absurd to call our moral faculties virtuous or vicious, morally good or evil. These qualities belong to the objects of those faculties, not to the faculties themselves. If any man, therefore, was so absurdly constituted as to approve of cruelty and injustice as the highest virtues, and to disapprove of equity and humanity as the most pitiful vices, such a constitution of mind might indeed be regarded as inconvenient both to the individual and to the society, and likewise as strange, surprising, and unnatural in itself; but it could not, without the greatest absurdity, be denominated vicious or morally evil.

26. Illustrations upon the Moral Sense. Sect. 1. p. 237, et seq. Third Edition.

Yet surely if we saw any man shouting with admiration and applause at a barbarous and unmerited execution, which some insolent tyrant had ordered, [360] we should not think we were guilty of any great absurdity in denominating this behaviour vicious and morally evil in the highest degree, though it expressed nothing but depraved moral faculties, or an absurd approbation of this horrid action, as of what was noble, magnanimous, and great. Our heart, I imagine, at the sight of such a spectator, would forget for a while its sympathy with the sufferer, and feel nothing but horror and detestation, at the thought of so execrable a wretch. We should abominate him even more than the tyrant who might be goaded on by the strong passions of jealousy, fear, and resentment, and upon that account be more excusable. But the sentiments of the spectator would appear altogether without cause or motive, and therefore most perfectly and completely detestable. There is no perversion of sentiment or affection which our heart would be more averse to enter into, or which it would reject with greater hatred and indignation than one of this kind; and so far from regarding such a constitution of mind as being merely something strange or inconvenient, and not in any respect vicious or morally evil, we should rather consider it as the very last and most dreadful stage of moral depravity.

Correct moral sentiments, on the contrary, naturally appear in some degree laudable and morally good. The man, whose censure and applause are upon all occasions suited with the greatest accuracy to the value or unworthiness of the object, seems to deserve a degree even of moral approbation. We admire the delicate precision of his moral sentiments: they lead our own judgments, and, upon account of their uncommon and surprising justness, they even excite our wonder and applause. We cannot indeed 361 be always sure that the conduct of such a person would be in any respect correspondent to the precision and accuracy of his judgments concerning the conduct of others. Virtue requires habit and resolution of mind, as well as delicacy of sentiment; and unfortunately the former qualities are sometimes wanting, where the latter is in the greatest perfection. This disposition of mind, however, though it may sometimes be attended with imperfections, is incompatible with any thing that is grossly criminal, and is the happiest foundation upon which the superstructure of perfect virtue can be built. There are many men who mean very well, and seriously purpose to do what they think their duty, who notwithstanding are disagreeable on account of the coarseness of their moral sentiments.

It may be said, perhaps, that though the principle of approbation is not founded upon any power of perception that is in any respect analogous to the external senses, it may still be founded upon a peculiar sentiment which answers this one particular purpose and no other. Approbation and disapprobation, it may be pretended, are certain feelings or emotions which arise in the mind upon the view of different characters and actions; and as resentment might be called a sense of injuries, or gratitude a sense of benefits, so these may very properly receive the name of a sense of right and wrong, or of a moral sense.

But this account of things, though it may not be liable to the same objections with the foregoing, is exposed to others which are equally unanswerable.

361 First of all, whatever variations any particular emotion may undergo, it still preserves the general features which distinguish it to be an emotion of such a kind, and these general features are always more striking and remarkable than any variation which it may undergo in particular cases. Thus anger is an emotion of a particular kind: and accordingly its general features are always more distinguishable than all the variations it undergoes in particular cases. Anger against a man, is, no doubt, somewhat different from anger against a woman, and that again from anger against a child. In each of those three cases, the general passion of anger receives a different modification from the particular character of its object, as may easily be observed by the attentive. But still the general features of the passion predominate in all these cases. To distinguish these, requires no nice observation: a very delicate attention, on the contrary, is necessary to discover their variations: every body takes notice of the former: scarce any body observes the latter. If approbation and disapprobation, therefore, were, like gratitude and resentment, emotions of a particular kind, distinct from every other, we should expect that in all the variations which either of them might undergo, it would still retain the general features which mark it to be an emotion of such a particular kind, clear, plain, and easily distinguishable. But in fact it happens quite otherwise. If we attend to what we really feel when upon different occasions we either approve or disapprove, we shall find that our emotion in one case is often totally different from that in another, and that no common features can possibly be discovered between them. Thus the approbation 363 with which we view a tender, delicate, and humane sentiment, is quite different from that with which we are struck by one that appears great, daring, and magnanimous. Our approbation of both may, upon different occasions, be perfect and entire; but we are softened by the one and we are elevated by the other, and there is no sort of resemblance between th

emotions which they excite in us. But, according to that system which I have been endeavouring to establish, this must necessarily be the case. As the emotions of the person whom we approve of, are, in those two cases, quite opposite to one another, and as our approbation arises from sympathy with those opposite emotions, what we feel upon the one occasion, can have no sort of resemblance to what we feel upon the other. But this could not happen if approbation consisted in a peculiar emotion which had nothing in common with the sentiments we approved of, but which arose at the view of those sentiments, like any other passion at the view of its proper object. The same thing holds true with regard to disapprobation. Our horror for cruelty has no sort of resemblance to our contempt for mean-spiritedness. It is quite a different species of discord which we feel at the view of those two different vices, between our minds and those of the person whose sentiments and behaviour we consider.

Secondly, I have already observed, that not only the different passions or affections of the human mind which are approved or disapproved of appear morally good or evil, but that proper and improper approbation appear, to our natural sentiments, to be stampt with the same characters. I would ask, 364 therefore, how it is, that, according to this system, we approve or disapprove of proper or improper approbation. To this question, there is, I imagine, but one reasonable answer, which can possibly be given. It must be said, that when the approbation with which our neighbour regards the conduct of a third person coincides with our own, we approve of his approbation, and consider it as, in some measure, morally good; and that on the contrary, when it does not coincide with our own sentiments, we disapprove of it, and consider it as, in some measure, morally evil. It must be allowed, therefore, that, at least in this one case, the coincidence or opposition of sentiments, between the observer and the person observed, constitutes moral approbation or disapprobation. And if it does so in this one case, I would ask, why not in every other? to what purpose imagine a new power of perception in order to account for those sentiments?

Against every account of the principle of approbation, which makes it depend upon a peculiar sentiment, distinct from every other, I would object; that it is strange that this sentiment, which Providence undoubtedly intended to be the governing principle of human nature, should hitherto have been so little taken notice of, as not to have got a name in any language. The word moral sense is of very late formation, and cannot yet be considered as making part of the English tongue. The word approbation has but within these few years been appropriated to denote peculiarly any thing of this kind. In propriety of language we approve of whatever is entirely to our satisfaction, of the form of a building, of the contrivance of a machine, of 365 the flavour of a dish of meat. The word conscience does not immediately denote any moral faculty by which we approve or disapprove. Conscience supposes, indeed, the existence of some such faculty, and properly signifies our consciousness of having acted agreeably or contrary to its directions. When love, hatred, joy, sorrow, gratitude, resentment, with so many other passions which are all supposed to be the subjects of this principle, have made themselves considerable enough to get titles to know them by, is it not surprising that the sovereign of them all should hitherto have been so little heeded, that, a few philosophers excepted, no body has yet thought it worth while to bestow a name upon it?

When we approve of any character or action, the sentiments which we feel, are, according to the foregoing system, derived from four sources, which are in some respects different from one another. First, we sympathize with the motives of the agent; secondly, we enter into the gratitude of those who receive the benefit of his actions; thirdly, we observe that his conduct has been agreeable to the general rules by which those two sympathies generally act; and, last of all, when we consider such actions as making part of a system of behaviour which tends to promote the happiness either of the individual or of the society, they appear to derive a beauty from this utility, not unlike that which we ascribe to any well contrived machine. After deducting, in any one particular case, all that must be acknowledged to proceed from some one or other of these four principles, I should be glad to know what remains, and I shall freely allow this overplus to be ascribed to a moral sense, or to any other peculiar faculty, 366 provided any body will ascertain precisely what this overplus is. It might be expected, perhaps, that if there was any such peculiar principle, such as this moral sense is supposed to be, we should feel it, in some particular cases, separated and detached from every other, as we often feel joy, sorrow, hope, and fear, pure and unmixed with any other emotion. This however, I imagine, cannot even be pretended. I have never heard any instance alleged in which this principle could be said to exert itself alone and unmixed with sympathy or antipathy, with gratitude or resentment, with the perception of the agreement or disagreement of any action to an established rule, or last of all with that general taste for beauty and order which is excited by inanimated as well as by animated objects.

II. There is another system which attempts to account for the origin of our moral sentiments from sympathy distinct from that which I have been endeavouring to establish. It is that which places virtue in utility, and accounts for the pleasure with which the spectator surveys the utility of any quality from sympathy with the happiness of those who are affected by it. This sympathy is different both from that by which we enter into the motives of the agent, and from that by which we go along with the gratitude of the persons who are benefited by his actions. It is the same principle with that by which we approve of a well contrived machine. But no machine can be the object of either of those two last mentioned sympathies. I have already, in the fourth part of this discourse, given some account of this system.

367

SECTION IV.
Of the manner in which different authors have treated of the practical rules of morality.

It was observed in the third part of this discourse, that the rules of justice are the only rules of morality which are precise and accurate; that those of all the other virtues are loose, vague, and indeterminate; that the first may be compared to the rules of grammar, the others to those which critics lay down for the attainment of what is sublime and elegant in composition, and which present us rather with a general idea of the perfection we ought to aim at, than afford us any certain and infallible directions for acquiring it.

As the different rules of morality admit such different degrees of accuracy, those authors who have endeavoured to collect and digest them into systems have done it in two different manners; and one set has followed thro' the whole that loose method to which they were naturally directed by the consideration of one species of virtues; while another has as universally endeavoured to introduce into their precepts that sort of accuracy of which only some of them are susceptible. The first have wrote like critics, the second like grammarians.

I. The first, among whom we may count all the ancient moralists, have contented themselves with describing in a general manner the different vices and virtues, and with pointing out the deformity and misery of the one disposition as well as the propriety and happiness of the other, but have not affected to lay down many precise rules that are to hold good unexceptionably in all particular cases. They have only endeavoured to ascertain, as far as language is capable of ascertaining, first, wherein consists the sentiment of the heart, upon which each particular virtue is founded, what sort of internal feeling or emotion it is which constitutes the essence of friendship, of humanity, of generosity, of justice, of magnanimity, and of all the other virtues, as well as of the vices which are opposed to them: and, secondly, What is the general way of acting, the ordinary tone and tenour of conduct to which each of those sentiments would direct us, or how it is that a friendly, a generous, a brave, a just, and a humane man, would, upon ordinary occasions, chuse to act.

To characterize the sentiment of the heart, upon which each particular virtue is founded, though it requires both a delicate and accurate pencil, is a talk, however, which may be executed with some degree of exactness. It is impossible, indeed, to express all the variations which each sentiment either does or ought to undergo, according to every possible variation of circumstances. They are endless, and language wants names to mark them by. The sentiment of friendship, for example, which we feel for an old man is different from that which we feel for a young: that which we entertain for an austere man different from that which we feel for one of softer and gentler manners: and that again from what we feel for one of gay vivacity and spirit. The friendship which we conceive for a man is different from that with which a woman affects us, even where there is no mixture of any grosser passion. What author could enumerate and ascertain these and all the other infinite varieties which this sentiment is capable of undergoing? But still the general sentiment of friendship and familiar attachment which is common to them all, may be ascertained with a sufficient degree of accuracy. The picture which is drawn of it, though it will always be in many respects incomplete, may, however, have such a resemblance as to make us know the original when we meet with it, and even distinguish it from other sentiments to which it has a considerable resemblance, such as good-will, respect, esteem, admiration.

To describe, in a general manner, what is the ordinary way of acting to which each virtue would prompt us, is still more easy. It is, indeed, scarce possible to describe the internal sentiment or emotion upon which it is founded, without doing something of this kind. It is impossible by language to express, if I may say so, the invisible features of all the different modifications of passion as they show themselves within. There is no other way of marking and distinguishing them from one another, but by describing the effects which they produce without, the alterations which they occasion in the countenance, in the air and external behaviour, the resolutions they suggest, the actions they prompt to. It is thus that Cicero, in the first book of his Offices, 370 endeavours to direct us to the practice of the four cardinal virtues, and that Aristotle in the practical parts of his Ethics, points out to us the different habits by which he would have us regulate our behaviour, such as liberality, magnificence, magnanimity, and even jocularity and good humour, qualities, which that indulgent philosopher has thought worthy of a place in the catalogue of the virtues, though the lightness of that approbation which we naturally bestow upon them, should not seem to entitle them to so venerable a name.

Such works present us with agreeable and lively pictures of manners. By the vivacity of their descriptions they inflame our natural love of virtue, and increase our abhorrence of vice: by the justness as well as delicacy of their observations they may often help both to correct and to ascertain our natural sentiments with regard to the propriety of conduct, and suggesting many nice and delicate attentions, form us to a more exact justness of behaviour, than what, without such instruction, we should have been apt to think of. In treating of the rules of morality, in this manner, consists the science which is properly called Ethics, a science, which though like criticism, it does not admit of the most accurate precision, is, however, both highly useful and agreeable. It is of all others the most susceptible of the embellishments of eloquence, and by means of them of bestowing, if that be possible, a new importance upon the smallest rules of duty. Its precepts, when thus dressed and adorned, are capable of producing upon the flexibility of youth, the noblest and most lasting impressions, and as they fall in with the natural magnanimity of that generous 371 age, they are able to inspire, for a time at least, the most heroic resolutions, and thus tend both to establish and confirm the best and most useful habits of which the mind of man is susceptible. Whatever precept and exhortation can do to animate us to the practice of virtue, is done by this science delivered in this manner.

II. The second set of moralists, among whom we may count all the casuists of the middle and latter ages of the christian church, as well as all those who in this and in the preceding century have treated of what is called natural jurisprudence, do not content themselves with characterizing in this general manner that tenour of conduct which they would recommend to us, but endeavour to lay down exact and precise rules for the direction of every circumstance of our behaviour. As justice is the only virtue with regard to which such exact rules can properly be given; it is this virtue, that has chiefly fallen under the consideration of those two different sets of writers. They treat of it, however, in a very different manner.

Those who write upon the principles of jurisprudence, consider only what the person to whom the obligation is due, ought to think himself entitled to exact by force; what every impartial spectator would approve of him for exacting, or what a judge or arbiter, to whom he had submitted his case, and who had undertaken to do him justice, ought to oblige the other person to suffer or to perform. The casuists, on the other hand, do not so much examine what it is, that might properly be exacted by force, as what it is, that the person who owes the obligation 372 ought to think himself bound to perform from the most sacred and scrupulous regard to the general rules of justice, and from the most conscientious dread, either of wronging his neighbour, or of violating the integrity of his own character. It is the end of jurisprudence to prescribe rules for the decisions of judges and arbiters. It is the end of casuistry to prescribe rules for the conduct of a good man. By observing all the rules of jurisprudence, supposing them ever so perfect, we should deserve nothing but to be free from external punishment. By observing those of casuistry supposing them such as they ought to be, we should be entitled to considerable praise by the exact and scrupulous delicacy of our behaviour.

It may frequently happen that a good man ought to think himself bound, from a sacred and conscientious regard to the general rules of justice to perform many things which it would be the highest injustice to extort from him, or for any judge or arbiter to impose on him by force. To give a trite example; a highwayman, by the fear of death, obliges a traveller to promise him a certain sum of money. Whether such a promise, extorted in this manner by unjust force, ought to be regarded as obligatory, is a question that has been very much debated.

If we consider it merely as a question of jurisprudence, the decision can admit of no doubt. It would be absurd to suppose that the highwayman can be entitled to use force to constrain the other to perform. To extort the promise was a crime which deserved the highest punishment, and to extort the performance would only be adding a new crime to [373] the former. He can complain of no injury who has been only deceived by the person by whom he might justly have been killed. To suppose that a judge ought to enforce the obligation of such promises, or that the magistrate ought to allow them to sustain an action at law, would be the most ridiculous of all absurdities. If we consider this question, therefore, as a question of jurisprudence, we can be at no loss about the decision.

But if we consider it as a question of casuistry, it will not be so easily determined. Whether a good man, from a conscientious regard to that most sacred rule of justice, which commands the observance of all serious promises, would not think himself bound to perform, is at least much more doubtful. That no regard is due to the disappointment of the wretch who brings him into this situation, that no injury is done to the robber, and consequently that nothing can be extorted by force, will admit of no sort of dispute. But whether some regard is not, in this case, due to his own dignity and honour, to the inviolable sacredness of that part of his character which makes him reverence the law of truth, and abhor every thing that approaches to treachery and falsehood, may, perhaps, more reasonably be made a question. The casuists accordingly are greatly divided about it. One party, with whom we may count Cicero among the ancients, among the moderns, Puffendorf, Barbeyrac his commentator, and above all the late Dr. Hutcheson, one who in most cases was by no means a loose casuist, determine, without any hesitation, that no sort of regard is due to any such promise, and that to think otherwise is [374] mere weakness and superstition. Another party, among whom we may reckon [z] some of the ancient fathers of the church, as well as some very eminent modern casuists, have been of another opinion, and have judged all such promises obligatory.

z. St. Augustine, la Placette.

If we consider the matter according to the common sentiments of mankind, we shall find that some regard would be thought due even to a promise of this kind; but that it is impossible to determine how much, by any general rule that will apply to all cases without exception. The man who was quite frank and easy in making promises of this kind, and who violated them with as little ceremony, we should not choose for our friend and companion. A gentleman who should promise a highwayman five pounds and not perform, would incur some blame. If the sum promised, however, was very great, it might be more doubtful, what was proper to be done. If it was such, for example, that the payment of it would entirely ruin the family of the promiser, if it was so great as to be sufficient for promoting the most useful purposes, it would appear in some measure criminal, at least extremely improper, to throw it, for the sake of a punctilio, into such worthless hands. The man who should beggar himself, or who should throw away an hundred thousand pounds, though he could afford that vast sum, for the sake of observing such a parole with a thief, would appear to the common sense of mankind, absurd and extravagant in the highest degree. Such profusion would seem inconsistent with his duty, with what he owed both to himself and 375 others, and what, therefore, regard, to a promise extorted in this manner, could by no means authorize. To fix, however, by any precise rule, what degree of regard ought to be paid to it, or what might be the greatest sum which could be due from it, is evidently impossible. This would vary according to the characters of the persons, according to their circumstances, according to the solemnity of the promise, and even according to the incidents of the rencounter: and if the promiser had been treated with a great deal of that sort of gallantry, which is sometimes to be met with in persons of the most abandoned characters, more would seem due than upon other occasions. It may be said in general, that exact propriety requires the observance of all such promises, whenever it is not inconsistent with some other duties that are more sacred; such as regard to the public interest, to those whom gratitude, whom natural affection, or whom the laws of proper beneficence should prompt us to provide for. But, as was formerly taken notice of, we have no precise rules to determine what external actions are due from a regard to such motives, nor, consequently, when it is that those virtues are inconsistent with the observance of such promises.

It is to be observed, however, that whenever such promises are violated, though for the most necessary reasons, it is always with some degree of dishonour to the person who made them. After they are made, we may be convinced of the impropriety of observing them. But still there is some fault in having made them. It is at least a departure from the highest and noblest maxims of magnanimity and honour. 376 A brave man ought to die, rather than make a promise which he can neither keep without folly, nor violate without ignominy. For some degree of ignominy always attends a situation of this kind. Treachery and falsehood are vices so dangerous, so dreadful, and, at the same time, such as may so easily, and, upon many occasions, so safely be indulged, that we are more jealous of them than of almost any other. Our imagination therefore attaches the idea of shame to all violations of faith, in every circumstance and in every situation. They resemble, in this respect, the violations of chastity in the fair sex, a virtue of which, for the like reasons, we are excessively jealous; and our sentiments are not more delicate with regard to the one than with regard to the other. Breach of chastity dishonours irretrievably. No circumstances, no solicitation can excuse it; no sorrow, no repentance atone for it. We are so nice in this respect that even a rape dishonours, and the innocence of the mind cannot in our imagination, wash out the pollution of the body. It is the same case with the violation of faith, when it has been solemnly pledged, even to the most worthless of mankind. Fidelity is so necessary a virtue, that we apprehend it in general to be due even to those to whom nothing else is due, and whom we think it lawful to kill and destroy. It is to no purpose that the person who has been guilty of the breach of it, urges that he promised in order to save his life, and that he broke his promise because it was inconsistent with some other respectable duty to keep it. These circumstances may alleviate, but cannot entirely wipe out his dishonour. He appears to have been guilty of an action with which, in the imaginations of men, some degree of shame is inseparably connected. He 377 has broke a promise which he had solemnly averred he would maintain and his character, if not irretrievably stained and polluted, has at least a ridicule affixed to it, which it will be very difficult entirely to efface; and no man, I imagine, who had gone through an adventure of this kind, would be fond of telling the story.

This instance may serve to show wherein consists the difference between casuistry and jurisprudence, even when both of them consider the obligations of the general rules of justice.

But though this difference be real and essential, though those two sciences propose quite different ends, the sameness of the subject has made such a similarity between them, that the greater part of authors whose professed design was to treat of jurisprudence, have determined the different questions they examine, sometimes according to the principles of that science, and sometimes according to those of casuistry, without distinguishing, and, perhaps, without being themselves aware when they did the one, and when the other.

The doctrine of the casuists, however, is by no means confined to the consideration of what a conscientious regard to the general rules of justice, would demand of us. It embraces many other parts of Christian and moral duty. What seems principally to have given occasion to the cultivation of this species of science was the custom of auricular confession, introduced by the Roman Catholic superstition, in times of barbarism and ignorance. By that institution, the most secret actions, and even the thoughts of every person, which could be suspected of receding in the smallest degree from the rules of Christian purity, were to be revealed to the confessor. The confessor informed his penitents whether, and in what respect they had violated their duty, and what penance it behoved them to undergo, before he could absolve them in the name of the offended Deity.

The consciousness, or even the suspicion of having done wrong, is a load upon every mind, and is accompanied with anxiety and terror in all those who are not hardened by long habits of iniquity. Men, in this, as in all other distresses, are naturally eager to disburthen themselves of the oppression which they feel upon their thoughts, by unbosoming the agony of their mind to some person whose secrecy and discretion they can confide in. The shame, which they suffer from this acknowledgment, is fully compensated by that alleviation of their uneasiness which the sympathy of their confident seldom fails to occasion. It relieves them to find that they are not altogether unworthy of regard, and that however their past conduct may be censured, their present disposition is at least approved of, and is perhaps sufficient to compensate the other, at least to maintain them in some degree of esteem with their friend. A numerous and artful clergy had, in those times of superstition, insinuated themselves into the confidence of almost every private family. They possessed all the little learning which the times could afford, and their manners, though in many respects rude and disorderly, were polished and regular compared with those of the age they lived in. They were regarded, therefore, not only as the great directors of all religious, but of all moral duties. Their familiarity gave reputation to whoever was so happy as to possess it, and every mark of their disapprobation stamped the deepest ignominy upon all who had the misfortune to fall under it. Being considered as the great judges of right and wrong, they were naturally consulted about all scruples that occurred, and it was reputable for any person to have it known that he made those holy men the confidents of all such secrets, and took no important or delicate step in his conduct without their advice and approbation. It was not difficult for the clergy, therefore, to get it established as a general rule, that they should be entrusted with what it had already become fashionable to entrust them, and with what they generally would have been entrusted though no such rule had been established. To qualify themselves for confessors became thus a necessary part of the study of churchmen and divines, and they were thence led to collect what are called cases of conscience, nice and delicate situations, in which it is hard to determine whereabouts the propriety of conduct may lie. Such works, they imagined, might be of use both to the directors of consciences and to those who were to be directed; and hence the origin of books of casuistry.

The moral duties which fell under the consideration of the casuists were chiefly those which can, in some measure at least, be circumscribed within general rules, and of which the violation is naturally attended with some degree of remorse and some dread of suffering punishment. The design of that institution which gave occasion to their works, was to appease those terrors of conscience which attend upon 380 the infringement of such duties. But it is not every virtue of which the defect is accompanied with any very severe compunctions of this kind, and no man applies to his confessor for absolution, because he did not perform the most generous, the most friendly, or the most magnanimous action which, in his circumstances, it was possible to perform. In failures of this kind, the rule that is violated is commonly not very determinate, and is generally of such a nature too, that though the observance of it might entitle to honour and reward, the violation seems to expose to no positive blame, censure, or punishment. The exercise of such virtues the casuists seem to have regarded as a sort of works of supererogation, which could not be very strictly enacted, and which it was therefore unnecessary for them to treat of.

The breaches of moral duty, therefore, which came before the tribunal of the confessor, and upon that account fell under the cognizance of the casuists, were chiefly of three different kinds.

First and principally, breaches of the rules of justice. The rules here are all express and positive, and the violation of them is naturally attended with the consciousness of deserving, and the dread of suffering punishment both from God and man.

Secondly, breaches of the rules of chastity. These in all grosser instances are real breaches of the rules of justice, and no person can be guilty of them without doing the most unpardonable injury to some other. In smaller instances, when they amount only to a violation of those exact decorums which ought 381 to be observed in the conversation of the two sexes, they cannot indeed justly be considered as violations of the rules of justice. They are generally, however, violations of a pretty plain rule, and, at least in one of the sexes, tend to bring ignominy upon the person who has been guilty of them, and consequently to be attended in the scrupulous with some degree of shame and contrition of mind.

Thirdly, breaches of the rules of veracity. The violation of truth, it is to be observed, is not always a breach of justice, though it is so upon many occasions, and consequently cannot always expose to any external punishment. The vice of common lying, though a most miserable meanness, may frequently do hurt to no person, and in this case no claim of vengeance or satisfaction can be due either to the persons imposed upon, or to others. But though the violation of truth is not always a breach of justice, it is always a breach of a very plain rule, and what naturally tends to cover with shame the person who has been guilty of it. The great pleasure of conversation, and indeed of society, arises from a certain correspondence of sentiments and opinions, from a certain harmony of minds, which like so many musical instruments coincide and keep time with one another. But this most delightful harmony cannot be obtained unless there is a free communication of sentiments and opinions. We all desire, upon this account, to feel how each other is affected, to penetrate into each other's bosoms, and to observe the sentiments and affections which really subsist there. The man who indulges us in this natural passion, who invites us into his heart, who, as it were, sets open the gates of his breast to us, seems to exercise [382] a species of hospitality more delightful than any other. No man, who is in ordinary good temper, can fail of pleasing, if he has the courage to utter his real sentiments as he feels them, and because he feels them. It is this unreserved sincerity which renders even the prattle of a child agreeable. How weak and imperfect soever the views of the open-hearted, we take pleasure to enter into them, and endeavour, as much as we can, to bring down our own understanding to the level of their capacities, and to regard every subject in the particular light in which they appear to have considered it. This passion to discover the real sentiments of others is naturally so strong, that it often degenerates into a troublesome and impertinent curiosity to pry into those secrets of our neighbours which they have very justifiable reasons for concealing, and, upon many occasions, it requires prudence and a strong sense of propriety to govern this, as well as all the other passions of human nature, and to reduce it to that pitch which any impartial spectator can approve of. To disappoint this curiosity, however, when it is kept within proper bounds, and aims at nothing which there can be any just reason for concealing, is equally disagreeable in its turn. The man who eludes our most innocent questions, who gives no satisfaction to our most inoffensive inquiries, who plainly wraps himself up in impenetrable obscurity, seems, as it were, to build a wall about his breast. We run forward to get within it, with all the eagerness of harmless curiosity, and feel ourselves all at once pushed back with the rudest and most offensive violence. If to conceal is so disagreeable, to attempt to deceive us is still more disgusting, even though we could possibly suffer nothing by the success of the fraud. If we see that our [383] companion wants to impose upon us, if the sentiments and opinions which he utters appear evidently not to be his own, let them be ever so fine, we can derive no sort of entertainment from them; and if something of human nature did not now and then transpire through all the covers which falsehood and affectation are capable of wrapping around it, a puppet of wood would be altogether as pleasant a companion as a person who never spoke as he was affected. No man ever deceives, with regard to the most insignificant matters, who is not conscious of doing something like an injury to those he converses with; and who does not inwardly blush and shrink back with shame and confusion even at the secret thought of a detection. Breach of veracity, therefore, being always attended with some degree of remorse and self-condemnation, naturally fell under the cognizance of the casuists.

The chief subjects of the works of the casuists, therefore, were the conscientious regard that is due to the rules of justice; how far we ought to respect the life and property of our neighbour; the duty of restitution; the laws of chastity and modesty, and wherein consisted what, in their language, are called the sins of concupiscence: the rules of veracity, and the obligation of oaths, promises, and contracts of all kinds.

It may be said in general of the works of the casuists that they attempted, to no purpose, to direct by precise rules what belongs to feeling and sentiment only to judge of. How is it possible to ascertain by rules the exact point at which, in every case, a delicate sense of justice begins to run into a frivolous and [384] weak scrupulosity of conscience? When it is that secrecy and reserve begin to grow into dissimulation? How far an agreeable irony may be carried, and at what precise point it begins to degenerate into a detestable lie? What is the highest pitch of freedom and ease of behaviour which can be regarded as graceful and becoming, and when it is that it first begins to run into a negligent and thoughtless licentiousness? With regard to all such matters, what would hold good in any one case would scarce do so exactly in any other, and what constitutes the propriety and happiness of behaviour varies in every case with the smallest variety of situation. Books of casuistry, therefore, are generally as useless as they are commonly tiresome. They could be of little use to one who should consult them upon occasion, even supposing their decisions to be just; because, notwithstanding the multitude of cases collected in them, yet upon account of the still greater variety of possible circumstances, it is a chance, if among all those cases there be found one exactly parallel to that under consideration. One, who is really anxious to do his duty, must be very weak, if he can imagine that he has much occasion for them; and with regard to one who is negligent of it, the style of those writings is not such as is likely to awaken him to more attention. None of them tend to animate us to what is generous and noble. None of them tend to soften us to what is gentle and humane. Many of them, on the contrary, tend rather to teach us to chicane with our own consciences, and by their vain subtilties serve to authorize innumerable evasive refinements with regard to the most essential articles of our duty. That frivolous accuracy which they attempted to introduce into subjects which do not admit of 385 it, almost necessarily betrayed them into those dangerous errors, and at the same time rendered their works dry and disagreeable, abounding in abstruse and metaphysical distinctions, but incapable of exciting in the heart any of those emotions which it is the principal use of books of morality to excite.

The two useful parts of moral philosophy, therefore, are Ethics and Jurisprudence: casuistry ought to be rejected altogether, and the ancient moralists appear to have judged much better, who, in treating of the same subjects, did not affect any such nice exactness, but contented themselves with describing, in a general manner, what is the sentiment upon which justice, modesty, and veracity are founded, and what is the ordinary way of acting to which those virtues would commonly prompt us.

Something, indeed, not unlike the doctrine of the casuists, seems to have been attempted by several philosophers. There is something of this kind in the third book of Cicero's Offices, where he endeavours like a casuist to give rules for our conduct in many nice cases, in which it is difficult to determine whereabouts the point of propriety may lie. It appears too, from many passages in the same book, that several other philosophers had attempted something of the same kind before him. Neither he nor they, however, appear to have aimed at giving a complete system of this sort, but only meant to show how situations may occur, in which it is doubtful, whether the highest propriety of conduct consists in observing or in receding from what, in ordinary cases, are the rules of duty.

386 Every system of positive law may be regarded as a more or less imperfect attempt towards a system of natural jurisprudence, or towards an enumeration of the particular rules of justice. As the violation of justice is what men will never submit to from one another, the public magistrate is under a necessity of employing the power of the commonwealth to enforce the practice of this virtue. Without this precaution, civil society would become a scene of bloodshed and disorder, every man revenging himself at his own hand whenever he fancied he was injured. To prevent the confusion which would atten

upon every man's doing justice to himself, the magistrate, in all governments that have acquired any considerable authority, undertakes to do justice to all, and promises to hear and to redress every complaint of injury. In all well-governed states too, not only judges are appointed for determining the controversies of individuals, but rules are prescribed for regulating the decisions of those judges; and these rules are, in general, intended to coincide with those of natural justice. It does not, indeed, always happen that they do so in every instance. Sometimes what is called the constitution of the state, that is, the interest of the government; sometimes of the interest of particular orders of men who tyrannize the government, warp the positive laws of the country from what natural justice would prescribe. In some countries, the rudeness and barbarism of the people hinder the natural sentiments of justice from arriving at that accuracy and precision which, in more civilized nations, they naturally attain to. Their laws are, like their manners, gross and rude and undistinguishing. In other countries the unfortunate constitution of their courts of judicature hinders any regular system of jurisprudence from ever establishing itself among them, though the improved manners of the people may be such as would admit of the most accurate. In no country do the decisions of positive law coincide exactly, in every case, with the rules which the natural sense of justice would dictate. Systems of positive law, therefore, though they deserve the greatest authority, as the records of the sentiments of mankind in different ages and nations, yet can never be regarded as accurate systems of the rules of natural justice.

It might have been expected that the reasonings of lawyers, upon the different imperfections and improvements of the laws of different countries, should have given occasion to an inquiry into what were the natural rules of justice independent of all positive institution. It might have been expected that these reasonings should have led them to aim at establishing a system of what might properly be called natural jurisprudence, or a theory of the general principles which ought to run through and be the foundation of the laws of all nations. But tho' the reasonings of lawyers did produce something of this kind, and though no man has treated systematically of the laws of any particular country, without intermixing in his work many observations of this sort; it was very late in the world before any such general system was thought of, or before the philosophy of law was treated of by itself, and without regard to the particular institutions of any one nation. In none of the ancient moralists, do we find any attempt towards a particular enumeration of the rules of justice. Cicero in his Offices, and Aristotle in his Ethics, treat of justice in the same general manner in which they treat of all the other virtues. In the laws of Cicero and Plato, where we might naturally have expected some attempts towards an enumeration of those rules of natural equity, which ought to be enforced by the positive laws of every country, there is however, nothing of this kind. Their laws are laws of police, not of justice. Grotius seems to have been the first, who attempted to give the world any thing like a system of those principles which ought to run through, and be the foundation of the laws of all nations; and his treatise of the laws of war and peace, with all its imperfections, is perhaps at this day the most complete work that has yet been given upon this subject. I shall in another discourse endeavour to give an account of the general principles of law and government, and of the different revolutions they have undergone in the different ages and periods of society, not only in what concerns justice, but in what concerns police, revenue, and arms, and whatever else is the object of law. I shall not, therefore, at present enter into any further detail concerning the history of jurisprudence.

THE END.

CONSIDERATIONS
Concerning the FIRST
FORMATION of LANGUAGES,
AND THE
Different Genius of original and compounded LANGUAGES.

The assignation of particular names, to denote particular objects, that is, the institution of nouns substantive, would, probably, be one of the first steps towards the formation of language. Two savages, who had never been taught to speak, but had been bred up remote from the societies of men, would naturally begin to form that language by which they would endeavour to make their mutual wants intelligible to each other, by uttering certain sounds, whenever they meant to denote certain objects. Those objects only which were most familiar to them, and which they had most frequent occasion to mention, would have particular names assigned to them. The particular cave whose covering sheltered them from the weather, the particular tree whose fruit relieved their hunger, the particular fountain whose water allayed their thirst, would first be denoted by the words *cave, tree, fountain*, or by whatever other 390 appellations they might think proper, in that primitive jargon, to mark them. Afterwards, when the more enlarged experience of these savages had led them to observe, and their necessary occasions obliged them to make mention of, other caves, and other trees, and other fountains, they would naturally bestow, upon each of those new objects, the same name, by which they had been accustomed to express the similar object they were first acquainted with. The new objects had none of them any name of its own, but each of them exactly resembled another object, which had such an appellation. It was impossible that those savages could behold the new objects, without recollecting the old ones; and the name of the old ones to which the new bore so close a resemblance. When they had occasion, therefore, to mention, or to point out to each other, any of the new objects, they would naturally utter the name of the correspondent old one, of which the idea could not fail, at that instant, to present itself to their memory in the strongest and liveliest manner. And thus, those words, which were originally the proper names of individuals, would each of them insensibly become the common name of a multitude. A child that is just learning to speak calls every person who comes to the house its papa or its mama; and thus bestows upon the whole species those names which it had been taught to apply to two individuals. I have known a clown, who did not know the proper name of the river which ran by his own door. It was *the river*, he said, and he never heard any other name for it. His experience, seems, had not led him to observe any other river. The general word *river*, therefore, was, it is evident, in his acceptance of it, a proper name, signifying an individual object. If this [391]person had been carried to another river, would he not readily have called it a river? Could we suppose any person living on the banks of the Thames so ignorant, as not to know the general word *river*, but to be acquainted only with the particular word *Thames*, if he was brought to any other river, would he not readily call it a *Thames*? This, in reality, is no more than what they, who are well acquainted with the general word, are very apt to do. An Englishman, describing any great river which he may have seen in some foreign country, naturally says, that it is another Thames. The Spaniards, when they first arrived upon the coast of Mexico, and observed the wealth, populousness, and habitations of that fine country, so much superior to the savage nations which they had been visiting for some time before, cried out, that it was another Spain. Hence it was called New Spain; and this name has stuck to that unfortunate country ever since. We say, in the same manner, of a hero, that he is an Alexander; of an orator, that he is a Cicero; of a philosopher, that he is a Newton. This way of speaking, which the grammarians call an Antonomasia, and which is still extremely common, though now not at all necessary, demonstrates how much mankind are naturally disposed to give to one object the name of any other, which nearly resembles it, and thus to denominate a multitude, by what originally was intended to express an individual.

It is this application of the name of an individual to a great multitude of objects, whose resemblance naturally recalls the idea of that individual, and of the name which expresses it, that seems originally to have given occasion to the formation of those classes [392]and assortments, which, in the schools, are called genera and species, and of which the ingenious and eloquent M. Rousseau of Geneva[28], finds himself so much at a loss to account for the origin. What constitutes a species is merely a number of objects, bearing a certain degree of resemblance to one another, and on that account denominated by a single appellation, which may be applied to express any one of them.

28. Origine de l'Inegalité. Partie premiere, p. 376, 377, Edition d'Amsterdam, des Oeuvres diverses de J. J. Rousseau.

When the greater part of objects had thus been arranged under their proper classes and assortments, distinguished by such general names, it was impossible that the greater part of that almost infinite number of individuals, comprehended under each particular assortment or species, could have any peculiar or proper names of their own, distinct from the general name of the species. When there was occasion, therefore, to mention any particular object, it often became necessary to distinguish it from the other objects comprehended under the same general name, either, first, by its peculiar qualities; or, secondly, by the peculiar relation which it stood in to some other things. Hence the necessary origin of two other sets of words, of which the one should express quality; the other relation.

Nouns adjective are the words which express quality considered as qualifying, or, as the schoolmen say, in concrete with, some particular subject. Thus the word *green* expresses a certain quality considered as qualifying, or as in concrete with, the particular [393]subject to which it may be applied. Words of this kind, it is evident, may serve to distinguish particular objects from others comprehended under the same general appellation. The words *green tree*, for example, might serve to distinguish a particular tree from others that were withered or blasted.

Prepositions are the words which express relation considered, in the same manner, in concrete with the co-relative object. Thus the prepositions *of, to, for, with, by, above, below,* &c. denote some relation subsisting between the objects expressed by the words between which the prepositions are placed; and they denote that this relation is considered in concrete with the co-relative object. Words of this kind serve to distinguish particular objects from others of the same species, when those particular objects cannot be so properly marked out by any peculiar qualities of their own. When we say, *the green tree of the meadow,* for example, we distinguish a particular tree, not only by the quality which belongs to it, but by the relation which it stands in to another object.

As neither quality nor relation can exist in abstract, it is natural to suppose that the words which denote them considered in concrete, the way in which we always see them subsist, would be of much earlier invention, than those which express them considered in abstract, the way in which we never see them subsist. The words *green* and *blue* would, in all probability, be sooner invented than the words *greenness* and *blueness*; the words *above* and *below*, than the words *superiority* and *inferiority*. To invent words of the latter kind requires a much greater effort of 394 abstraction than to invent those of the former. It is probable, therefore, that such abstract terms would be of much later institution. Accordingly, their etymologies generally show that they are so, they being generally derived from others that are concrete.

But though the invention of nouns adjective be much more natural than that of the abstract nouns substantive derived from them, it would still, however, require a considerable degree of abstraction and generalization. Those, for example, who first invented the words, *green, blue, red,* and the other names of colours, must have observed and compared together a great number of objects, must have remarked their resemblances and dissimilitudes in respect of the quality of colour, and must have arranged them, in their own minds, into different classes and assortments, according to those resemblances and dissimilitudes. An adjective is by nature a general, and in some measure, an abstract word, and necessarily presupposes the idea of a certain species or assortment of things, to all of which it is equally applicable. The word *green* could not, as we were supposing might be the case of the word *cave*, have been originally the name of an individual, and afterwards have become, by what grammarians call an Antonomasia the name of a species. The word *green* denoting, not the name of a substance, but the peculiar quality of a substance, must from the very first have been a general word, and considered as equally applicable to any other substance possessed of the same quality The man who first distinguished a particular object by the epithet of *green*, must have observed other objects that were not *green*, from 395 which he meant to separate it by this appellation. The institution of this name, therefore, supposes comparison. It likewise supposes some degree of abstraction. The person who first invented this appellation must have distinguished the quality from the object to which it belonged, and must have conceived the object as capable of subsisting without the quality. The invention, therefore even of the simplest nouns adjective, must have required more metaphysics than we are apt to be aware of. The different mental operations, of arrangement or classing, or comparison, and of abstraction, must all have been employed, before even the names of the different colours, the least metaphysical of all nouns adjective, could be instituted. From all which I infer, that when languages were beginning to be formed, nouns adjective would by no means be the words of the earliest invention.

There is another expedient for denoting the different qualities of different substances, which as it requires no abstraction, nor any conceived separation of the quality from the subject, seems more natural than the invention of nouns adjective, and which, upon this account, could hardly fail, in the first formation of language, to be thought of before them. This expedient is to make some variation upon the noun substantive itself, according to the different qualities which it is endowed with. Thus, in many languages, the qualities both of sex and of the want of sex, are expressed by different terminations in the nouns substantive, which denote objects so qualified. In Latin, for example, *lupus, lupa; equus, equa; juvencus, juvenca; Julius, Julia; Lucretius, Lucretia,* &c. denote the qualities of male and female in the animals and persons to whom such appellations belong, without needing the addition of any adjective for this purpose. On the other hand, the words *forum, pratum, plaustrum,* denote by their peculiar termination the total absence of sex in the different substances which they stand for. Both sex, and the want of all sex, being naturally considered as qualities modifying and inseparable from the particular substances to which they belong, it was natural to express them rather by a modification in the noun substantive, than by any general and abstract word expressive of this particular species of quality. The expression bears, it is evident, in this way, a much more exact analogy to the idea or object which it denotes, than in the other. The quality appears, in nature, as a modification of the substance, and as it is thus expressed, in language, by a modification of the noun substantive, which denotes that substance, the quality and the subject are, in this case, blended together, if I may say so, in the expression, in the same manner, as they appear to be in the object and in the idea. Hence the origin of the masculine, feminine, and neutral genders, in all the ancient languages. By means of these, the most important of all distinctions, that of substances into animated and inanimated, and that of animals into male and female, seem to have been sufficiently marked without the assistance of adjectives, or of any general names denoting this most extensive species of qualifications.

There are no more than these three genders in any of the languages with which I am acquainted; that is to say, the formation of nouns substantive, can, by itself, and without the accompaniment of adjectives, express no other qualities but those three above-mentioned, the qualities of male, of female, of neither male nor female. I should not, however, be surprised, if, in other languages with which I am unacquainted, the different formations of nouns substantive should be capable of expressing many other different qualities. The different diminutives of the Italian, and of some other languages, do, in reality, sometimes, express a great variety of different modifications in the substances denoted by those nouns which undergo such variations.

It was impossible, however, that nouns substantive could, without losing altogether their original form, undergo so great a number of variations, as would be sufficient to express that almost infinite variety of qualities, by which it might, upon different occasions, be necessary to specify and distinguish them. Though the different formation of nouns substantive, therefore, might, for some time, forestall the necessity of inventing nouns adjective, it was impossible that this necessity could be forestalled altogether. When nouns adjective came to be invented, it was natural that they should be formed with some similarity to the substantives, to which they were to serve as epithets or qualifications. Men would naturally give them the same terminations with the substantives to which they were first applied, and from that love of similarity of sound, from that delight in the returns of the same syllables, which is in the foundation of analogy in all languages, they would be apt to vary the termination of the same adjective, according as they had occasion to apply it to a masculine, to a feminine, or to a neutral substantive. 398 They would say, *magnus lupus, magna lupa, magnum pratum*, when they meant to express a great he wolf, a great *she wolf*, a great *meadow*.

This variation, in the termination of the noun adjective, according to the gender of the substantive, which takes place in all the ancient languages, seems to have been introduced chiefly for the sake of a certain similarity of sound, of a certain species of rhyme, which is naturally so very agreeable to the human ear. Gender, it is to be observed, cannot properly belong to a noun adjective, the signification of which is always precisely the same, to whatever species of substantives it is applied. When we say, *a great man, a great woman*, the word *great* has precisely the same meaning in both cases, and the difference of the sex in the subjects to which it may be applied, makes no sort of difference in its signification. *Magnus, magna, magnum*, in the same manner, are words which express precisely the same quality, and the change of the termination is accompanied with no sort of variation in the meaning. Sex and gender are qualities which belong to substances, but cannot belong to the qualities of substances. In general, no quality, when considered in concrete, or as qualifying some particular subject, can itself be conceived as the subject of any other quality; though when considered in abstract it may. No adjective therefore can qualify any other adjective. A *great good man*, means a man who is both *great* and *good*. Both the adjectives qualify the substantive; they do not qualify one another. On the other hand, when we say, the *great goodness* of the man, the word *goodness* denoting a quality considered in abstract, which may itself be the subject of other qualities, is upon that 399 account capable of being qualified by the word, *great*.

If the original invention of nouns adjective would be attended with so much difficulty, that of prepositions would be accompanied with yet more. Every preposition, as I have already observed, denotes some relation considered in concrete with the co-relative object. The preposition *above*, for example, denotes the relation of superiority, not in abstract, as it is expressed by the word *superiority*, but in concrete with some co-relative object. In this phrase, for example, *the tree above the cave*, the word *above*, expresses a certain relation between the *tree* and the *cave*, and it expresses this relation in concrete with the co-relative object, the *cave*. A preposition always requires, in order to complete the sense, some other word to come after it; as may be observed in this particular instance. Now, I say, the original invention of such words would require a yet greater effort o abstraction and generalization, than that of nouns adjective. First of all, a relation is, in itself, a more metaphysical object than a quality. Nobody can be at a loss to explain wha is meant by a quality; but few people will find themselves able to express, very distinctly what is understood by a relation. Qualities are almost always the objects of our externa senses; relations never are. No wonder, therefore, that the one set of objects should be s much more comprehensible than the other. Secondly, though prepositions always expres the relation which they stand for, in concrete with the co-relative object, they could no have originally been formed without a considerable effort of abstraction. A prepositio denotes a relation, and nothing but a relation. 400 But before men could institute a wor which signified a relation, and nothing but a relation, they must have been able, in some measure, to consider this relation abstractedly from the related objects; since the idea of those objects does not, in any respect, enter into the signification of the preposition. The invention of such a word, therefore, must have required a considerable degree of abstraction. Thirdly, a preposition is from its nature a general word, which, from its very first institution, must have been considered as equally applicable to denote any other similar relation. The man who first invented the word *above*, must not only have distinguished, in some measure, the relation of *superiority* from the objects which were so related, but he must also have distinguished this relation from other relations, such as, from the relation of *inferiority* denoted by the word *below*, from the relation of *juxtaposition*, expressed by the word *beside*, and the like. He must have conceived this word, therefore, as expressive of a particular sort or species of relation distinct from every other, which could not be done without a considerable effort of comparison and generalization.

Whatever were the difficulties, therefore, which embarrassed the first invention of nouns adjective, the same, and many more, must have embarrassed that of prepositions. If mankind, therefore, in the first formation of languages, seem to have, for some time, evaded the necessity of nouns adjective, by varying the termination of the names of substances, according as these varied in some of their most important qualities, they would much more find themselves under the necessity of evading, by some similar contrivance, the yet more difficult invention of prepositions. The different cases in the ancient languages is a contrivance of precisely the same kind. The genitive and dative cases, in Greek and Latin, evidently supply the place of the prepositions; and by a variation in the noun substantive, which stands for the co-relative term, express the relation which subsists between what is denoted by that noun substantive, and what is expressed by some other word in the sentence. In these expressions, for example, *fructus arboris*, *the fruit of the tree*; *sacer Herculi*, *sacred to Hercules*; the variations made in the co-relative words, *arbor* and *Hercules*, express the same relations which are expressed in English by the prepositions *of* and *to*.

To express a relation in this manner, did not require any effort of abstraction. It was not here expressed by a peculiar word denoting relation and nothing but relation, but by a variation upon the co-relative term. It was expressed here, as it appears in nature, not as something separated and detached, but as thoroughly mixed and blended with the co-relative object.

To express relation in this manner, did not require any effort of generalization. The words *arboris* and *Herculi*, while they involve in their signification the same relation expressed by the English prepositions *of* and *to*, are not, like those prepositions, general words, which can be applied to express the same relation between whatever other objects it might be observed to subsist.

To express relation in this manner did not require any effort of comparison. The words *arboris* and *Herculi* are not general words intended to denote a particular species of relations which the inventors of those expressions meant, in consequence of some sort of comparison, to separate and distinguish from every other sort of relation. The example, indeed, of this contrivance would soon probably be followed, and whoever had occasion to express a similar relation between any other objects would be very apt to do it by making a similar variation on the name of the co-relative object. This, I say, would probably, or rather certainly happen; but it would happen without any intention or foresight in those who first set the example, and who never meant to establish any general rule. The general rule would establish itself insensibly, and by slow degrees, in consequence of that love of analogy and similarity of sound, which is the foundation of by far the greater part of the rules of grammar.

To express relation therefore, by a variation in the name of the co-relative object, requiring neither abstraction, nor generalization, nor comparison of any kind, would, at first, be much more natural and easy, than to express it by those general words called prepositions, of which the first invention must have demanded some degree of all those operations.

The number of cases is different in different languages. There are five in the Greek, six in the Latin, and there are said to be ten in the Armenian language. It must have naturally happened that there should be a greater or a smaller number of cases, according as in the terminations of nouns substantive the first formers of any language happened to have established a greater or a smaller number of 403 variations, in order to express the different relations they had occasion to take notice of, before the invention of those more general and abstract prepositions which could supply their place.

It is, perhaps, worth while to observe that those prepositions, which in modern languages hold the place of the ancient cases, are, of all others, the most general, and abstract, and metaphysical; and of consequence, would probably be the last invented. Ask any man of common acuteness, What relation is expressed by the preposition *above*? He will readily answer, that of *superiority*. By the preposition *below*? He will as quickly reply, that of *inferiority*. But ask him, what relation is expressed by the preposition *of*, and, if he has not beforehand employed his thoughts a good deal upon these subjects, you may safely allow him a week to consider of his answer. The prepositions *above* and *below* do not denote any of the relations expressed by the cases in the ancient languages. But the preposition *of*, denotes the same relation, which is in them expressed by the genitive case; and which, it is easy to observe, is of a very metaphysical nature. The preposition of, denotes relation in general, considered in concrete with the co-relative object. It marks that the noun substantive which goes before it, is somehow or other related to that which comes after it, but without in any respect ascertaining, as is done by the preposition *above*, what is the peculiar nature of that relation. We often apply it, therefore, to express the most opposite relations; because, the most opposite relations agree so far that each of them comprehends in it the general idea or nature of a relation. We say, *the father of the son*, and *the son of the father*; the 404 *fir-trees of the forest*, and the *forest of the fir-trees*. The relation in which the father stands to the son, is, it is evident, a quite opposite relation to that in which the son stands to the father; that in which the parts stand to the whole, is quite opposite to that in which the whole stands to the parts. The word *of*, however, serves very well to denote all those relations, because in itself it denotes no particular relation, but only relation in general; and so far as any particular relation is collected from such expressions, it is inferred by the mind, not from the preposition itself, but from the nature and arrangement of the substantives, between which the preposition is placed.

What I have said concerning the preposition *of*, may in some measure be applied to the prepositions, *to, for, with, by*, and to whatever other prepositions are made use of in modern languages, to supply the place of the ancient cases. They all of them express ver abstract and metaphysical relations, which any man, who takes the trouble to try it, will find it extremely difficult to express by nouns substantive, in the same manner as we may express the relation denoted by the preposition *above*, by the noun substantive *superiority*. They all of them, however, express some specific relation, and are, consequently, none of them so abstract as the preposition *of*, which may be regarded as by far the most metaphysical of all prepositions. The prepositions therefore, which are capable of supplying the place of the ancient cases, being more abstract than the other prepositions, would naturally be of more difficult invention. The relations at the same time which those prepositions express, are, of all others, those which we have most frequent occasion to mention. [405]The prepositions *above, below, near, within, without, against*, &c. are much more rarely made use of, in modern languages, than the prepositions *of, to, for, with, from, by*. A preposition of the former kind will not occur twice in a page; we can scarce compose a single sentence without the assistance of one or two of the latter. If these latter prepositions, therefore, which supply the place of the cases, would be of such difficult invention on account of their abstractedness, some expedient, to supply their place, must have been of indispensable necessity, on account of the frequent occasion which men have to take notice of the relations which they denote. But there is no expedient so obvious, as that of varying the termination of one of the principal words.

It is, perhaps, unnecessary to observe, that there are some of the cases in the ancient languages, which, for particular reasons, cannot be represented by any prepositions. These are the nominative, accusative, and vocative cases. In those modern languages, which do not admit of any such variety in the terminations of their nouns substantive, the correspondent relations are expressed by the place of the words, and by the order and construction of the sentence.

As men have frequently occasion to make mention of multitudes as well as of single objects, it became necessary that they should have some method of expressing number. Number may be expressed either by a particular word, expressing number in general, such as the words *many, more*, &c. or by some variation upon the words which express the things numbered. It is this last expedient which [406]mankind would probably have recourse to, in the infancy of language. Number, considered in general, without relation to any particular set of objects numbered, is one of the most abstract and metaphysical ideas, which the mind of man is capable of forming; and, consequently, is not an idea, which would readily occur to rude mortals, who were just beginning to form a language. They would naturally, therefore, distinguish when they talked of a single, and when they talked of a multitude of objects, not by any metaphysical adjectives, such as the English, *a, an, many*, but by a variation upon the termination of the word which signified the objects numbered. Hence the origin of the singular and plural numbers, in all the ancient languages; and the same distinction has likewise been retained in all the modern languages, at least, in the greater part of words.

All primitive and uncompounded languages seem to have a dual, as well as a plural number. This is the case of the Greek, and I am told of the Hebrew, of the Gothic, and of many other languages. In the rude beginnings of society, *one, two*, and *more*, might possibly be all the numeral distinctions which mankind would have any occasion to take notice of. These they would find it more natural to express, by a variation upon every particular noun substantive, than by such general and abstract words as *one, two, three, four*, &c. These words, though custom has rendered them familiar to us, express, perhaps, the most subtile and refined abstractions, which the mind of man is capable of forming. Let any one consider within himself, for example, what he means |407| by the word *three*, which signifies neither three shillings, nor three pence, nor three men, nor three horses, but three in general; and he will easily satisfy himself that a word, which denotes so very metaphysical an abstraction, could not be either a very obvious or a very early invention. I have read of some savage nations, whose language was capable of expressing no more than the three first numeral distinctions. But whether it expressed those distinctions by three general words, or by variations upon the nouns substantive, denoting the things numbered, I do not remember to have met with any thing which could determine.

As all the same relations which subsist between single, may likewise subsist between numerous objects, it is evident there would be occasion for the same number of cases in the dual and in the plural, as in the singular number. Hence the intricacy and complexness of the declensions in all the ancient languages. In the Greek there are five cases in each of the three numbers, consequently fifteen in all.

As nouns adjective, in the ancient languages, varied their terminations according to the gender of the substantive to which they were applied, so did they likewise, according to the case and the number. Every noun adjective in the Greek language, therefore, having three genders, and three numbers, and five cases in each number, may be considered as having five and forty different variations. The first formers of language seem to have varied the termination of the adjective, according to the case and the number of the substantive, for the same reason |408| which made them vary according to the gender; the love of analogy, and of a certain regularity of sound. In the signification of adjectives there is neither case nor number, and the meaning of such words is always precisely the same, notwithstanding all the variety of termination under which they appear. *Magnus vir, magni viri, magnorum virorum; a great man, of a great man, of great men* in all these expressions the words *magnus, magni, magnorum*, as well as the word *great*, have precisely one and the same signification, though the substantives to which they are applied have not. The difference of termination in the noun adjective is accompanied with no sort of difference in the meaning. An adjective denotes the qualification of a noun substantive. But the different relations in which that noun substantive may occasionally stand, can make no sort of difference upon its qualification.

If the declensions of the ancient languages are so very complex, their conjugations are infinitely more so. And the complexness of the one is founded upon the same principle with that of the other, the difficulty of forming, in the beginnings of language, abstract and general terms.

Verbs must necessarily have been coeval with the very first attempts towards the formation of language. No affirmation can be expressed without the assistance of some verb. We never speak but in order to express our opinion that something either is or is not. But the word denoting this event, or this matter of fact, which is the subject of our affirmation, must always be a verb.

|409| Impersonal verbs, which express in one word a complete event, which preserve in the expression that perfect simplicity and unity, which there always is in the object and in the idea, and which suppose no abstraction, or metaphysical division of the event into its several constituent members of subject and attribute, would, in all probability, be the

species of verbs first invented. The verbs *pluit, it rains*; *ningit, it snows*; *tonat, it thunders*; *lucet, it is day*; *turbatur, there is a confusion*, &c. each of them express a complete affirmation, the whole of an event, with that perfect simplicity and unity with which the mind conceives it in nature. On the contrary, the phrases, *Alexander ambulat, Alexander walks*; *Petrus sedet, Peter sits*, divide the event, as it were, into two parts, the person or subject, and the attribute, or matter of fact, affirmed of that subject. But in nature, the idea or conception of Alexander walking, is as perfectly and completely one single conception, as that of Alexander not walking. The division of this event, therefore, into two parts, is altogether artificial, and is the effect of the imperfection of language, which, upon this, as upon many other occasions, supplies, by a number of words, the want of one, which could express at once the whole matter of fact that was meant to be affirmed. Every body must observe how much more simplicity there is in the natural expression, *pluit*, than in the more artificial expressions, *imber decidit, the rain falls*; or, *tempestas est pluvia, the weather is rainy*. In these two last expressions, the simple event, or matter of fact, is artificially split and divided, in the one, into two; in the other, into three parts. In each of them it is expressed by a sort of grammatical circumlocution, [410] of which the significancy is founded upon a certain metaphysical analysis of the component parts of the idea expressed by the word *pluit*. The first verbs, therefore, perhaps even the first words, made use of in the beginnings of language, would in all probability be such impersonal verbs. It is observed accordingly, I am told, by the Hebrew Grammarians, that the radical words of their language, from which all the others are derived, are all of them verbs, and impersonal verbs.

It is easy to conceive how, in the progress of language, those impersonal verbs should become personal. Let us suppose, for example, that the word *venit, it comes*, was originally an impersonal verb, and that it denoted, not the coming of something in general, as at present, but the coming of a particular object, such as *the Lion*. The first savage inventors of language, we shall suppose, when they observed the approach of this terrible animal, were accustomed to cry out to one another, *venit*, that is, *the lion comes*; and that this word thus expressed a complete event, without the assistance of any other. Afterwards, when, on the further progress of language, they had begun to give names to particular substances, whenever they observed the approach of any other terrible object, they would naturally join the name of that object to the word *venit*, and cry out, *venit ursus, venit lupus*. By degrees the word *venit* would thus come to signify the coming of any terrible object, and not merely the coming of the lion. It would now therefore, express, not the coming of a particular object, but the coming of an object of a particular kind. Having become more general in its signification, it could no longer represent [411] any particular distinct event by itself, and without the assistance of a noun substantive, which might serve to ascertain and determine its signification. It would now, therefore, have become a personal, instead of an impersonal verb. We may easily conceive how, in the further progress of society, it might still grow more general in its signification, and come to signify, as at present, the approach of any thing whatever, whether good, bad, or indifferent.

It is probably in some such manner as this, that almost all verbs have become personal, and that mankind have learned by degrees to split and divide almost every event into a great number of metaphysical parts, expressed by the different parts of speech, variously combined in the different members of every phrase and sentence.[20] The same sort of progress seems to have been made in the art of speaking as in the art of writing. When mankind first began to attempt to express their ideas by writing, every character represented a whole word. But the number of words being almost infinite, the memory found itself quite loaded and oppressed by the multitude of 412 characters which it was obliged to retain. Necessity taught them, therefore, to divide words into their elements, and to invent characters which should represent, not the words themselves, but the elements of which they were composed. In consequence of this invention, every particular word came to be represented, not by one character, but by a multitude of characters; and the expression of it in writing became much more intricate and complex than before. But though particular words were thus represented by a greater number of characters, the whole language was expressed by a much smaller, and about four and twenty letters were found capable of supplying the place of that immense multitude of characters, which were requisite before. In the same manner, in the beginnings of language, men seem to have attempted to express every particular event, which they had occasion to take notice of, by a particular word, which expressed at once the whole of that event. But as the number of words must, in this case, have become really infinite, in consequence of the really infinite variety of events, men found themselves partly compelled by necessity, and partly conducted by nature, to divide every event into what may be called its metaphysical elements, and to institute words, which should denote not so much the events, as the elements of which they were composed. The expression of every particular event, became in this manner more intricate and complex, but the whole system of the language became more coherent, more connected, more easily retained and comprehended.

29. As the far greater part of Verbs express, at present, not an event, but the attribute of an event, and, consequently, require a subject, or nominative case, to complete their signification, some grammarians, not having attended to this progress of nature, and being desirous to make their common rules quite universal, and without any exception, have insisted that all verbs required a nominative, either expressed or understood; and have, accordingly put themselves to the torture to find some awkward nominatives to those few verbs, which still expressing a complete event, plainly admit of none. *Pluit*, for example, according to *Sanctius*, means *pluvia pluit*, in English, *the rain rains*. See Sanctii Minerva, l. 3. c. 1.

When verbs, from being originally impersonal had thus, by the division of the event into its metaphysical 413 elements, become personal, it is natural to suppose that they would first be made use of in the third person singular. No verb is ever used impersonally in our language, nor, so far as I know, in any other modern tongue. But in the ancient languages, whenever any verb is used impersonally, it is always in the third person singular. The termination of those verbs, which are still always impersonal, is constantly the same with that of the third person singular of personal verbs. The consideration of these circumstances, joined to the naturalness of the thing itself, may serve to convince us that verbs first became personal in what is now called the third person singular.

But as the event, or matter of fact, which is expressed by a verb, may be affirmed either of the person who speaks, or of the person who is spoken to, as well as of some third person or object, it became necessary to fall upon some method of expressing these two peculiar relations of the event. In the English language this is commonly done, by prefixing, what are called the personal pronouns, to the general word which expresses the event affirmed. *I came, you came, he* or *it came*; in these phrases the event of having come is in the first, affirmed of the speaker; in the second, of the person spoken to; in the third of some other person, or object. The first formers of language, it may be imagined, might have done the same thing, and prefixing in the same manner the two first personal pronouns, to the same termination of the verb, which expressed the third person singular, might have said, *ego venit, tu venit*, as well as *ille* or *illud venit*. And I make no doubt 414 but they would have done so, if at the time when they had first occasion to express these relations of the verb, there had been any such words as either *ego* or *tu* in their language. But in this early period of the language, which we are now endeavouring to describe, it is extremely improbable that any such words would be known. Though custom has now rendered them familiar to us, they, both of them, express ideas extremely metaphysical and abstract. The word *I*, for example, is a word of a very particular species. Whatever speaks may denote itself by this personal pronoun. The word *I*, therefore, is a general word, capable of being predicated, as the logicians say, of an infinite variety of objects. It differs, however, from all other general words in this respect; that the objects of which it may be predicated, do not form any particular species of objects distinguished from all others. The word *I*, does not, like the word *man*, denote a particular class of objects, separated from all others by peculiar qualities of their own. It is far from being the name of a species, but, on the contrary, whenever it is made use of, it always denotes a precise individual, the particular person who then speaks. It may be said to be, at once, both what the logicians call, a singular, and what they call, a common term; and to join in its signification the seemingly opposite qualities of the most precise individuality, and the most extensive generalization. This word, therefore, expressing so very abstract and metaphysical an idea, would not easily or readily occur to the first formers of language. What are called the personal pronouns, it may be observed, are among the last words of which children learn to make use. A child, speaking of itself, 415 says, *Billy walks, Billy sits*, instead of *I walk, I sit*. As in the beginnings of language, therefore, mankind seem to have evaded the invention of at least the more abstract proportions, and to have expressed the same relations which these *now* stand for, by varying the termination of the co-relative term, so they likewise would naturally attempt to evade the necessity of inventing those more abstract pronouns by varying the termination of the verb, according as the event which it expressed was intended to be affirmed of the first, second, or third person. This seems, accordingly, to be the universal practice of all the ancient languages. In Latin, *veni, venisti, venit*, sufficiently denote, without any other addition, the different events expressed by the English phrases, *I came, you came*, he, or *it came*. The verb would, for the same reason, vary its termination, according as the event was intended to be affirmed of the first, second, or third persons plural; and what is expressed by the English phrases, *we came, ye came, they came*, would be denoted by the Latin words, *venimus, venistis, venerunt*. Those primitive languages, too, which, upon account of the difficulty of inventing numeral names, had introduced a dual, as well as a plural number, into the declension of their nouns substantive, would probably, from analogy, do the same thing in the conjugations of their verbs. And thus in all those original languages, we might expect to find, at least six, if not eight or nine variations, in the termination of every verb, according as the event which it denoted was meant to be affirmed of the first, second, or third persons singular, dual, or plural. These variations again being repeated, along with others, through all its different tenses, modes and voices, must necessarily 416 have rendered their conjugations still more intricate and complex than their declensions.

Language would probably have continued upon this footing in all countries, nor would ever have grown more simple in its declensions and conjugations, had it not become more complex in its composition, in consequence of the mixture of several languages with one another, occasioned by the mixture of different nations. As long as any language was spoke by those only who learned it in their infancy, the intricacy of its declensions and conjugations could occasion no great embarrassment. The far greater part of those who had occasion to speak it, had acquired it at so very early a period of their lives, so insensibly and by such slow degrees, that they were scarce ever sensible of the difficulty. But when two nations came to be mixed with one another, either by conquest or migration, the case would be very different. Each nation, in order to make itself intelligible to those with whom it was under the necessity of conversing, would be obliged to learn the language of the other. The greater part of individuals too, learning the new language, not by art, or by remounting to its rudiments and first principles, but by rote, and by what they commonly heard in conversation, would be extremely perplexed by the intricacy of its declensions and conjugations. They would endeavour, therefore, to supply their ignorance of these, by whatever shift the language could afford them. Their ignorance of the declensions they would naturally supply by the use of prepositions; and a Lombard, who was attempting to speak Latin, and wanted to express that such a person was a citizen of Rome, or a benefactor to Rome, 417 if he happened not to be acquainted with the genitive and dative cases of the word *Roma*, would naturally express himself by prefixing the prepositions *ad* and *de* to the nominative; and, instead of *Romæ*, would say, *ad Roma*, and *de Roma*. *Al Roma* and *di Roma*, accordingly, is the manner in which the present Italians, the descendants of the ancient Lombards and Romans, express this and all other similar relations. And in this manner prepositions seem to have been introduced, in the room of the ancient declensions. The same alteration has, I am informed, been produced upon the Greek language, since the taking of Constantinople by the Turks. The words are, in a great measure, the same as before; but the grammar is entirely lost, prepositions having come in the place of the old declensions. This change is undoubtedly a simplification of the language, in point of rudiments and principle. It introduces, instead of a great variety of declensions, one universal declension, which is the same in every word, of whatever gender, number, or termination.

A similar expedient enables men, in the situation above-mentioned, to get rid of almost the whole intricacy of their conjugations. There is in every language a verb, known by the name of the substantive verb; in Latin, *sum*; in English, *I am*. This verb denotes not the existence of any particular event, but existence in general. It is, upon this account, the most abstract and metaphysical of all verbs; and, consequently, could by no means be a word of early invention. When it came to be invented, however, as it had all the tenses and modes of any other verb, by being joined with the passive participle, it was capable of supplying the place of 418 the whole passive voice, and of rendering this part of their conjugations as simple and uniform, as the use of prepositions had rendered their declensions. A Lombard, who wanted to say, *I am loved*, but could not recollect the word *amor*, naturally endeavoured to supply his ignorance, by saying, *ego sum amatus*. *Io sono amato*, is at this day the Italian expression, which corresponds to the English phrase above-mentioned.

There is another verb, which, in the same manner, runs through all languages, and which is distinguished by the name of the possessive verb; in Latin, *habeo*; in English, *I have*. This verb, likewise, denotes an event of an extremely abstract and metaphysical nature, and, consequently, cannot be supposed to have been a word of the earliest invention.

When it came to be invented, however, by being applied to the passive participle, it was capable of supplying a great part of the active voice, as the substantive verb had supplied the whole of the passive. A Lombard, who wanted to say, *I had loved*, but could not recollect the word *amaveram*, would endeavour to supply the place of it, by saying either *ego habebam amatum*, or *ego habui amatum*. *Io avevá amato*, or *Io ebbi amato*, are the correspondent Italian expressions at this day. And thus upon the intermixture of different nations with one another, the conjugations, by means of different auxiliary verbs, were made to approach towards the simplicity and uniformity of the declensions.

In general it may be laid down for a maxim, that the more simple any language is in its composition, 419 the more complex it must be in its declensions and conjugations; and, on the contrary, the more simple it is in its declensions and conjugations, the more complex it must be in its composition.

The Greek seems to be, in a great measure, a simple, uncompounded language, formed from the primitive jargon of those wandering savages, the ancient Hellenians and Pelasgians, from whom the Greek nation is said to have been descended. All the words in the Greek language are derived from about three hundred primitives, a plain evidence that the Greeks formed their language almost entirely among themselves, and that when they had occasion for a new word, they were not accustomed, as we are, to borrow it from some foreign language, but to form it, either by composition or derivation from some other word or words, in their own. The declensions and conjugations, therefore, of the Greek are much more complex than those of any other European language with which I am acquainted.

The Latin is a composition of the Greek and of the ancient Tuscan languages. Its declensions and conjugations accordingly are much less complex than those of the Greek: it has dropt the dual number in both. Its verbs have no optative mood distinguished by any peculiar termination. They have but one future. They have no aorist distinct from the preterit-perfect; they have no middle voice; and even many of their tenses in the passive voice are eked out, in the same manner as in the modern languages, by the help of the substantive verb joined to the passive participle. In both the voices, the number of infinitives 420 and participles is much smaller in the Latin than in the Greek.

The French and Italian languages are each of them compounded, the one of the Latin, and the language of the ancient Franks, the other of the same Latin and the language of the ancient Lombards. As they are both of them, therefore, more complex in their composition than the Latin, so are they likewise more simple in their declensions and conjugations. With regard to their declensions, they have both of them lost their cases altogether; and with regard to their conjugations, they have both of them lost the whole of the passive, and some part of the active voices of their verbs. The want of the passive voice they supply entirely by the substantive verb joined to the passive participle; and they make out part of the active, in the same manner, by the help of the possessive verb and the same passive participle.

The English is compounded of the French and the ancient Saxon languages. The French was introduced into Britain by the Norman conquest, and continued, till the time of Edward III. to be the sole language of the law as well as the principal language of the court. The English, which came to be spoken afterwards, and which continues to be spoken now, is a mixture of the ancient Saxon and this Norman French. As the English language, therefore, is more complex in its composition than either the French or the Italian, so is it likewise more simple in its declensions and conjugations. Those two languages retain, at least, a part of the distinction of genders, and their adjectives vary their termination [421] according as they are applied to a masculine or to a feminine substantive. But there is no such distinction in the English language, whose adjectives admit of no variety of termination. The French and Italian languages have, both of them, the remains of a conjugation, and all those tenses of the active voice, which cannot be expressed by the possessive verb joined to the passive participle, as well as many of those which can, are, in those languages, marked by varying the termination of the principal verb. But almost all those other tenses are in the English eked out by other auxiliary verbs, so that there is in this language scarce even the remains of a conjugation. *I love, I loved, loving*, are all the varieties of termination which the greater part of English verbs admit of. All the different modifications of meaning, which cannot be expressed by any of those three terminations, must be made out by different auxiliary verbs joined to some one or other of them. Two auxiliary verbs supply all the deficiencies of the French and Italian conjugations; it requires more than half a dozen to supply those of the English, which besides the substantive and possessive verbs, makes use of *do, did; will, would; shall, should; can, could; may, might*.

It is in this manner that language becomes more simple in its rudiments and principles, just in proportion as it grows more complex in its composition, and the same thing has happened in it, which commonly happens with regard to mechanical engines. All machines are generally, when first invented, extremely complex in their principles, and there is often a particular principle of motion for every particular [422] movement which, it is intended, they should perform. Succeeding improvers observe, that one principle may be so applied as to produce several of those movements, and thus the machine becomes gradually more and more simple, and produces its effects with fewer wheels, and fewer principles of motion. In language, in the same manner, every case of every noun, and every tense of every verb, was originally expressed by a particular distinct word, which served for this purpose and for no other. But succeeding observation discovered that one set of words was capable of supplying the place of all that infinite number, and that four or five prepositions, and half a dozen auxiliary verbs, were capable of answering the end of all the declensions, and of all the conjugations in the ancient languages.

But this simplification of languages, though it arises, perhaps, from similar causes, has by no means similar effects with the correspondent simplification of machines. The simplification of machines renders them more and more perfect, but this simplification of the rudiments of languages renders them more and more imperfect and less proper for many of the purposes of language: and this for the following reasons.

First of all, languages are by this simplification rendered more prolix, several words having become necessary to express what could have been expressed by a single word before. Thus the words, *Dei* and, *Deo*, in the Latin, sufficiently show, without any addition, what relation, the object signified is understood to stand in to the object expressed by the other words in the sentence. But to express the same [423] relation in English, and in all other modern languages, we must make use of, at least, two words, and say, *of God, to God*. So far as the declensions are concerned, therefore, the modern languages are much more prolix than the ancient. The difference is still greater with regard to the conjugations. What a Roman expressed by the single word, *amavissem*, an Englishman is obliged to express by four different words, *I should have loved*. It unnecessary to take any pains to show how much this prolixness must enervate the eloquence of all modern languages. How much the beauty of any expression depends upon its conciseness, is well known to those who have any experience in composition.

Secondly, this simplification of the principles of languages renders them less agreeable to the ear. The variety of termination in the Greek and Latin, occasioned by their declensions and conjugations, give a sweetness to their language altogether unknown to ours, and a variety unknown to any other modern language. In point of sweetness, the Italian, perhaps, may surpass the Latin, and almost equal the Greek; but in point of variety, it is greatly inferior to both.

Thirdly, this simplification, not only renders the sounds of our language less agreeable to the ear, but it also restrains us from disposing such sounds as we have, in the manner that might be most agreeable. It ties down many words to a particular situation, though they might often be placed in another with much more beauty. In the Greek and Latin, though the adjective and substantive were separated 424 from one another, the correspondence of their terminations still showed their mutual reference, and the separation did not necessarily occasion any sort of confusion. Thus in the first line of Virgil:

Tityre tu patulæ recubans sub legmine fagi.

We easily see that *tu* refers to *recubans*, and *patulæ* to *fagi*; though the related words are separated from one another by the intervention of several others: because the terminations, showing the correspondence of their cases, determine their mutual reference. But if we were to translate this line literally into English, and say, *Tityrus, thou of spreading reclining under the shade beech*, Œdipus himself could not make sense of it; because there is here no difference of termination, to determine which substantive each adjective belongs to. It is the same case with regard to verbs. In Latin the verb may often be placed, without an inconveniency or ambiguity, in any part of the sentence. But in English its place is almost always precisely determined. It must follow the subjective and precede the objective member of the phrase in almost all cases. Thus in Latin whether you say, *Joannem verberavit Robertus*, or *Robertus verberavit Joannem*, the meaning is precisely the same, and the termination fixes John to be the sufferer in both cases. But in English *John beat Robert*, and *Robert beat John*, have by no means the same signification. The place therefore of the three principal members of the phrase is in the English, and for the same reason in the French and Italian languages almost always precisely determined; whereas in the ancient languages a greater latitude is 425 allowed, and the place of those members is often, in a great measure, indifferent. We must have recourse to Horace, in order to interpret some parts of Milton's literal translation;

Who now enjoys thee credulous all gold,
Who always vacant, always amiable
Hopes thee; of flattering gales
Unmindful.

are verses which it is impossible to interpret by any rules of our language. There are no rules in our language, by which any man could discover, that, in the first line, *credulous* referred to *who*, and not to *thee*; or, that *all gold* referred to any thing; or, that in the fourth line, *unmindful*, referred to *who*, in the second, and not to *thee* in the third; or, on the contrary, that, in the second line *always vacant, always amiable*, referred to *thee* in the third, and not to *who* in the same line with it. In the Latin, indeed, all this is abundantly plain.

Qui nunc te fruitur credulus aureâ,
Qui semper vacuam, semper amabilem
Sperat te; nescius auræ fallacis.

Because the terminations in the Latin determine the reference of each adjective to its proper substantive, which it is impossible for any thing in the English to do. How much this power of transposing the order of their words must have facilitated the composition of the ancients, both in verse and prose, can hardly be imagined. That it must greatly have facilitated their versification it is needless to observe; and in 426 prose, whatever beauty depends upon the arrangement and construction of the several members of the period, must to them have been acquirable with much more ease, and to much greater perfection, than it can be to those whose expression is constantly confined by the prolixness, constraint and monotony of modern languages.

FINIS.

Made in the USA
Columbia, SC
18 January 2023

10615976R00107